A brief history of
COCAINE

Steven B. Karch, M.D.

CRC Press
Boca Raton Boston London New York Washington, D.C.

Acquiring Editor: *Paul Petralia*
Project Editor: *Susan Fox*
Cover Design: *Dawn Boyd*
Prepress: *Kevin Luong and Carlos Esser*

Library of Congress Cataloging-in-Publication Data

Karch, Steven B.
   A brief history of cocaine / by Steven B. Karch.
     p.   cm.
   Includes bibliographical references and index.
   ISBN 0-8493-4019-5
   1. Cocaine—History I. Title.
QP801.C68K369 1997
362.29'8'09—dc21

             97-35399
             CIP

PREFACE

In 1986, I was a visiting fellow in Margaret Billingham's cardiac pathology laboratory at Stanford University. I was studying the cellular changes that occur in the heart during cardiac arrest. It seemed to me that, if we could characterize the changes that occurred at the microscopic level, we might be able to understand what was happening to the whole patient, and devise better ways to treat them. While examining sections of heart from a group of cardiac arrest victims, I noticed some peculiar changes, and asked Professor Billingham about them. She explained that the changes I had identified were characteristically associated with stress, and with high levels of adrenaline, i.e., the stress hormone.

A few weeks later, I saw the same peculiar changes in the heart of a young San Francisco housewife who had collapsed and died while using cocaine. She had no known medical problems; however, she and her husband had been "experimenting" with cocaine for about a year. When I examined her heart, I noticed that it was enlarged, and its walls thickened. I also noticed an unusual, gritty, feeling when I cut into the heart. I processed several portions of the heart for examination under the microscope. One week later, when I finally had time to look at the sections, I was astonished to see how badly scarred the heart was.

Although not particularly interested, or knowledgeable, about the medical complications of drug abuse, I did know that cocaine affected the stress hormones, and I wondered whether some abnormality, having to do with high levels of adrenaline, might not have been responsible for the woman's death. I contacted the San Francisco Medical Examiner, Dr. Boyd Stephens, and asked him if I could review any similar cases which had occurred in his jurisdiction. He invited me to come and take a look.

We found some 30 similar cases which had occurred over a 2-year period. We compared the appearance of the cocaine users' hearts to those of a control group. There was no question that the same stress hormone-related changes were present in the cocaine users' hearts, and absent in the controls. A paper was soon written by the members of our group, and quickly accepted by *Human Pathology*. The paper received quite a bit of attention, partially because of the death of Len Bias, an extremely talented young basketball player. Bias died while using cocaine a few weeks after our paper was published. His heart showed exactly the same changes we had seen and described.

Months later, while looking for a book in the stacks at Stanford's Lane Library, I found a copy of *Der Kokainismus*, a book published in Germany in 1926. Written by Hans Maier, a Swiss author-psychiatrist, it chronicled the medical and social history of cocaine-related disease. A chapter on the medical consequences of chronic cocaine abuse contained illustrations made by two Italian pathologists, Eugenio Bravetta and Giuseppe Invernizzi, in 1922. The illustrations depicted the changes they observed in the hearts of experimental animals, and in a man who died as a consequence of chronic cocaine abuse. I was astonished to notice that the illustrations showed exactly the same changes our San Francisco group had observed.

Our original observations were not quite as original as we thought they were. I was concerned lest anyone think we had appropriated the work of other earlier researchers, and passed it off as our own. And so I started to write a letter to the journal that had published our paper, with the intention of acknowledging the earlier work of Bravetta and Invernizzi, and pointing out that we had not been aware that other researchers had ever looked at the problem. But, after reading more of Professor Maier's book, I became fascinated with the story of cocaine abuse at the turn of the century, and started reading more of the old literature. The Stanford Medical Library has a complete collection of medical journals dating from the mid-1880s. It did not take a great deal of research to find that not only had the pathology of cocaine-related heart disease been studied, but cocaine-related heart attacks and strokes had been reported in large numbers, long before the turn of the century.

What started out as a letter acknowledging the work of the earlier researchers turned into a short history of the medical problems associated with cocaine use (The history of cocaine toxicity, in *Human Pathology*, 20(11) 1037-1039, 1989). The paper is still occasionally quoted, but even while writing it, I wondered how much of the problem of cocaine abuse had already been solved by earlier researchers, whose work was now completely ignored, just because it had been published a long time ago, in another language. It turns out, quite a bit.

I discovered that not only has past medical research been ignored, but there was extensive literature dealing with many other aspects of the cocaine problem, all written before World War II, with much of it written before World War I. Earlier researchers had not just confined their attentions to the medical complications of cocaine abuse, they had also analyzed the agriculture, botany, chemistry, and political science of coca. Much of what I read sounded like it could have been written today.

In particular, neither the language, nor the proposals of politicians wrestling with ways to control the spread of cocaine in the 1920s, differed in any important respects from what is being said and proposed today. The only real difference between political leaders then and now is that political leaders at the turn of the century did not have to speak in 15-second sound bites for television screens, and did not have 75 years of experience to guide them. I hope that, with the publication of this book, some of that information will become more accessible, and perhaps even used.

Steven B. Karch, M.D.
Berkeley, California

INTRODUCTION

Coca will never cease to be esteemed. There are men in Spain who have grown wealthy through buying and selling this coca and trading in the Indian markets

From *Crónicas de la Conquista*, Pedro Cieza de León, 1550

The quote may be over four centuries old, but it is as accurate now as it was in 1550. Financial considerations made coca production an important feature in Spain's new world colonies. Today, the economic distortions produced by the cocaine industry continue to hamper development in Colombia and Peru. What has changed during those four centuries is the science of coca growing and cocaine production. These developments have been paid scant attention, yet they are vitally important. In a very real and important sense, the economics of the illegal cocaine trade are, and always have been, determined by technology. The impact of cocaine abuse on society, not to mention the impact of cocaine use on the death rate, can be accurately related to technical advances that have increased the amount of cocaine that cocaine users can get into their bodies.

The cocaine problem may fairly be said to have begun with the Spanish occupation of Peru, but most of the important technical advances have occurred within the last 100 years. Europeans, in large numbers, did not hear about coca until the late 1800s, and selling cocaine did not become an important business until the 20th century. If, as many claim, current drug policy is flawed, the flaws may be explained by the fact that policymakers seem to care little, and know less, about the cocaine business during that period. Overwhelmed by the vast quantities of cocaine flooding our country, they continue to seek political solutions, for what is, in the final analysis, a medical problem, and an old one at that.

Proposed solutions to the cocaine problem generally consist of four elements: (1) aggressive local policing with crop eradication, (2) crop substitution, (3) international cooperation, and (4) the establishment of tighter border controls. The rationale for these proposals appears to be that once the total output of coca leaf is decreased, there will be less cocaine produced, and interdiction of the remainder will be more feasible. This line of thinking equates solving the cocaine problem with solving the coca cultivation problem.

Anyone who has ever actually read such proposals, or listened to the speeches of leaders who want to escalate the drug war, will have noticed a certain sameness about them. The sameness is simply explained; the proposals are very old and they have been heard time and time again. Political leaders might be shocked if they knew just how old some of their ideas are. The Second Marqués de Cañete, the Spanish Viceroy in Peru from 1555 to 1560, was the first to pass laws requiring crop substitution. His attempts at limiting coca production were as ineffectual then as they appear to be now. Current leaders might be forgiven for not knowing about the Marqués de Cañete, but it is hard to excuse their fixation on controlling coca production in South America. At one time, more coca leaf was exported from Indonesia than from Peru. It could happen again.

Coca leaf has been grown commercially in Nigeria, Sri Lanka, Malaysia, Indonesia, Taiwan, and Iwo Jima. Furthermore, the first cocaine cartel was formed in Amsterdam, not in Cali, and its members included Hoffman-LaRoche, Sandoz, Merck, and other drug companies that are now household names. If, as it seems, no one knows that the Southeast Asian cocaine industry existed, then it is even less likely anyone would know that the varieties of coca grown in Taiwan and Java contained more than twice as much cocaine as the varieties grown in the Andes. If planners did know, they might wonder whether, given sufficient financial incentive, these areas could again become coca producers. Indonesia, after all, has nearly 14,000 islands spread over 3,200 miles. A prohibition on coca growing would be impossible to enforce, even if there was a will to do so.

Policymakers also tend to overrate the effectiveness of the third and fourth components of their control programs, i.e., international regulation and border controls. The few successes that have been realized as a result of organized international efforts came about only because of some unique features of the drugmaking business which no longer exist. During the first half of this century, international treaties did lead to reductions in cocaine production, but only because all the cocaine was being manufactured by legitimate, if somewhat rapacious, pharmaceutical houses. The clandestine drug lab was yet to be invented, and government agencies knew where the crops were being grown. Today, virtually all cocaine is made clandestinely, and the rules are different.

In 1925, when treaty requirements for import and export controls forced legitimate drugmakers, such as Merck, out of the cocaine business, their place was taken by other legitimate drug producers in Japan. Prior to World War II, Japan signed a series of international drug control treaties, originated and sponsored by the United States. Japan actively participated in the League of Nations drug control efforts, and gave lip service to firm drug control measures. But evidence presented at the Tokyo War Crimes Trials held in 1946, clearly demonstrated that international laws do not prevent outlaw states from selling drugs. The government of Japan, in partnership with Japan's largest private businesses, sold drugs by the ton in occupied China. Sumitomo and Mitsubishi banks even underwrote a bond offering guaranteed by narcotic sales in China. After World War II, Japan was charged with crimes against humanity, not just for the Nanking massacre, and other assorted atrocities, but also for its adventures in the drug trade.

If policymakers seem uninformed about the past history of the cocaine business, they appear to know even less about what happens to cocaine users. Fifty years ago, the common varieties of South American coca leaf contained less than .5% cocaine, and the low cocaine content acted as a safeguard. Cocaine-related heart attacks and strokes were, and still are, uncommon among the Aymara Indians. The reason is simply that there is a limit to the number of leaves that even the most determined users can chew. The physical constraints of leaf chewing limit the amount of cocaine that can get into the bloodstream. That limit acts as a safeguard against toxicity. When Merck and Company began to manufacture refined cocaine in 1862, that safeguard began to erode. Commercially produced hypodermic syringes became available a few years later, totally eliminating all of the safeguards. The first cocaine-related heart attacks were reported in 1885, just a few months after physicians began injecting cocaine as a local anesthetic.

The likelihood of becoming addicted to cocaine also has to do with cocaine blood levels. Within certain limits, increasing the amount of cocaine administered increases the amount entering the bloodstream, and, ultimately, the amount that reaches the brain. During the last decade, drug users have been able to get more cocaine more cheaply than ever before. According to figures released by the White House in 1996, the true price of cocaine has declined by nearly 75% during the last 15 years (from $587 to $137, the amount of money necessary to buy enough street drug to yield one gram of pure cocaine).

Between 1884, the year that Karl Koller discovered that cocaine was an effective local anesthetic, and 1984, when the first crack smokers began appearing at medical clinics on the island of Jamaica, there have been important advances in the way cocaine is grown, refined, distributed, and used. Smoking a given amount of cocaine ("crack") will produce a much higher blood level than snorting the same amount of drug. In a very real sense, "crack" smoking represents a technical advance. The net impact of all these improvements has been to increase the amount of cocaine that gets into the bloodstream of cocaine users. These "improvements" translate into increased toxicity and increased potential for addiction.

The early history of the cocaine market was characterized by shortages of the raw material, and attempts at finding new sources. The later history is best described as an orderly progression from excess production to market manipulation, and eventually to diversion of the drug to the black market. The chapters that follow describe key events in the history of the cocaine business. This story begins with the Spanish Conquest of Peru, and ends with the Tokyo War Crimes Trials, held at the end of World War II. The chapters in-between chronicle the growth of the cocaine industry, from its inception until the end of World War II.

Chapter 1 describes what happened when the Europeans arrived in the New World. Coca had been cultivated in Peru for at least one thousand years before the Spanish arrived, but it was only after the Spanish Conquest of Peru that coca became a cash crop and a medium of exchange. Supplying coca to laborers in the silver and mercury mines became a hugely profitable undertaking. Even the Bishop of Cuzco couldn't resist the opportunity to earn extra income. There was so much money to be made growing coca that farmers stopped growing other crops. The second Spanish Viceroy passed laws limiting the acreage that could be devoted to coca. Other regulations were designed to encourage crop substitution, but the measures proved to be ineffective.

The Spanish Court tried to monopolize trade with, and knowledge about, its New World possessions. Books by Spanish historians accurately describe the practice of coca chewing, but they were rigidly censored by the Casa de Contratación (Trade/Monopoly Board), the Inquisition, and King Phillip, himself. It was not until late in the 16th century that other Europeans had the opportunity to read about coca and its marvelous powers, and later still that specimens from the New World began to appear at Botanical Gardens in Germany, France, and the Netherlands. Academics may have known about coca, but the general public did not. Coca was so popular in Peru, there was no surplus to export.

If coca leaves had been smuggled out of South America by European merchantmen, in contravention of the Spanish embargo, they would have traveled poorly. The cocaine content of samples that did make their way back to Europe would have been very low, and results of their use disappointing. In 1708, Boerhaave, the famous Dutch physician, recommended coca in one of his books. But mentions of coca in his later works were conspicuously absent, probably because his supply was unreliable. The European coca supply was destined to remain unreliable for another 150 years, until the mid-1800s.

Chapter 2 describes the events that transformed coca growing from a South American monopoly to a worldwide industry. King George (1738-1820) of England realized that the New World plants were worth money, and he expanded his Royal Botanic Gardens at Kew, outside of London, to take advantage of that fact. He effectively created the infrastructure necessary for the systematic discovery and exploitation of New World plants. His programs were wildly successful. Seedlings of the cinchona tree, the source of quinine, were smuggled out of Ecuador and transplanted in India. Within a few years, quinine was transformed from one of the world's most expensive drugs to one of the cheapest. The same approach was planned for coca, but with not quite the same results. The plants selected to start British coca plantations in Jamaica's Blue Mountains, and Ceylon, Malaya, and Australia grew leaves with a relatively low cocaine content — between 0.25 and 0.5%. Almost certainly by accident, plantation owners in Indonesia, and later in Japan and Taiwan, managed to acquire a strain that produced three or four times as much cocaine as the South American variety, although it was much harder to extract cocaine from the coca leaves grown in Indonesia than the varieties grown in the Andes. The Southeast Asian cocaine industry did not take off until German chemists developed an economical way to process coca grown in Asia.

Chapter 3 is about Angelo Mariani, the man credited with the invention of coca wines. These wines were very popular in Europe during the 1870s and 1880s, and were not, as far as anyone knows, ever associated with any toxic side effects. The amount of cocaine in Mariani's wines was limited by the chemistry of coca. Large scale commercial production of purified cocaine did not begin until the mid-1880s. Thus, the only way to add more cocaine to the wine was to add more leaves. But adding too many leaves ruined the taste. The main reason for the wine's success was not the modest amount of cocaine it contained. The reason was Mariani himself.

It was Mariani who first invented the celebrity endorsement. And it was Mariani who first printed advertising supplements that were inserted into newspapers. Another reason for the success of coca wines has recently become apparent; when alcohol and cocaine are consumed at the same time, a new compound, called cocaethylene is formed. Cocaethylene has all the same properties as cocaine, except that it lasts much longer. Its formation could explain why the wines, which had such a low cocaine content, were nonetheless so popular.

The legacies of Sigmund Freud and Karl Koller are considered in Chapter 4. Neither Freud nor Koller could have achieved fame, or even notoriety, if chemists at Merck and Parke, Davis & Company had not already mastered the chemistry of commercial cocaine production. Freud believed that he could cure morphine addicts by treating them with cocaine. He got his ideas from an American journal, the *Therapeutic Gazette*, and quoted from the *Gazette* when he wrote his famous paper about cocaine. The *Gazette* was, in fact, an advertising vehicle for Parke, Davis products and it was owned by Parke, Davis & Company. Freud seems to have been unaware that he was quoting from an advertisement, although he certainly must have known what he was doing when he later received payment from Parke, Davis to endorse its brand of cocaine over Merck's.

Karl Koller's idea that a cocaine solution could be used to prevent the pain of eye surgery had a profound effect on modern medicine. But, like Freud, his success would not have been possible without the help of Merck of Darmstadt, the famous drug company. Researchers before Koller had speculated about cocaine's local anesthetic properties, but none of the researchers had access to a reliable source of coca leaf or purified cocaine. Their experiments failed because the cocaine solutions they used usually contained no cocaine, at least until the Merck family began selling purified cocaine.

Chapter 5 shows how the medical complications associated with cocaine use can be related to the cocaine supply. As cocaine supplies increased, physicians had the opportunity to experiment with using cocaine in treating a variety of conditions. The first deaths and medical problems were reported almost as soon as physicians began experimenting with purified cocaine. The complications consisted mainly of seizures, heart attacks, and strokes which occurred when doctors administered too much cocaine at one time. A second wave of deaths occurred around 1910, a result of drug abuse, not medical treatment. The underlying mechanisms were different, with death occurring when abusers took too much cocaine over too long a period. Such an indulgence only became possible as cocaine became more readily available.

One of the most dramatic consequences of using large amounts of cocaine for long periods is agitated delirium. Victims become wildly psychotic, appear to be immune to pain, and die suddenly. Agitated delirium only occurs in individuals with a preexisting genetic propensity. The number of individuals with that propensity appears to be quite small; thus, the incidence of agitated delirium within any given community can be used as a reliable indicator of cocaine availability within that community. No new cases of agitated delirium were reported in the United States between the 1920s and 1985 when the disorder reappeared in Miami. It is now increasingly common in large cities where cocaine supplies are abundant.

Chapter 6 describes the founding of the coca industry in Java. Fortunately for the Dutch growers, their root stock came from a source in Belgium, not Kew Gardens in England. The strain supplied from

Belgium was harder to refine than South American coca, but it contained much more cocaine. Just before the turn of the century, a German chemical company, Farbwerke, patented a way to refine Javanese coca leaf. The Dutch Colonial Development Board then helped finance a coca refinery, based on the Farbwerke process, in Amsterdam. In 1903, when the Farbwerke patent ran out, other German chemical makers also began to use Java leaf, further increasing the demand for Java leaf and further increasing the amount of cocaine on the market. By 1910, the Dutch refinery was producing several tons of refined cocaine per year.

The greatest demand for Java leaf was in Japan. The major pharmaceutical companies in Japan were all cocaine producers. At first they imported large quantities of coca leaf from Dutch growers in Java. Later, Japanese firms bought out existing Javanese plantations. Ultimately, the Japanese drug houses planted their own plantations in Taiwan, Okinawa, and Iwo Jima. By 1925, when the Taiwanese plantations were firmly established, the Japanese government had already begun to limit imports from Java. When the Netherlands signed the Geneva Convention, which required import and export controls, and limited production to what could be justified by medical needs, it became impossible for Dutch growers to find buyers for Java coca. Legitimate producers, except those in Japan, were effectively forced out of business.

Chapter 7 charts the rise of the great pharmaceutical houses. At first, their cocaine dealings were entirely legitimate, although their business practices were somewhat less so. Merck provided Freud with funds, presumably to help cover research costs, but quite possibly also to stop Freud from making unfavorable comments about its products. Parke, Davis paid Freud to endorse their brand of cocaine too, but passed the endorsement off as legitimate scientific opinion. Freud's role was pivotal in the development of the industry. His advocacy of cocaine as a treatment for morphine addiction gave a significant, if short-lived, boost to sales.

The first cocaine cartel was founded in 1910 by a group of eight European drug manufacturers. Members included most of Europe's important pharmaceutical houses. Cartel members may, or may not, have fixed prices, but they certainly did not sponsor any price wars either. On several occasions, they acted as a group to force down the price of raw cocaine coming from South American suppliers. They did not have similar leverage in Southeast Asia; Java growers and producers, with the help of the Dutch Colonial Development Bank, had formed their own cartel.

Chapter 8 describes the less than predictable legislative responses to the predictable medical problems associated with unlimited access to cocaine. As the pharmaceutical houses increased production, prices dropped, allowing the makers of various snake oil and quack medicines, in all parts of the world, to incorporate combinations of cocaine and alcohol in their remedies. The commonly held view is that reformers, such as novelist Upton Sinclair, raised public awareness and forced the passage of the Pure Food and Drug Act of 1906. In reality, the food and drug industries themselves had as much to do with passage of the new law as the reformers. The real focus of the 1906 bill was meat and foodstuffs, not drugs. Still, there can be little question that the Act marked the beginning of the regulation for the drug industry. It also marked the beginning of what has now become a common practice: the use of bad science to support perceived social good.

In 1911, the Coca-Cola Company found itself in court with the U.S. government because Coca-Cola contained caffeine, even though caffeine was, at the time, a perfectly legal drug. The company was also accused of false advertising because Coca-Cola did not contain any cocaine. Harvey Wiley, the head government chemist at the Department of Agriculture, was convinced that caffeine was bad, even if he could not provide the science to back up his contentions. At trial, government scientists had to content themselves with introducing evidence showing that when they filled the lungs of rabbits with Coca-Cola syrup, the animals always died. The government eventually won its case, but had to drop its plans for a nationwide team of inspectors who would visit soda fountains weekly to ferret out caffeine-containing soft drinks.

Chapter 9 describes attempts by the United States to set limits on drug use and the drug industry. After the passage of the Pure Food and Drug Act in 1906, America undertook a series of drug control initiatives. In reality, these initiatives were little more than exercises in international relations. They were designed to serve American political needs, more than to solve any particular domestic drug problem. Almost entirely at U.S. insistence, a series of international agreements curbing drug abuse were negotiated and implemented. Viewpoints about the drug problem were entirely different in Europe than in the United States. The Europeans, particularly the British, believed that the only way to solve the problem was by placing strict controls on the drug manufacturing process. Representatives of the United States insisted that control could be achieved only by stopping production of the raw materials: opium and coca.

Chapter 10 describes Japan's adventures in the cocaine trade. While American diplomats were negotiating a series of measures designed to control the proliferation of drug use, the Japanese cocaine industry was quietly maturing. There was a peculiarity about Japanese law that favored drug dealing — the laws applied only to opium. Heroin and cocaine production was not specifically mentioned in any part of the legal code. For all intents and purposes, regulations applicable to the production and sale of morphine, heroin, and cocaine were nonexistent. Japan's cocaine industry flourished.

Evidence introduced at the Tokyo War Crimes Trials showed that Korekiyo Takahashi, the Japanese Minister of Finance, owned a major portion of the largest Taiwan cocaine refinery. Other evidence suggests Takahashi was acting as a front man for Mitsui, the largest company in Japan (and today probably the largest company in the world). Mitsui and the Mitsubishi Company fought a hotly contested trade battle for the rights to sell drugs in Japan-occupied China. The situation became so contentious that the Foreign Office finally had to step in and mediate. While the central government was sorting out squabbles among its drug dealers on the one hand, it was signing international drug control treaties with the other hand.

Japan signed all of the important international agreements, including The Hague International Opium Convention of 1912, the Geneva International Opium Convention of 1925, and the Convention for Limiting the Manufacture and Regulating the Distribution of Narcotic Drugs of 1931. In spite of the reporting and limitation agreements, Japan's official reports understated actual production by more than one half, permitting Japanese drugmakers to divert tons of cocaine onto the black market. Just to be on the safe side, however, Japanese drug control bureaucrats kept two sets of books. One recorded actual production. In the second set, totals were adjusted to agree with production and export quotas set by the League of Nations. Since there was no effective means of enforcement, the treaties never did much to retard the growth of the drug industry. In fact, they left a production vacuum that Japanese drugmakers were eager and ready to fill.

Chapter 11 presents data that proves creative report writing was just a part of Japan's approach to drug control. As the Japanese Army took ever tighter control of Japan's government, drug sales in occupied China were not only encouraged, but they were also regulated by the Japanese government. During the war, supplies of coca leaf were limited by Allied contention of the sea lanes, but Japan still managed to procure adequate supplies of raw opium, and to build the world's largest heroin refinery at Mukden. Raw materials were shipped to the factory by Japan's Navy, and the finished product was distributed by the Japanese Army's "special services branch".

Virtually all aspects of the Japanese government were involved, and the largest companies in Japan, not to mention individual members of the government and armed forces, profited. Yet, until three years before the bombing of Pearl Harbor, Japanese representatives attended every meeting of the League of Nations Opium Committee. The pretense stopped when Japan's Privy Counsel terminated all relations with the League of Nations on November 2, 1938.

And there, the history of the first century of the cocaine business ends. The afterword contains some additional information about cocaine production today. From the public health standpoint, the numbers are distressing. Diplomats in Europe and America were concerned about the cocaine "menace" when worldwide production amounted to less than 10 tons per year. What would they think about the more than 750 tons of refined cocaine produced in South America in 1996?

Some might say that a 7500% increase in cocaine availability is proof that the attempts at solving the problem by controlling production, either of raw materials or finished product, have not worked very well. The "supply side" strategy may work for economists, but it has not proved to be a very effective way to control drug use, at least during the first four centuries of its application.

THE AUTHOR

Dr. Karch received his bachelors degree from Brown University, did graduate work in cell biology and biophysics at Stanford, and attended Tulane University Medical School. He studied neuropathology at the Barnard Baron Institute in London, and cardiac pathology at Stanford. During the 1970s, he was a Medical Advisor for Bechtel in Southeast Asia. It was during that time when he first heard about the Javanese coca plantations. He is an Assistant Medical Examiner in San Francisco, where he consults on cases of drug-related death. His textbook, *The Pathology of Drug Abuse*, is used around the world, and is generally considered the standard reference on the subject. He and his wife, Donna, live in Berkeley, California.

ACKNOWLEDGMENTS

John Taylor, the military historian at the National Archives, gave me invaluable help. Until I met him, I had never heard of "Purple", let alone "The Red Intercepts", and I knew nothing about navigating my way through the miles of documents that Mr. Taylor seems to know by heart. In England, Cheryl Piggott, the former archivist at Kew Gardens, was kind enough to ferret out workbooks and correspondence, mostly uncatalogued, describing the early days of the coca business. Dr. J. T. Omtzigt, from the Gerechtelijk Laboratorium in the Netherlands, uncovered much of the material about the Colonial Development Bank and the Cocaine Producers Cartel, and was even kind enough to translate it, and portions of Marcel de Kort's thesis, for me. Dr. Kari Blaho, at the University of Tennessee found the material on Harvey Wiley's plan to police America's soda fountains. Thanks also to Joe Bono, of the DEA's Special Testing Lab for finding a way to get me a copy of *La Coca De Java* — no easy task since there appears to be only two in the United States. Professor Rudolph Steiner, of the Political Science Department at Stanford, who actually attended the Tokyo War Crimes Trials, and who knows more about them than anyone else, took the time to read the Japan chapters and point me in the right direction when I began to wander.

Eva Rigney helped with some of the German translations. Bill Keach, a reference librarian with the Providence Public Libraries was able to supply references, and unearth obscure statistics, faster than I ever thought possible. Without his help, this book would have taken even longer to write, and would not have been nearly as accurate. Sara Morabito read all of the versions and always had helpful comments to make, even though we do not always agree politically. Fellow 1K flyer Richard G. McCracken also provided encourgement and much appreciated help with the final manuscript.

Thanks, too, to Professor Paul Gootenberg and the Russell Sage Foundation, for inviting me to participate in their workshop on cocaine. Some of the thoughts we shared have helped make this a better book.

Hardwin Meade and Roger Winkle continue to make their own unique contributions. Thanks also to Professor Rob Sprinkle in the School of Public Affairs at the University of Maryland. Because he took the time and trouble to read and review my first attempts, this final version is much improved. And my wife, Donna, who was not only patient with me during the process, but who also helped wade through the miles of documents we reviewed. It is a good thing we both like old books.

DEDICATION

For my Uncle, Stanley Shlosman on his 85th. Governor Long may
have had the first word, but you had the last, and I'm glad. And for Sara
Morabito, the best proofreader a son-in-law could ask for.

TABLE OF CONTENTS

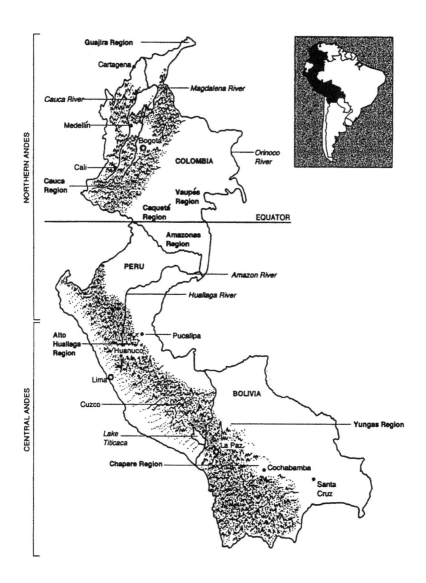

Map of primary coca-producing areas: It is based on surveys performed by the U.S.
Office of Technology Assessment in 1993, and is probably accurate, so far as it goes.
However, the map fails to indicate that the coca was once, and presumably could be
again, grown in Southeast Asia and Africa. Early in this century, Japanese drug
traffickers established large coca plantations in Taiwan, Okinawa, and Iwo Jima.

Chapter 1

THE FIRST DRUG DEALERS

The cultivation and trade of coca is a very important enterprise and of the greatest significance...

Juan Matienzo, lobbyist for the coca growers, in a letter to King Phillip II in 1566

Coca is a thing without benefit and...takes the lives of many.

From a summary of the Second Council of Lima, submitted to King Phillip II in 1569

Cash flow is not a problem for drug dealers, and they rarely worry about balancing their budgets. Most governments are not so fortunate. And, that may explain why the leaders of so many countries have willingly used drug sales to pay the bills. No one knows which government first conceived the idea, but 16th century bureaucrats, sent by Spain to administer her possessions in the New World, certainly were among the first. They balanced their budgets by taxing and selling coca leaf. To their credit, the Spanish were, at least, ambivalent about it.

Coca grows wild in the Andes, particularly in the section of mountains extending from Colombia to Bolivia. But in the early years, coca cultivation was carried out on a small scale. It was not until the time of the Incas that plantations dedicated to coca growing were finally established (2). Coca chewing was used in South America long before the first European ever set foot in the New World. Radiocarbon dating of chewing paraphernalia from Southwestern Ecuador and Northern Chile, confirms that the practice is more than 2000 years old.

Sixteenth-century Spanish historians wrote at length about Inca history, and even dealt specifically with the issue of coca production (1)(3)(4). But the picture presented by these historical accounts is confusing at best. Most of the historians who discussed coca had a stake in the business, either for or against coca consumption. The writers were, after all, Jesuit missionaries writing polemics. Depending on how they felt about the issue, their accounts were colored accordingly (5). Still,

1

there is broad agreement that under the Incas, coca growing was never the source of much revenue. The situation changed rather rapidly after the Europeans arrived.

When Pizzaro first led his armies into Peru, agricultural development was not the project foremost on his mind. But after the initial shipments of gold had been sent back to Seville, entrepreneurs and skilled workers from Europe started to arrive in large numbers. Land grants were handed out by the King, complete with laborers to work the land. Plantations were developed.

Farther south, in Brazil, sugar became the main cash crop, and an important export (6)(7). It was highly proxed in Europe and easy to ship.

In Peru, where the coca plant thrived, the quickest way to make money was by growing coca. Inca-owned coca plantations were turned over to the holders of Spanish land grants, and tax laws were revised to permit land owners to make their tax payments in coca leaves. In 1539, the Bishop of Cuzco began to tithe coca, taking one tenth of the value of each crop (5). Coca production in Peru expanded so rapidly that, within a few years, there was a temporary glut of leaf on the market and price competition forced a drop in the earnings of Spanish coca producers (1).

Before the arrival of the Spanish, coca was used sparingly, often as a reward. After the conquest, coca chewing became widespread, and coca, itself, became a medium of exchange. In mid-sixteenth century Peru, the importance of coca, both as a commodity and as a means of exchange, became even greater when silver was discovered. Huge silver deposits were discovered at Potosí (Bolivia) in 1545, and in Zacatecas (Mexico) in 1546 (8). Silver soon replaced gold as the most important export. The Crown cut taxes on silver mining revenues from 20 to 10%, in hopes of encouraging investors to commit the large sums required to develop the new mines. The incentives worked. From 1546 to 1601, the mines surrounding Potosí produced more than half of the world's silver supply. Once the silver reached Spain, it was either sold on the open market as a luxury item, or used to pay off heavy debts that had been incurred by the Crown (6). There was only one problem; the Potosí mines were located 13,780 feet above sea level.

Living conditions at Potosí were, at best, inhospitable. Nothing grew in the sparse soil and thin air. Everything required for everyday life, not to mention whatever was needed to run a mining operation, had to be imported by pack train. As often as not, the packs were carried on the backs of Indian porters. Conditions in the mines themselves were intolerably cold and damp, and the mortality rate among the workers was high. To assure a steady supply of workers at the mines, and of porters to supply the miners, the Spanish Viceroy established a system of forced labor, known as the *mita*. Up to one-seventh of the inhabitants of any given region could be called for temporary work outside of their community (9). Most of the *mita* workers were sent to the mines. The miners may have been ill-housed, poorly fed, and forced to work in dangerous conditions, but they were kept well supplied with coca leaves.

So much money could be made selling coca in Potosí that many merchants were attracted to the business. Native workers at Potosí spent nearly twice as much on coca leaves as they did on food and clothing. Coca leaves that were bought for a few pesos in Cuzco could be sold for ten to eleven pesos in Potosí (5). A street in Potosí was even named for the coca merchants. There was a coca producers lobby at the court, and its leader estimated that at least 2000 Spaniards (roughly 8% of the Europeans living in Peru) were involved in the coca trade.

Shipments from Cuzco, the coca-producing hub, to Potosí, required hundreds of pack animals and porters to carry thousands of baskets of coca leaves. According to a 16th-century history of the region, the value of one such shipment was 7500 pesos, equivalent in value to just over 34 kg of gold. The value of such purchases was placed at more than one million pesos per year (more than 4500 kg of gold) (10). In Potosí, produce and other commodities were taxed at a rate of 2%, but a much higher rate of 5% applied to coca sales. Even the Bishop of Cuzco profited handsomely by organizing coca deliveries to the mines (9).

Most, but far from all (3), of the churchmen were opposed to coca chewing. Opponents waged a long, and not entirely unsuccessful campaign against the practice; however, they did succeed in forcing a series of government reforms. The reforms were designed to protect the rights of Indians drafted to work in the mines and on the coca plantations. Unfortunately, these measures remained largely unenforced. Attempts at an outright ban on the use of coca were unsuccessful. Fearing for both the health of the Indians, and for the health of the local economy, the Marqués de Cañete, viceroy from 1555 to 1560, promulgated land reform measures designed to limit the number of acres devoted to coca cultivation. Cañete even created financial incentives to encourage the substitution of food crops for coca, but the Peruvian government's attempts were unsuccessful (5).

Spanish missionaries believed that coca use interfered with the conversion of the natives. The same charges were repeated 400 years later, by British and American missionaries, working in China at the turn of the century. The only difference was that the modern missionaries blamed opium for their lack of success (11). Some of the more extreme coca prohibitionists argued that the Spanish had promoted coca chewing in order to break the will of the people, and make them easier to subjugate (5)(12). That same refrain was also repeated 400 years later at the Tokyo War Crimes Trials, which were held at the end of World War II. The Allies charged Japan with trying to undermine the will of the Chinese by selling them heroin and cocaine (See Chapters 10 and 11). Evidence for the 16th-century accusations was just as unconvincing as the evidence brought forth in Tokyo. What appears to have transpired in both cases was that the colonial governments were short on cash. Taxes on drugs provided revenues. The Spaniards also had another reason for tolerating the drug trade; the colonial administrators, including King Phillip II, appear to have genuinely believed that without coca to chew, the silver miners would be unable to work. They believed that without coca, there would be no silver from Potosí.

Silver was the ideal export. It was compact, easy to ship, and worth enough in Europe to make the expense of the trans-Atlantic crossing worthwhile. Tobacco and sugar fulfilled the same criteria. There was sufficient demand in Europe, and sufficient output in Peru, to make exports feasible. But there was virtually no demand in Europe for coca. And the reasons that a European market for coca did not exist in the 16th and 17th centuries was that, with few exceptions, no one in Europe knew about the value of coca. Spain kept knowledge of its new territories largely to itself.

The kings of Portugal and Spain, with the blessings of Pope Alexander, divided Africa and South America. The division was decreed in a Papal bull issued after Columbus's first voyage, and later codified in the Treaty of Tordesillas, signed on June 7, 1494. Under that agreement, a north–south line was drawn 370 leagues west of Cape Verde (in other words, between 48° and 49° west of Greenwich)(7). Everything east of the line, including most of Brazil and all of Africa, belonged to Portugal. Everything to the west of that line became the exclusive property of Spain.

Neither Spain nor Portugal was particularly keen to share knowledge about, or profits from, their newly acquired possessions. In Spain, books about the New World were subject to rigid censorship not only by the King, but also by the Holy Office of the Inquisition, the Council of the Indies, and the Casa de Contratación. The latter was a semi-autonomous agency founded in 1503. It regulated all trade between Spain and its New World possessions. It licensed ships, inspected cargoes, and collected taxes. It advised the King on trade matters and also functioned as a sort of trade court. But mostly what it did, or tried to do, was ensure that Spain maintained a strict monopoly on New World trade.

New World imports and exports were funneled though Seville, and a handful of ports in South America. Vessels bound for the New World were only allowed to dock in Cartagena in New Granada (Columbia), Puerto Bello in Panama, and Vera Cruz in Mexico. Only goods made in

Spain could be imported into the New World colonies, and they had to be transported on Spanish ships. Ships from other countries were excluded (13). Jesuit missionaries and explorers documented events and discoveries in South America in great detail, down to and including coca production and how it was used. First hand, accurate accounts, were provided by Amerigo Vespucci in 1505, by G. Fernandez de Oviedo in 1535, and by Nicholas Monardes in 1565 (14). But very few people in the rest of Europe were to read their accounts. Rumors about what transpired in the New World were limited by the lack of commercial contact, and the first accounts of coca were not translated into Latin from the Spanish until 1574. The first English translation appeared three years later.

Actually, the trade and knowledge embargo was never as strict as the Spanish Crown would have preferred, and it was almost non-existent in the Portuguese-held territories. As commerce developed in the New World, Spain was unable to supply booming New World colonies with the goods that were needed. Because Spanish law prevented other countries from trading with New World colonies, Spanish merchants frequently found themselves acting as illegal intermediaries. In order to circumvent the Casa de Contratación, trading houses in Seville and Cadiz would, for a fee, put their names on goods made by producers in France, Italy, and England. The goods were then placed on Spanish ships and transported to the New World as if they had been produced in Spain (13).

On the opposite side of the Atlantic, traffic in contraband flourished. Port officials were often corrupt, and ships from England, France, and the Netherlands began to call at ports all along the Pacific coast of South America. Buenos Aires became an unofficial free trade zone. European goods shipped to Buenos Aires, and carted into Peru, avoided Casa de Contratación restrictions and taxes. Dutch merchants had been the main source of funding for Brazil's sugar industry (6), and almost from the very beginning, significant numbers of Dutchmen and non-Spanish Europeans lived in Buenos Aires. These merchants had firsthand knowledge of developments in the New World, and they took this knowledge back to Europe with them.

Spain's commercial rivals also set up shop in the Caribbean - Jamaica and Curacao - trading European manufactured goods for Peruvian gold and silver. Such incursions were, of course, resisted by the Spanish (7). Holland proved to be the main conduit through which stories about coca managed to make their way back to Europe. In 1630, the Dutch seized Pernambuco, a rich sugar growing region on Brazil's northeast coast. Even though the Portuguese eventually reclaimed Pernambuco, for 24 years the Dutch and the Dutch West India Company maintained a foothold in the New World. Dutch technicians learned enough about sugar cane to establish a Dutch-owned sugar industry in the Caribbean (15). From 1637 to 1644, the Dutch governor in occupied Brazil, Count Johan Maurits of Nassau-Siegen, sent a steady supply of New World plants and animals for further study (16). Maurits also commissioned several artists and scientists to record and catalog the exotic people, animals, and plants living in the area. They produced an extraordinary body of art that is still impressive today.

The University at Leiden, near Amsterdam, was an indirect beneficiary of the new Dutch colony at Pernambuco. The university was well known for its botanical garden (17), and also for the famous botanists who created and managed the garden. European scholars had their first chance to read about New World plants only after Monardes' text on coca, and other medicinal plants of the New World, was annotated and translated into Latin. The translation appeared in 1574. It was translated by the first director of Leiden's botanical garden, Charles de L'Écluse (known to botanists by his Latinized name, Clasius). In 1582, eight years after publishing his translation of Monardes' book, L'Écluse translated another book on Peruvian medicinal plants. This book had been written by the Jesuit Cristóbal Acosta. The same year that L'Écluse published the Acosta translation, he published *Aliquot notae in garciae aromatum historiam*, a book based on notes about the western coast of America which had been written by Francis Drake.

During the early 1560s, L'Écluse had traveled extensively in Spain, which, no doubt, was where he obtained the material he later translated(18). Whether Count Maurits, or any of the other Dutch merchants ever sent back samples of coca, or whether L'Écluse ever saw an actual coca leaf, is not known. If he did, they could not have been from living plants, since the first heated greenhouses, necessary for growing tropical plants, were not installed at Leiden until 1709 (17).

Monardes' book was translated into several European languages. An Italian version, translated by Annibale Briganti, appeared in Venice in 1576. An English translation of Monardes' book was first published in London the following year (19). The translation was produced by John Frampton, a British merchant who had lived and worked in Spain. Frampton had taken up translation as a hobby after his retirement, and translated Marco Polo's book into English just two years after completing the Monardes' project. Even though the Frampton's translation of Monardes' book appears to have been widely read, the topic of coca evoked little interest.

More than 80 years elapsed between the time that Frampton first translated Monardes' book, and the first independent mention of coca in the English literature. This occurred when the poet, Abraham Cowley (1616-1667), wrote a poem about coca leaf. Cowley, whose poetry is not as well remembered as that of his famous contemporary, John Milton, was mainly a dramatist and satirist. He studied medicine at Oxford and, along with his friend, Christopher Wren, helped found the British Royal Society. In all probability, Cowley was also a spy for the Royalists opposing Cromwell. He was a secretary to the secretary of Queen Henrietta Maria, Lord Jermyn. Cowley spent 12 years living with the exiled Queen in Paris, translating coded messages, and accompanying Lord Jermyn on "dangerous journeys (20)."

Cowley might have gained his knowledge of coca in either England or France, but since French bankers and merchants were already underwriting trade ventures in the New World, the latter seems more likely. Cowley's poem, "A Legend of Coca," appeared in a collection of poems about plants that was published in 1662 (*A. Covleii Plantarum Libri Duo*). The last paragraph of the poem begins *"Nor Coca only useful art at Home, A famous Merchandize thou art become..."* But none of the "merchandise" made it back to Europe. A few people may have known about the plant, but there was hardly enough demand to warrant large scale exports. Even if demand had been great, coca was so popular in Peru there would have been little excess leaf to export.

If there had been ample leaf for export, shipping it would have been a problem. Coca leaf does not travel well. Unless considerable care was taken, the cocaine content of the dried leaves brought back by travelers was likely to have been nil. Europeans who had heard of the magical leaves would, more than likely, have been disappointed if they had actually had the chance to have chewed some of the much traveled leaves. That probably accounts for Herman Boerhaave's (1668-1738) experiences with coca. Boerhaave was placed in charge of Leiden's "physik" garden in 1709, exactly 100 years after the death of its founder, L'Écluse, in 1609 (17).

Boerhaave, like L'Écluse before him, and the other famous botanists of the 16th and 17th centuries, was a physician as well as a botanist. Physicians at that time had to be botanists because plants constituted the raw materials used to produce medications. Boerhaave was certainly the most famous and respected physician of his time, and his writings prove that he had an extensive knowledge of New World plants, including Peruvian Bark (quinine) and coca (21). How much of that knowledge came from reading L'Écluse's translations of Monardes and Acosta, how much came from knowledge gained in correspondence with other botanists such as Linneaus, and how much came from the examination of real specimens, is hard to say. Boerhaave made mention of coca in a materia medica, *Institutiones Medicae*, published in 1708, but not in any of his later writings (21). Coca is not listed in his materia medica published in 1755 (22), and is not included in the list of his personal collection of plants that was auctioned after his death (17). Boerhaave's apparent loss of interest in the subject suggests that coca was not grown in Leiden, and that adequate supplies were either unavailable or, more likely, of poor quality and ineffective.

Linneaus and other French scientists finally got their chance to see real coca plants, but only after Boerhaave had died. The French Academy of Science sponsored an expedition to the New World in 1735 (23). The expedition was prompted by a debate between Isaac Newton and Jacques Cassini. Newton maintained that the earth was an oblate spheroid (slightly flattened at the poles), and Cassini, the Royal Astronomer of France, maintained that the earth was a prolate spheroid (slightly constricted at the equator). The debate soon came to be perceived as a matter of national honor. In 1734, in order to settle the debate once and for all, the French Academy decided to send simultaneous expeditions to the Arctic and the equator. The meridian of an arc of a degree of latitude was to be measured at both locations. If Newton's theory was correct, an arc of a degree of latitude should be slightly longer in the Arctic (24). By that time, Spain's grip on its new territories had loosened somewhat, and Phillip V, in spite of vocal objections from the Council of the Indies, decided that, after 250 years, it would allow the French to visit the Andes. But just to be on the safe side, he sent along two Spanish Naval officers to act as chaperones. He also sent messages to local officials in Peru advising them to be helpful, but not overly informative (*"poner los ojos en la Tierra"*) to the visitors.

The Academy's expedition to the equator sailed on May 16, 1735. It was headed by Charles-Marie de La Condamine, a mathematician and friend of Voltaire, himself an avid supporter of Newton's theories. Crew members included a watchmaker, a draftsman, a mathematician, the nephew of the treasurer of the Academy (who appears to have had no scientific qualifications) and botanist Joseph de Jussieu (1704-1779). de Jussieu was one of a family of French botanists and physicians and a cousin to Antoine de Jussieu, member of the same family, and an even better known botanist. Joseph spent 36 years in Peru. Unfortunately, the specimens he collected, including samples of the coca plant, never made it back to Europe. According to one account, the samples that de Jussieu had collected for La Condamine were packed in crates, and the crates taken to the pier to await loading. Thieves, thinking that the crates contained something valuable, broke into them. When they found only plants, they were so angry they tossed the crates into the water, where they promptly sank. de Jussieu did not take the loss at all well and apparently suffered a nervous breakdown. He must have recovered at some point, however, because in 1750 he successfully shipped samples of coca back to his uncle, Antoine (25). Along with the dried coca plants, de Jussieu also sent seeds of fragrant heliotrope which, because of its intense fragrance, quickly became popular in Europe (26)(27).

La Condamine was much more successful. In March of 1743, he made his measurements. But before he returned to France, La Condamine and Pedro Maldonado navigated the length of the Amazon in a small boat. The trip to Pará, on the Atlantic, took four months, long enough for La Condamine to acquire samples of rubber and quinine, which he carried home with him. La Condamine arrived back in Paris in the spring of 1745, 10 years after he departed.

The coca plants sent by de Jussieu, after being examined by Antoine, were donated to the Museum of Natural History in Paris, where they were examined by Carl von Linnaeus, and, subsequently by Lamarck. The plant illustrated in Lamarck's encyclopedia, which was published in 1786, appears in every way to be identical to other plants which eventually found their way to England. Pictures of this plant eventually appeared in a British publication, giving the English public its first glimpse of the coca plant. While there is no doubt that the plant illustrated in the English journal and the plant illustrated by Lamarck were the same plant, it is now clear that that particular variety of coca plant was not the variety of coca plant commonly chewed by the Indians. Nor was it the same variety commonly sold by exporters (28). This discrepancy proved to be a major factor in the development of the cocaine industry.

TAB. XXI.

Erythroxylon Coca.

<u>Coca leaves</u>: After hearing rumors about coca for several centuries, Englishmen finally got to see an accurate rendering in 1835. This illustration was drawn by Sir William Hooker, then the Director of Kew Gardens. Hooker's drawing appeared in the *Companion to the Botanical Magazine* (Volume I:161-175, 1835). It accompanied Hooker's translation of a German naturalist's account of life on the Amazon. For his model, Hooker used a specimen collected in the neighborhood of Chincheros, Peru. It had been sent back to Kew by a botanist named James Matthews. It later became apparent that this was not the best variety for producing cocaine.

Chapter 2

BOTANISTS AND PEDESTRIANS

Surely it is a thyung of greate consideration, to see how the Indians are so desirous to bee deprived of their wittes, and be without understanding.

Nicolas Monardes, writing of coca, circa 1565 (1)

The first European entrepreneurs to appreciate coca's commercial potential were the managers of The Royal Botanical Gardens at Kew. Known today mainly for its collections of exotic flowers, the gardens at Kew were once an important resource for the economic exploitation of New World discoveries. Located on the south bank of the Thames River in Surrey, six miles by road west—southwest of Hyde Park Corner, the first Kew Gardens occupied only 11 acres. It was laid out by Lord Capel of Tewkesbury in 1721. Capel's Gardens consisted of little more than some pretty ornamental plants and a few vegetables for the Tewkesbury kitchen. The gardens were later enlarged by the Princess Dowager, widow of Frederick, Prince of Wales. The Princess had an interest in pretty plants, but not particularly in the science of botany. King George III, however, had different plans for the garden (2).

George III may have had periods of "madness", but he was sane enough to accept advice from his friend, Sir Joseph Banks, the botanist who accompanied Captain Cook on his first voyage. Banks served for 42 years as the President of the Royal Society, and it was obvious to Banks that some of the plants being discovered in the new colonies were worth money. Banks convinced King George III to make Kew Gardens a repository for exotic new plant life from the colonies, and to use Kew as a training center for young botanists, who could then go out and collect more new specimens. The King agreed. One of the botanists selected had the misfortune to accompany Captain Bligh, and to die from exposure when Bligh and his party were set adrift in a long boat. But, those who did survive brought thousands of plants back to England. Before the economic potential of any of these new plants could really be exploited, work on the Gardens abruptly halted. Kew's fortunes and England's economy both suffered setbacks when King George III died in January 1820. Sir Banks died in June of the same year. Succeeding administrators did not share the visions of either man. (2)(3).

Without Bank's and the King's support, very little happened at Kew Gardens until 1841. In that year, a government-appointed committee recommended that the original plans for Kew Gardens, as envisioned by Banks and King George, be revived. Sir William Hooker (1785-1865) was appointed as director of the gardens. Hooker immediately ordered the construction of a giant new herbarium and, at the same time, initiated an exhaustive survey of plant life across the English Empire. Under Hooker's leadership, Kew Gardens expanded to occupy over 300 acres. Hooker sent Kew-trained botanists and gardeners around the world, and he contracted with other explorers who catalogued and sent back to England any newly discovered plants that looked as if they might have some value. Kew scientists, under Hooker's leadership, were the real inventors of "economic botany". Two of the botanists associated with Hooker, Richard Spruce (1817-1893) and Clement Markham (1830-1916), succeeded in smuggling cinchona plants (the source of quinine) out of South America, and in establishing new cinchona plantations in occupied India. On later trips, they supplied Kew Gardens with coca seedlings (4).

Markham went to Peru in 1860 and brought living cinchona plants back to Kew. After allowing the plants to recover for a few months, Markham took the seedlings to India, where they were planted at Nilghiri Hills, a steep plateau in Southwest Madras which has average heights of over 6,500 feet. Today, the area consists mostly of coffee and tea plantations, but when Markham first planted his cinchona plants, little else was growing there. Hooker was concerned that the species of cinchona chosen by Markham might not be hardy enough to survive in India. Hooker wrote to Richard Spruce, who was in the lower Amazon gathering plants. Hooker asked Spruce to travel to Ecuador and obtain an additional supply of cinchona seeds. Hooker sent Robert Mackenzie Cross, a Kew gardener, to assist Spruce in this task.

In Ecuador, the local residents jealously guarded their cinchona trees. So, it was at some risk to Spruce's life that he managed to gather enough cuttings to start a garden. With a civil war raging around them, Spruce and Cross retreated to a remote area in the foothills, planted the cuttings, and patiently waited for more than a year until they flowered and produced seeds. More than 100,000 seeds were accumulated over the course of a year. Getting the seeds back to the coast, and on board a ship, was problematic. The final leg of the saga involved a three-day whitewater rafting trip downriver to Guayaquil. Two days later, Cross, with the cinchona seeds, boarded a ship for England, and then sailed on to India. Spruce went back to plant collecting in the Amazon. Before Spruce's success, the Bengal government had been paying £40,000 per year for imported quinine. By 1893, quinine could be purchased for pennies at any post office in Bengal (4).

Given Kew's success with cinchona, it was only natural to suppose that the same process could be repeated with coca. But early attempts were hampered by a lack of knowledge about the plant. Until the mid-1800s, the main reference was Nicholas B. Monardes' work on New World plants (5)(6).

The Latin version of Monardes' text was never a best seller, but in 1582 a London merchant named John Frampton translated it into English (7). Frampton retitled it "Joyfulle news out of the new founde worlde, wherein is declared the virtues of herbs, treez, oyales, plantes and stones." Frampton's version, possibly because of its catchy title, became the 16th-century equivalent of a best seller. The translation of Monardes' book contained accurate descriptions of the plant, and the way the leaves of the plant were used. Monardes also commented on coca's potential toxicity. Monardes even mused about why people would want to use the drug in the first place. He wrote, "*Surely it is a thyung of greate consideration, to see how the Indians are so desirous to bee deprived of their wittes, and be without understanding.*" Frampton's translation even contained illustrations. Some of the wood cuts were more detailed than Monardes' original drawings, suggesting that Frampton truly knew his botany (1).

The first picture to appear in the popular English press was drawn by Sir William Hooker. It appeared in the *Companion to the Botanical Magazine* for 1836, a semi-official publication of Kew Gardens, which was edited by Hooker. For his model, Hooker used a specimen that had been sent back to Kew by a botanist named James Matthews. According to Matthews, the plant had been collected in the neighborhood of Chincheros, Peru, an area that lies about halfway between Cuzco in the south and Lima in the north (8).

Seeds from the commercial variety of coca arrived at Kew in 1869. They were collected from somewhere in the Huánuco Valley area just to the south of Cuzco, Peru, a location nearly 200 miles from where the first Kew specimens had been collected. These first seeds to arrive at Kew were continuously cultivated there for at least 40 years. The plants that grew from the seeds were identical in appearance to specimens collected by Kew botanists during the 1850s in the Valley of the Magdalena River in Colombia (then known as New Granada), more than 2000 miles north of where de Jussieu's and Kew's first specimens were found. Hence the title, E. coca Novo Granatense (9).

Officials at Kew shipped seeds from these plants to botanical research stations around the British Empire. Samples were sent to India,

Africa, Ceylon, Malaya, and even Jamaica (10)(13). But they were never sent to Java, which was just as well for the Dutch growers. The variety distributed from Kew contained only a fraction of the cocaine found in the variety grown in Java (14)(16). The sources for the Java variety have never been clearly identified. We do know, though, that the seeds, themselves, were obtained from Herman Linden and Company in Ghent, Belgium. However, the trail ends there (16). Published descriptions of the plants grown in Java match those of specimens collected by Richard Spruce in 1854, before he was dispatched to Ecuador to collect cinchona. At the time, Spruce was collecting specimens along the banks of the Rio Negro River, hundreds of miles from where the variety grown at Kew was collected, and thousands of miles from where the de Jussieu specimens were originally collected (17). Whatever the origin of the Java seedlings, when processed correctly, they were capable of yielding more than twice as much cocaine as leaves cultivated in South America, or leaves grown at any of Kew's branches in English colonies around the world. More than any other single factor, the high cocaine content of the Java plant made possible the later development of Japan's illegal drug trade.

The active principle of coca leaves is, of course, cocaine. But for many years, European scientists were in no position to determine that because there was just not enough leaf to analyze. This was certainly the case at Kew, where only a handful of coca plants were grown, and also in the rest of Europe where coca leaf was even less available. Given the state of analytic chemistry in the mid-1800s, many pounds of dried leaves were needed in order to carry out any type of successful analysis. The relative shortage of raw material probably explains why initial advances in the field of cocaine chemistry were made in Germany, and not in England. German chemists had an edge because German naturalists supplied them with enough coca leaf to analyze.

One of the most famous German naturalists was Johan von Tschudi. von Tschudi made several trips to Peru (18). His primary interest was the classification of animal life, but he also recorded observations on cinchona, balsam, and coca. von Tschudi wrote extensively about his travels. One of his books contains many anecdotes about coca use in the Andes. His general impression was that coca use "may even be very conducive to health", but one anecdote in particular seems to have struck a responsive cord among Europeans. In 1857, at the completion of one of his trips, just before he was to return to Germany, von Tschudi visited Enrique Pizzi, a professor of chemistry and pharmacology at the University of La Paz. von Tschudi convinced Pizzi to try isolating coca's active principle. Pizzi claimed he had succeeded, and gave von Tschudi a sample to take home with him (19)(20).

When von Tschudi got back to Göttingen, he immediately went to visit his friend, Fredrich Wöhler, chairman of the Chemistry Department at Göttingen. Wöhler (1800-1882) was not just any ordinary organic chemist. He and his sometime friend and collaborator, Justus von Liebig, practically laid the foundations of modern organic chemistry. In 1825, when he was a chemistry instructor at the Berlin Trade School, Wöhler synthesized urea, the first organic compound to be prepared from inorganic materials. Wöhler was appointed chairman of chemistry at Göttingen in 1836, and remained there for the rest of his career. He trained literally thousands of students, and made the University of Göttingen a major center for the study of chemistry. It was only natural that von Tschudi should take Professor Wöhler the sample to analyze (21).

Wöhler gave the sample to his graduate student, Albert Niemann, who analyzed it, and found it contained only gypsum. It remains an unanswered question whether Pizzi or Niemann was inept, but obviously someone made a mistake. Thirty years after the mixup, Pizzi's successor, Clemente Torretti, wrote a letter to the *American Druggist* magazine, claiming that he had found the original isolates prepared by Pizzi. Torretti had tested them, and found that they contained cocaine (19). By that time, of course, Niemann had already published a technique for the isolation of cocaine from coca leaf (20).

A few months later, Wöhler got another chance to find the active principle in coca when Austrian Arch Duke Ferdinand decided to send the frigate Novara on an around-the-world-cruise. Having men-of-war circumnavigate the globe was something of a craze during the mid-1800s, and Austria was not immune. However, the voyage of the Novara was more than an expensive way to show the colors; it was also a training cruise for young naval officers, and a scientific mission to relatively unexplored regions of South America and the Pacific. The peaceful intent of the voyage is clear from the way that the six-year-old, 165 foot, 2600 ton, Novara had been refitted. One third of the cannons were removed, the ship's gun room was converted into a library and reading room, and more staterooms were added. A distilling apparatus, manufactured by Rocher et Nantes was fixed on the gun deck. It could supply enough drinking water, so it was unnecessary to store large amounts of water. Having so much fresh water was an unheard of luxury for ships of the line, and so was the installation of crew showers on the deck and forecastle (22).

The German Imperial Academy of Science nominated two of the crew members while the Navy selected the remainder of the scientific team. In addition to the naval cadets, the crew included a botanist, a zoologist, an artist, and a "flower gatherer". Carl von Scherzer (1821-

1903) was one of those selected by the Imperial Academy. Just before the Novara sailed for Trieste on March 15, 1857, Wöhler contacted von Scherzer and asked for his help. If Wöhler was ever going to identify the active principle of coca, he needed a real supply of coca leaves, not just a handful. Wöhler estimated that he would need at least 50 or 60 pounds of leaf. von Scherzer promised he would try. He did, and was successful.

The Novara was recalled to Austria before it could reach Peru, so von Scherzer left the expedition at Valparaiso, on Chile's northern coast, and made his own way north to Lima. He wrote an account of his travels, but his book makes no mention of where he purchased the coca leaves. However, he did manage to acquire 60 pounds of leaves. von Scherzer packed half of the leaves in his luggage and made arrangements with two Austrian merchants living in Lima to forward the rest of them. von Scherzer then continued his journey overland to Panama, where he booked passage home. He delivered the leaves to Wöhler in September of 1859. Wöhler, again, gave them to Albert Niemann, his student, to analyze.

The analysis proved to be the basis for Niemann's doctoral thesis, which he successfully defended in 1860, the same year that Abraham Lincoln was elected president of the United States. Other than the fact that Niemann earned his doctorate by isolating cocaine from coca leaves, and that he carried out the work under Wöhler's guidance, not very much is known about Albert Niemann (1834-1861). His thesis was reprinted in a number of journals. Americans were first able to read it in 1861, when the *American Journal of Pharmacy* had it translated, and printed an abridged version.

Niemann began his thesis by acknowledging von Scherzer's efforts. He then went on to discuss the similarity of coca to other alkaloid stimulants such as coffee, tea, and tobacco. He pointed out that all of these chemicals appear to be used for roughly the same purpose — stimulants. Niemann reviewed the researches of earlier workers, including the much maligned Enrique Pizzi of La Paz, and then described the techniques he had used to isolate a compound he called cocaina. Except for the scale of their operations, the method devised by Niemann was not very different from the process still used today by clandestine chemists in the jungles of Peru. Neimann did not live to enjoy his discoveries. He died shortly after his thesis was published. There is nothing in the records to indicate the cause.

Note: Alcohol is relatively expensive and difficult to come by, so today's illegal refiners often substitute gasoline where Niemann used alcohol. The methodology is otherwise the same. Leaves are soaked in a dilute solution of water and strong alkali, usually lime, for three or four days. An organic solvent, gasoline, or kerosene, or even acetone, depending on availability, is then added to the mixture. Separation of cocaine from this mixture is based on the fact that solvents do not mix with water, and the fact that the cocaine molecule contains nitrogen, but many of the other components found in the leaf do not. When acid is added to the mixture, the nitrogen-containing molecules dissolve in the solvent. In order to separate cocaine from all of the other compounds in the leaf, all that needs to be done is to throw away the spent leaves, remove the organic solvent that has floated to the top, and add some alkali (more lime). Crude cocaine will fall to the bottom of the solution, after which it is collected and dried in the sun (23).

Niemann's discovery was greeted with modest enthusiasm, but 10 years went by before anyone even bothered to confirm his observation that cocaine crystals made the tongue numb (24), and almost a quarter of a century elapsed before Koller discovered that cocaine was an effective local anesthetic. The lack of interest is more apparent than real. Cocaine was simply not available. Very little leaf was being imported into Europe, and the technique devised by Niemann was, for those days, both cumbersome and unreliable. Physicians who wanted to experiment with coca leaves, or with refined cocaine, were never entirely sure what they were actually administering. Products billed as cocaine were, not infrequently, found to be inert. Leaves, claimed to be fresh from Peru, had often spent so much time in transit they contained too little cocaine to matter.

But other factors, still undefined, must have been involved. Had there been a demand for cocaine, chemists and drug manufacturers would have supplied it. Merck began producing cocaine just 18 months after Niemann published his method for extracting it from coca, but Merck's average production amounted to less than one quarter of a pound per year. Merck chemists certainly could have produced more, but there was simply no demand. That all changed when cocaine's local anesthetic properties were discovered. Less than two years after Koller's announcement that the use of cocaine drops permitted painless eye surgery, Merck was manufacturing cocaine by the ton (25).

For nearly a quarter of a century, from 1860 when Niemann's thesis was published, until Koller's paper was read at the Ophthalmology Congress at Heidelberg in 1884, coca and cocaine remained curiosities. What little interest there was centered almost entirely on coca's alleged abilities to enhance performance, increase endurance, and act as a "substance d'épargne", an agent that would allow individuals to go without food (26). This preoccupation with strength and endurance was partly the result of press coverage; stories about coca-induced feats of strength and endurance made fascinating reading. But it was also due to the teachings of one particular scientist: Justus von Liebig (1803–1874).

von Liebig was a brilliant chemist, born in Darmstadt, Germany, just after the turn of the century. He became Chairman of the Chemistry Department in Munich in 1852, as well as President of the German Imperial Academy of Sciences. von Liebig was the author of at least 317 separate papers and books, the founder of the *Annals of Chemistry*, and the editor of an encyclopedia of chemistry. Perhaps, more importantly, he was the first famous entrepreneur scientist. He exploited his reputation, and the growing respect with which the public viewed science, to make money. von Liebig invented the bouillon cube (27).

von Liebig believed, quite incorrectly, that the energy required for muscles to contract was produced by oxidizing (burning up) portions of the muscle itself. In order to maintain the ability to work, destroyed muscle had to be constantly replenished. He was convinced that the only way to do that was to take in nitrogen-containing compounds in amounts equal to the amount destroyed. Carbohydrates and fats, he thought, were only used to generate heat and to support respiration. In 1847, von Liebig published a paper describing the components of a rational diet (28). One component was a meat extract, called extractum carnis. It amounted to little more than what we today call bouillon. Bouillon was soon being sold as a cure-all under the name, "Liebig's extract of meat". Advertisements made outrageous claims for the product, and von Liebig, who got a percentage of sales for lending his name to the product, made an outrageous amount of money.

Probably as a result of his closeness with Wöhler, von Liebig knew about coca and was interested in its effects, to the extent that he gave some to his students and studied the effects it had on them (29). Given the rumors about coca's effects on performance, Liebig must have been fascinated by the possibilities, and would certainly have communicated this interest to his students. By the late 1870s, other physiologists, including many of his own students, began to reject von Liebig's theory.

But even though von Liebig's theories about performance were in decline, people still believed that particular substances could have a profound and immediate effect on performance. The scientific community and the popular press remained fascinated with coca's effects on strength and endurance. It is hardly surprising then, that the first reported case of sports "doping" involved athletes chewing coca leaves. The first known athlete to cheat by using drugs was an American.

During the latter part of the 19th century, race walking was a popular sport in England and the United States. During most of the 1870s, the reigning champion was Edward P. Weston, an American. In 1876, Weston sailed to England to challenge England's race walking champion. The challenge took the form of a 24-hour, 115-mile, ultra marathon. The race began on the evening of February 8, 1876, at the

Royal Agricultural Hall on Liverpool Road in Islington, a London suburb.

Weston was described as a "spare" man, 37-years-old, 5 feet 7.5 inches high, and weighing "a little under" 140 pounds. Weston's English opponent was a faster walker, but lacked Weston's endurance. Foot pain caused the Englishman to quit 14 hours into the race after he had covered only 65.5 miles. When examined immediately afterwards, he did not look well. His pulse and temperature were elevated, his blood pressure was too low, and his feet were extensively blistered.

Weston, however, kept walking through the heat of the poorly ventilated arena, in spite of foot blisters that caused him to pause briefly after 17 hours. After a short rest, he continued walking until the full 24 hours had elapsed, and he had covered 109.5 miles. During the race, Weston fortified himself with liquids, primarily tea and coffee, along with egg yolks and Liebig extract (30). He also chewed coca leaf during much of the race. When reporters found out that Weston had been chewing coca leaf, it caused something of a furor (31). The results of the race, however, were never disputed. In a letter to the *British Medical Journal*, Weston admitted he had been using coca but said that he did not believe it had helped him. In fact, he claimed, it made him sleepy (32).

The connection between coca and performance was so widely accepted that race walkers still relied on coca 10 years after Weston's victory. In 1885, Dr. Palmer, a coca advocate from Louisville, Kentucky, published a description of another race. This race involved six female "pedestrianists" who were to run 350 miles in seven days (33). Dr. Palmer stopped in on Day Six of the race and noticed one contestant, a 120-pound 17-year-old woman named "L.C.", who appeared to be imminently in danger of collapse. Palmer administered a glass of Fraser's Wine of Coca, which the woman drank stating that it tasted "elegant". She did not win the race, but she did finish the 350 miles in just under seven days, in spite of the fact that someone had stolen her bottle of coca wine, and that she had fallen down and sprained her ankle.

Weston and the women "pedestrianists" were neither the first, the only, nor the most prominent, to study coca's effects on performance. Sir Robert Christison, president of the Scottish Medical Association and Professor of Materia Medica at Edinburgh (a combination of medicinal chemistry and botany) experimented on some of his students in 1870, and on himself in 1875. In the first set of experiments, Christison observed that students who drank coca extract reported increased feelings of well being. A second set of experiments was conducted with leaves that one of his students, Alexander Bennett, had obtained in Paris (see below). In the first experiment, Christison gave coca extracts to students who then took 20- to 30-mile hikes; the students reported they felt no fatigue. Christison was so enthused with these results that on September 15, 1875 he climbed Ben Vorlich, a small (3,224 feet) mountain in Scotland. The climb presented no challenge, and Christison enjoyed himself so much that he increased the dose of coca and repeated the climb again eight days later (34). While the height of Ben Vorlich is not all that impressive, Christison's age, 78 years, was. Similar reports were published by other researchers that same year (35).

As the reports by Christison and the other researchers clearly demonstrated, coca was still a novelty in the 1870s. For whatever reason, very little coca made its way to either England, or to the United States. Coca's scarcity, especially in England, is evident from the medical literature. In 1874, a Doctor Sieveking wrote to the *British Medical Journal* that "I have never had the good fortune to meet with any medical man who had a personal acquaintance with it (coca)", but he went on to add that he expected it would prove to be "a very valuable restorative (36)." Sieveking's letter prompted responses from several pharmacists saying that they carried the leaves (37), and others wrote to the journal confirming Sieveking's impressions (38).

Coca was so scarce it was hardly ever mentioned in the medical literature, which suggests it was very scarce indeed. (Today, a report describing a patient who died of a cocaine-related heart attack would almost automatically be rejected by medical journals because cocaine-related heart attacks are so common that another anecdotal report would not be considered worth publishing. However, the same report, had it been submitted in 1975, would surely have been accepted. Cocaine-related heart attacks were rare then, and, therefore, newsworthy.) By definition, anecdotal medical reports are about uncommon events. In the English literature, at least, from the time of Niemann's discovery, until the time of Koller's announcements, all of the reports were anecdotal.

In 1873, Alexander Bennett published his doctoral thesis in the *Edinburgh Medical Journal*. He compared the effects of cocaine, caffeine, and other alkaloids on experimental animals. Bennett complained that in order to find the coca leaves to make cocaine he had to go to Paris. "In this country," he wrote, "the coca leaves are rare, and even in Paris, where they can be obtained, they are very expensive (39)." In 1876, Allan Hamilton, a physician working at a hospital for neurological disease in New York, wrote a letter to the *British Medical Journal*, and described how he felt after he drank an extract of coca leaves. Hamilton was only able to experiment on himself because someone had given him a pound of dried coca leaf as a gift (40).

In 1876, in a speech given before the Botanical Society of Edinburgh, Sir Robert Christison, then president of the Scottish Medical Association, outlined the history of coca and described some of the experiments he had done in 1870. The 1870 experiments used coca leaf which had been sent to Christison by a London merchant six years earlier. Even in 1876, Christison stated, "Cuca is not yet a regular commercial article in this country (34)." Why was coca leaf available in Paris, and not in London? Surprisingly, the explanation had little to do with trends in scientific research. Rather, it was the result of financial considerations, and the efforts of a self-promoting pharmacist manufacturer named Angelo Mariani.

Newspaper advertisment for Vin Mariani: Angelo Mariani was a master at self-promotion, and it is difficult to decide for which of his two great inventions he should be remembered: the popularization of coca wine, or the invention of the modern publicity campaign. *Vin Mariani* was immensely popular. Mariani would send cases of free wine to celebrities, who would then write thank-you notes, or even endorsements which Mariani collected and published. Thomas Edison and Sarah Bernhardt wrote endorsements, as did Pope Leo, III. President William McKinley's secretary, John Addison Porter, wrote Mariani to thank him. Porter assured Mariani that the wine would be used whenever the occasion required. This advertisement, with a picture of the Pope, appeared in a London newspaper in 1899.

Chapter 3

CELEBRITY DRUG ENDORSEMENTS

The literature of cocaine is more voluminous than valuable, more expectant than exact.

J.T. Brown, 1886 (1)

Question: What is your opinion of coca leaf? from J.K. of Visalia, California

Answer: The virtues of coca leaves have probably been exaggerated; but in our opinion, nevertheless, they possess very remarkable properties... Although we have had no personal experience, we consider the reports in their favor sufficient to warrant giving them a trial...

From a letter to the editor of the *Druggists Circular and Chemical Gazette*, September 1876 (2)

In the 1880s, the name most often associated with coca, at least as far as the public was concerned, belonged neither to Sigmund Freud nor Karl Koller, the inventor of local anesthesia. The name that most people thought of was that of Angelo Mariani, and his coca-based wine, Vin Mariani. Mariani was a Corsican, born at Pero-Casevecchie in 1838. He died in 1914 at his villa in Saint-Raphaél, outside of Paris. The history of Mariani's early years is vague, made more vague by Mariani's penchant for self-promoting publicity. It can be said, with reasonable certainty, that Mariani worked as an apprentice pharmacist in Paris at Chantrels, a pharmacy located on the Rue de Clichy. Sometime during his apprenticeship years, Mariani moved to another pharmacy in Saint Germain. He always claimed that he was a certified pharmacist, and his death certificate supports his assertions. But, there is no record that he ever passed his certification examinations (3).

Mariani created coca wine while working as an assistant at Chantrels in late 1868 or early 1869. At Chantrels, one of his assigned duties was to assist in the preparation of "wine tonics". At the time, many medications were prescribed in the form of wine mixtures. Many of the drugs, then popular, were foul tasting, and the wine made drugs more palatable. As a practical matter, most of the medications were dissolved in alcohol, rather than in water. A French pharmacopoeia, which was published in 1844, listed 100 medicinal wines. By 1884, 40 years later, that number had grown to 154. Mariani had read about the miraculous properties of the coca leaf, and was surprised that no one had yet conceived the idea of combining coca with wine. When a famous actress of the Comédie-Francaise came to Chantrels complaining of depression, Mariani took it upon himself to recommend a coca wine. The depressed actress improved rapidly and soon was recommending Mariani's mixture to her friends. At some point, and it is not exactly clear when, Mariani decided to leave the pharmacy and go into business for himself. By 1870, Vin Mariani was offered for sale throughout France. Mariani's Paris office was located at 41 Boulevard Haussmann. As sales increased, he opened additional branch offices, including one in London and another in New York City.

Most of what Mariani knew about coca he probably learned from his cousin, Charles Fauvel. Fauvel was born in Amiens, France, in 1830, and trained in medicine. Fauvel became one of the era's first ear, nose, and throat specialists. He had a celebrity practice, and treated many famous singers and opera stars. One of the reasons for Fauvel's success was the good results he achieved with his patients. And the reason his results were so good was that he had found a way to effectively anesthetize the throat. With adequate anesthesia, it became possible to do more thorough examinations and perform more extensive surgical procedures.

Although Koller quite justly received credit for discovering that cocaine drops could anesthetize the eye, Fauvel observed, almost a quarter of a century earlier, that applying a tincture of coca (an alcohol solution in which coca leaves had been dissolved) made painless throat surgery possible. Surgeons came from the United States and other countries to study Fauvel's techniques. Freud gave Fauvel due credit when he wrote his famous paper, *On Coca*, which included a history of cocaine use. For some reason, Fauvel did not receive much recognition but Mariani, largely by virtue of his own efforts, became famous. Mariani was a master at self-promotion, and it is difficult to decide for which of his two great inventions he should be remembered: the discovery of coca wine, or the invention of the modern publicity campaign.

Liebig may have been the first famous scientist to make money by promoting his own product line, but Mariani was the first to collect celebrity endorsements and use them to sell his own product. Mariani's early advertising campaigns were aimed mainly at doctors. He sent out free wine samples and solicited endorsements in return. By 1902, Mariani had received letters of praise from more than 8000 physicians and other happy clients from around the world. Many of these endorsements were then included in other Mariani publications. Mariani wrote and printed scientific brochures and monographs, which he distributed free of charge to physicians. The brochures invariably contained endorsements, if not from media stars and artists, then from physicians claiming impressive cures. Mariani also purchased advertising space in the Paris newspapers. Well-known graphic artists of the era, such as Chéret and Robida, were commissioned to produce graphics for the newspapers (4). The artists were also paid to draw posters which were, in turn, displayed around Paris. Mariani also produced a line of medallions and plaques, each with a different Vin Mariani endorsement.

Competitors entered the market, and product recognition became a problem. (Modern winemakers in California, who have sued one another for appropriating the distinctive shapes of their wine bottles, may be surprised to learn that similar scenarios had been played out more than a century ago.) Mariani had a bottle especially designed for his Vin Mariani, and he never changed its shape. Even though Vin Mariani spawned a host of imitators during its time, the Mariani wine bottle was as recognizable as the Coca-Cola bottle is today. Advertisements in medical journals warned members of the medical profession about the "disappointment and annoyance caused by imitations and substitutions" and advised them to "impress on patients to accept only Mariani Wine (5)."

Mariani shamelessly courted artists and writers. He often rented Ledoyen, a well-known restaurant, and served opulent dinners to members of the Society of French Artists. Menus for these gatherings were, of course, fashioned by leading art nouveau illustrators. A painting of one of these dinners by the artist Grun, shows Mariani seated among the famous guests. Mariani also hired well-known writers, paying them handsomely to write stories about the marvelous effects of coca and his wine. Not surprisingly, the artists and writers also wrote enthusiastic endorsements for Mariani's products.

Mariani did not just lavishly entertain and employ artists, he also flattered the artists by publishing lithographed albums about them. Each album contained biographic notes, photographs, autographs, and accounts of the wonderful experiences enjoyed by the artists while they were drinking Vin Mariani. According to Joseph Uzanne, Mariani's secretary and publicity director, the letters were at first sent spontaneously by the artists (3). Later they were solicited. From 1891 to 1913, Mariani published a series of albums. Each album contained a collection of 75 profiles. These profiles were lithographed by Lalauze, a well-known illustrator. Cheaper anthology additions were also produced.

A total of 1,086 celebrity portraits were published. Included among the celebrities were 3 popes, 16 kings and queens, and 6 presidents of the French Republic. There were also painters, composers, actors, politicians, generals, bishops, physicians, and respected scientists. The mix of celebrities was eclectic. Most of the celebrities who were profiled were French, but Americans were not totally ignored. Later editions included both Thomas Edison and Sarah Bernhardt. Different celebrities made different kinds of contributions. Author H.G. Wells drew two small cartoons of himself. In the first one, he was slouched and depressed. In the second drawing, a happy Wells is shown after drinking Vin Mariani. President William McKinley's secretary, John Addison Porter, wrote to Mariani and thanked him for the case of wine he had sent to the White House. Porter assured Mariani that the wine would be used whenever the occasion presented itself (6). A complete set of these endorsement albums is available for viewing at the British Museum.

The celebrity folios were expensive, and designed to reach an influential, if limited, audience. In order to increase product recognition, Mariani had extracts of the folios reprinted. Biographies of individual celebrities were republished and issued as bulletins. The bulletins were then inserted in local papers around Paris. These bulletins, or supplements, were similar to the promotions used by supermarkets and department stores today. The supplements were folded into the centers of leading Parisian newspapers under the title, *Contemporary Figures*. Each issue was 16 pages long, and measured 32 cm x 23 cm. Mariani printed 800,000 at one time, and had them inserted into *Le Journal, Le Monde, L'Eclair, Le Figaro*, and half a dozen other major newspapers. Over the 20 years of publication, more than 64 million issues of Mariani's *Contemporary Figures* were distributed (3)! Mariani squeezed additional mileage out of the supplements by taking individual photographs from the albums and reprinting them as postcards. Four series of 30 cards were printed and sold for ten cents a card.

In the final analysis, Mariani's advertising innovations were probably more important than his pharmaceutical or wine making skills. The precise formula for Vin Mariani was, of course, secret. All that Mariani would say was that the wine was made using a "fine" Bordeaux, and that only "the finest coca leaves" were added. Actually, the formula for coca wine was no big secret. The French government had set guidelines for its manufacture, and any pharmacist could produce it. Sixty grams of ground coca leaves were soaked for 10 hours in 1 L (2.1 pints) of red or white wine. The only requirement for the wine was that it contain 10 to 15% alcohol. Given an average cocaine content of .25 to .5% for Bolivian leaf (the only kind of leaf available in France at the time), 1 L of wine would have contained as little as 150 mg, and no more than 300 mg, of cocaine (7). By modern standards, Vin Mariani did not contain very much cocaine. One ounce of Mariani's tonic contained 6 mg of cocaine. Two glasses of wine would have contained less than 50 mg of cocaine, equivalent to one "line" of snorted cocaine. Even using today's sophisticated measuring techniques, 50 mg of cocaine is barely enough to cause measurable effects in humans.

Mariani had competitors in England, America, and France. In 1895, a representative of the Pharmaceutical Society of Lyon complained to the French government when one of its generals ordered a supply of Vin Mariani for his troops in Madagascar. The pharmacists argued there was no great secret to making coca wines, and any competent pharmacist could make wines as good as Mariani's. And, "since the general had not found it necessary to specify any particular non-coca-containing brands of Bordeaux of Champagne wine for the troops, it is equally undesirable that he should give one maker a monopoly of the supply of coca wine. (8)" The American brands tended to contain more cocaine (4.5 to 10.8 mg per ounce) than Vin Mariani. Wyeth & Brothers produced a sherry containing 15.2% alcohol with 4.5 mg of cocaine per ounce, while Metcalf & Company located at 39 Tremont Street in Boston, offered a Malaga (a kind of sherry) containing nearly 21% alcohol with 9.7 mg of cocaine per ounce. In contrast to Mariani's "fine Bordeaux", H. Caswell & Company used a generic "red wine" which contained nearly as much alcohol as Mariani's, and one-third more cocaine (11.5 mg) per ounce. Perhaps, as a competitive measure, the Vin Mariani exported to the United States contained slightly more cocaine than the variety sold in France (7.2 mg per ounce vs. 6 mg per ounce) (9).

The higher cocaine content of the American wines may have been their own undoing. Commercial quantities of refined cocaine did not become available until the late 1880s. Without the availability of refined cocaine to add to the wine, the only way to raise the wine's cocaine content was to soak more leaves in the wine. The problem with this approach was that other compounds, some of them not particularly tasty, were extracted into the wine as well; thus the higher the cocaine content, the worse the wines tasted. That observation probably explains the basis for certain rulings of the British Inland Revenue Service. Pharmacists in England were allowed to sell coca wines tax free ("non-excisable") provided that wines contained so much coca leaf extract (at least 30 mg per ounce), that they were guaranteed to taste terrible. Wines that contained lesser amounts of extract were considered beverages, not medications, and as such were taxable (10). If a pharmacist wanted to sell the good tasting wines, he had to purchase the equivalent of a liquor license. Enterprising pharmacists got around that law by selling concentrated essences to customers who could then add the "essence" to their own wine. One popular version of "essence" contained .25% cocaine, while other brands contained up to twice as much. When added to the customer's own bottle of port wine, for instance, the final product would have been hard to tell from any of the specially brewed coca wine products (11).

In later years, Mariani ridiculed competitors who simply added refined cocaine to wine. He maintained that other components of the leaf were needed for flavor and character, but the blend had to be balanced, otherwise it was not drinkable. If the history of the Coca-Cola Company is any indication, Mariani was probably correct. Sometime after 1901, Coca-Cola dropped cocaine from its formula, but continued to add an extract of coca leaves from which the cocaine had been removed. The decocainized leaves, referred to as "Merchandise No. 5" were prepared especially for Coca-Cola at the Shaeffer Chemical Manufacturing Facility in Maywood, New Jersey (12). Presumably, the decocainized leaves supplied the desirable flavoring to which Mariani had referred.

The advertising claims made by Mariani's American competitors largely repeated the claims for coca leaf made when European physicians first began experimenting with coca leaf extracts during the 1870s. Typical was an advertisement for Metcalf's Coca Wine:

> ...With stimulating and anodyne properties combined, Metcalf's Coca Wine acts without deliberating, being always uniform and therefore always reliable. For Athletes it is invaluable in imparting energy and resisting fatigue; Public Speakers and Singers find it indispensable as a "Voice Tonic," because being a "tensor" of the vocal chords, it greatly strengthens and increases the volume of the voice; and to the elderly it is a dependable aphrodisiac, superior to any other drug.

Metcalf's Coca Wine sold for one dollar a bottle (13).

Neither Mariani nor any of his competitors could possibly have had any idea of how or why their "anodyne" was so stimulating. More than a century passed before that secret was unraveled. In 1990, separate groups of researchers, one in Barcelona and one in Miami, discovered that the combination of alcohol and cocaine does more than make users feel good. It also produces a very unusual compound called cocaethylene. When cocaine is consumed in the absence of alcohol, it is broken down into two principal metabolites, one called benzoylecgonine and one called ecgonine methyl ester. In humans, at least, neither of the two metabolites has any stimulant or psychological effects, but cocaethylene does. In fact, cocaethylene produces nearly as much stimulation as cocaine itself (14). When cocaine and alcohol are consumed together, cocaine's stimulant effects are enhanced and prolonged. Vin Mariani drinkers were, in effect, getting more cocaine than either Mariani, or his competitors, thought they were providing. That may explain why Vin Mariani, and the other cocaine-containing wines, were so popular.

The discovery of cocaethylene also explains the puzzling observation that drinking relatively small amounts of coca wine seemed to cause an intense feeling of well being, out of proportion to the amount of cocaine consumed. Today's cocaine abusers often consume alcohol and cocaine, and the practice can be explained as an exercise in empirical pharmacology (15); users have found a way to get a more intense, or at least prolonged, stimulant effect for the same amount of money. The downside to this approach is that using cocaine and alcohol together appears to make cocaine more toxic.

Advertising claims made by Mariani and his competitors, were not nearly as outrageous as they seem today. The claims of the coca winemakers were entirely consistent with the ideas generally held by the medical community at the time. von Liebig's theory of nutrition, bizarre and flawed as it was, had many adherents in the 1870s and 1880s. There was a general feeling, shared by physicians and their patients, that many ailments were the result of "tissue wasting", and that "tissue wasting" occurred when certain vital, but uncharacterized, compounds were absent from the diet. von Liebig believed that nitrogen-containing compounds were the prime suspect. The fact that coca leaves contained nitrogen, albeit in small amounts, made them especially interesting to the medical community. Reports from early naturalists and explorers returning from the Amazon also made it seem likely that cocaine, or at least the coca plant, possessed real medicinal value.

Following the Napoleonic wars, the pace of exploration in South America noticeably increased, and a succession of European naturalists had the opportunity to explore the Amazon. Two of the earliest were Karl Fredrich Philip von Martius (1794-1868) and Johan Baptist von Spix (1781-1826). They sailed to Buenos Aires, then traveled by land to Chile and north to Ecuador. von Martius and von Spix completed their trip by canoeing down the Amazon River. The naturalists took botanical specimens back to Europe, but whether or not they shipped back any coca plants is unclear. von Martius, however, did make detailed observations of Indian life, especially the medicinal use of plants. He was fascinated by the diet of the Indians; noting they subsisted on only a few spoons of maize and water each day, and never complained, as long as they also had coca leaves to chew on (16).

Johan von Tschudi spent three years in Peru. His primary interest was animal life classification, but he also recorded detailed observations of sasparilla, cinchona, balsam, and coca. von Tschudi found the natives "unsocial and gloomy", and clearly did not like them very much. But, he was fascinated by some aspects of their lifestyle, particularly their use of coca. von Tschudi swore that chewing coca leaves could prevent "the difficulty of respiration felt in the rapid ascents of the Cordilleras...," a disorder known today as high altitude pulmonary edema. However, it was another part of von Tschudi's memoirs that really caught the attention of his readers. According to von Tschudi:

> *A cholo of Huarai, named Hatan Huamang, was employed by me in very laborious digging. During the five days and nights he was in my service he never tasted any food, and took only two hours sleep each night. But at intervals of two and a half or three hours he regularly chewed about half an ounce of coca leaves, and he kept an acullio (a wad of leaves) continually in his mouth. I was constantly beside him, and therefore I had the opportunity of closely observing him. The work for which I engaged him being finished, he accompanied me on a two days' journey of twenty-three leagues across the level heights. Though on foot, he kept up with the pace of my mule, and halted only for the chacchar (more coca leaves). On leaving me, he declared he would willingly engage himself again for the same amount of work, and that he would go through it without food, if I would but allow him a sufficient supply of coca. The village priest assured me that this man was sixty-two years of age, and that he had never known him to be ill, a day in his life (17).*

Such claims, and those made by others returning from South America, were taken quite seriously, and they were firmly lodged in the public's consciousness. Letters to the editors of the *Lancet* and the *British Medical Journal*, from military surgeons and team physicians, described how coca chewing could be used as a way to decrease thirst and increase endurance. In 1877, a Canadian physician described what happened when he gave coca leaves to members of the Toronto Lacrosse Club:

> *The day was exceedingly hot, the thermometer marking 110 °F in the sun. The antagonist of the club were men of sturdy build, of good physique, well trained in the game and, in general, connected with the mechanical trades, or with out-door avocations. In the latter particular they were in strong and apparently unfavorable contrast with the players of the Toronto club, whose occupations were all of a sedentary character. However, at the close of the day, during a short interval of rest between the games, I remarked that the men of the rival club were so thoroughly exhausted that it was with the utmost*

difficulty they could be roused by their field captain to take part in concluding the game, while the coca-chewers were as elastic and apparently as free from fatigue as at the commencement of play (18).

Given the known effects of cocaine, and ambient temperatures of 110°F the result is difficult, but not impossible, to believe. At the 1996 Olympic games in Atlanta, several Russian athletes were disqualified for using an amphetamine-like drug known as Bromantane. Although structurally different from cocaine, it exerts many of the same physiologic effects. The drug had, it transpires, been developed by Russian Army chemists searching for agents that would improve performance in hot, humid, climates.

Another group of coca enthusiasts described how chewing coca had helped them to climb Mont Blanc in Switzerland. Each of the climbers chewed a total of 5 g of dried coca leaf during the 10 hours required for the climb. They drank no water, no tea, and no coffee, though they did indulge in some wine. According to the climbers, the trip was made in "comparative comfort" (19). And there was, of course, the famous climb of a mountain in Scotland, made by the 78-year-old president of the Scottish Medical Association. He also claimed that chewing coca eliminated feelings of hunger and thirst (20). Given the quality and type of coca leaf that was available in Europe in 1882, it is unlikely that the Mont Blanc climbers could have ingested much more than 25 mg (.05% of 5 g) of cocaine, far too little to have produced any measurable physiologic effects. But, the climbers were so convinced of coca's powers they would probably have felt the same if the leaves they chewed contained no cocaine. In 1882, the placebo effect was yet to be recognized.

Surgeon-Major T. Edmonston Charles of the Indian Army wrote to the *Medical Times and Gazette* and recommended coca for "assuaging thirst during great exertion in hot countries". Charles went on to argue that a particularly famous military disaster in Afghanistan could have been averted had only the troops been supplied with coca (21). This preoccupation with endurance culminated with the publication of a paper from Germany which described what happened when a military surgeon secretly added cocaine to the drinking water of Prussian artillery men.

The physician was Theodore Aschenbrandt (1855-?). An Austrian, Aschenbrandt studied pharmacology in Würzburg from 1891 to 1892. The director of the Pharmacology Department at Würzburg, Dr. Michael Rossbach (1842-1894), was interested in cocaine research, and knowledgeable about the topic. Prior to Aschenbrandt's arrival in Würzburg, Professor Rossbach had supervised another student, Vassili von Anrep

(1852-1925), who was also interested in cocaine research. von Anrep had written an extensive review about cocaine's actions, and had suggested that cocaine might prove to be a useful anesthetic (22). von Anrep could well have become famous as the inventor of local anesthesia, but he did not capitalize on his findings. He was a good scientist, and he believed that the results of his animal experiments, at least as far as cocaine's anesthetic properties were concerned, were not as clear cut as they could be. von Anrep had planned to do a series of experiments in humans, but before he could do them, he returned to his home in St. Petersburg where he became a professor of pharmacology (23). Thus, Karl Koller received the credit for the discovery of local anesthetic in 1884, 14 years later.

Rossbach unsuccessfully tried to convince Aschenbrandt to continue von Anrep's work. Aschenbrandt never become an academic, but he did eventually contribute to the literature on cocaine. After receiving his degree, Aschenbrandt went into private practice and joined the Army Reserve. In 1883, while on summer maneuvers with the Bavarian Artillery, Aschenbrandt was called upon to treat a number of soldiers with heat exhaustion. Aschenbrandt went to the local pharmacy and purchased some cocaine. In the paper he subsequently published, he described the results in six cases (24). In one of the cases, he reported that when a soldier collapsed on the second day of a forced march, he was given one tablespoon of cocaine-containing solution. According to Aschenbrandt, "...he stood up of his own accord and traveled the distance to H., several kilometers, easily and cheerfully and with a pack on his back."

The success of Aschenbrandt's experiment was almost as miraculous as the success of the climbers on Mont Blanc. In reality, cocaine could only make heat exhaustion worse, and Aschenbrandt offered no proof that heat exhaustion was, in fact, the problem. The soldiers in question could simply have been tired, and if that was the case, the cocaine would almost certainly have helped alleviate their symptoms. Since cocaine increases the heart's workload and raises core body temperature, the later explanation seems more likely. Aschenbrandt saw what he wanted to see.

Cocaine's alleged ability to promote strength and endurance received most of the attention, but there were other recurring themes in the medical literature. Coca was believed to be an effective remedy for shyness, nervousness, and even stage fright. (Note: The latter notion is particularly strange because the symptoms of stage fright are the result of high circulating blood levels of stress hormones [the hormones epinephrine and norepinephrine]; coca actually increases the blood levels of those hormones. The modern treatment for those pathologically afraid of public speaking consists of giving drugs [beta blockers] that counter the effects of the stress hormones.) Another area of interest was the treatment of morphine addiction. Opium had been used sparingly in Europe during the Middle Ages, but its popularity increased during the Renaissance. By the dawn of the 19th century, opium addiction was a major problem (25). By the 1830s, case reports describing "morphia" toxicity were a regular feature in the medical journals. Almost as soon as coca leaf became commercially available, physicians began experimenting with it as a treatment for addiction. Given what was known about addiction in the late 1800s (basically nothing), the idea of treating opiate addiction with cocaine was not as bizarre as it sounds.

Addicts in the late 1800s differed from today's addicts in two very important respects: (1) they took opium, not morphine, and (2) they took it orally, not by injection. The distinctions may seem academic, but they are not. Opium taken by mouth is partly destroyed in the stomach, and partly detoxified before it reaches the brain. This means that addiction potential is much lower. The oral use of opium had, at least, built-in safeguards that made addiction less likely and toxicity harder to produce. The safeguards were partially eliminated when morphine, the active ingredient of opium, was successfully isolated from opium, by Sertürner, in 1803. In that year, Sertürner announced that he had isolated an alkaline base in opium which he called morphium. The event marked an important milestone for organic chemistry, and not just for addicts (26).

Prior to Sertürner's successful experiment, it was universally held that the chemicals isolated from plants could only be acids, and that only metals could be alkali. Sertürner's discovery put an end to those beliefs. More importantly, his discovery led, quite rapidly, to the successful isolation of dozens of other potent drugs from plants, all alkali. Quinine and cocaine were just two of the many useful molecules to be found in plants. They were referred to as "plant alkaloids". The founder of England's Royal Pharmaceutical Society, Thomas Morton, started to refine and purify morphine in 1821. Merck of Darmstadt started the following year (27).

The practice of injecting opium dates back to at least the 17th century, and perhaps earlier. Christopher Wren (1632-1723), best known as the architect who rebuilt St. Paul's Cathedral, designer of St. James of Piccadilly, and President of the Royal Society, was also a student of anatomy. In 1664, he helped Thomas Willis create the illustrations for his famous book on neuroanatomy (Note: The confluence of blood vessels at the base of the brain, the shape of which often determines outcome in cases of stroke and head trauma, was first described by Willis and is still referred to as "The Circle of Willis"), but Wren was interested in medical problems long before he became an illustrator for Willis. According to the history of the Royal Society, while Wren was a professor of Astronomy at Gresham College, Oxford, in 1656, he experimented giving intravenous opium injections to dogs. The hypodermic syringe had not yet been invented. Wren made do by attaching a quill to a small bladder which he filled with an opium solution. All of the experimental animals survived, and Wren was so encouraged by his preliminary results that he decided to repeat the experiment on a man. The services of a "delinquent servant" were offered by an ambassador to the Court of St. James. The servant survived, but things did not go quite as well as they had with the dogs, and Wren abandoned the project. The idea of injecting medications was all but abandoned for the next 150 years (28).

In the early 1850s, Alexander Wood, a Scottish physician, reasoned that the best way to relieve painful extremity injuries would be to inject morphine directly into the nerves that supplied the painful area. Even in the 1850s, syringes were clumsy affairs, and the technique did not work well. However, it quickly became apparent to Wood that the morphine he was trying to inject into the nerves was producing effects throughout the body. Wood's findings were published in 1855. "It is truly astonishing," he wrote, "how rapidly it affects the system. If you throw in a large quantity of morphine, you will see the eyes immediately injected and the patient narcotized... (29)". Wood carried out a number of experiments, mainly on his wife and himself. He proved that effective pain relief could be achieved by injecting morphine. In the course of his researches, Wood managed to addict both his wife and himself. Unfortunately, Wood's wife holds the distinction of being the first woman to die of an injected narcotic drug overdose (28).

A few years after Wood's paper was published, an American physician named Charles Hunter (1834 or 1835 - 1878), elaborated on Wood's original experiment. Hunter found that a small dose of morphine given hypodermically produced the very same effects as a large dose given orally (30). This is precisely why repeated small injections of morphine are much more likely to result in addiction than large doses of opium taken orally. By the beginning of the American Civil War, in 1861, commercially manufactured hypodermic syringes were available in America and Europe (31). The supply of syringes remained limited for much of the war, but by the war's conclusion in 1865, supplies of syringes were abundant, and so was the number of addicts. Addiction was extremely common and American physicians expended considerable effort to find ways to treat the problem.

Common though the condition may have been, physicians did not have the remotest idea of how morphine relieved pain, much less know how it caused addiction. Some misguided theorists even argued that hypodermic injection of morphine was less, rather than more, likely to produce addiction (32). Because cocaine's effects were so obviously opposite to those of morphine, many physicians concluded that cocaine would be an ideal treatment for morphine addicts. In this belief, they were encouraged by the drug companies that manufactured cocaine-containing products, particularly Parke, Davis & Company of Detroit, Michigan. George Davis, one of its owners, also owned a medical journal called the *Therapeutic Gazette*. Davis solicited articles from several physicians who claimed to have cured morphine addicts using Parke, Davis' tincture of coca. It was these articles that caught the attention of Sigmund Freud, and prompted him to experiment with cocaine.

Chapter 4

FREUD, KOLLER, AND THE MUMMY'S CURSE

The genies that they summoned up to help them turned into furies bearing misfortune and disaster (1)

Albert Erlenmeyer describing the events that occurred after Freud recommended cocaine as a treatment for morphine addiction

Good ideas can be slow to catch on, but if the history of cocaine is any example, bad ideas spread rapidly. There are, at least, good explanations why bad ideas about cocaine were so rapidly accepted. In 1884, Karl Koller assured his place in history and helped to usher in the era of modern surgery, when he announced his discovery that a few drops of cocaine solution could prevent the pain of eye surgery. Koller's observation, however, could hardly be called original. A succession of earlier physicians had noticed that cocaine had anesthetic effects. In fact, quite a few of them had already published papers on the subject.

In 1855, a paper was published in the *French Archives of Pharmacy* by a chemist named Gaedecke (2). Gaedecke described the small, needle-like crystals that he had been able to isolate from coca leaves. He called the crystals "Erythroxyline". There is no evidence that Samuel Percy of New York City had read Gaedecke's paper, or even heard of him, but in November of 1857, in a paper read at a meeting of the New York Academy of Medicine, Percy described how he had found crystals similar to those described by Gaedecke. Like Gaedecke, Percy also named the substance "Erythroxyline". Percy went on to suggest that these crystals may have useful anesthetic properties (3)(4). Bearing in mind that the accepted taxonomic name for the coca plant is Erythroxylin, it may have been a coincidence that both authors chose the same name. Then, again, it might not have been.

In 1860, Albert Niemann repeated and expanded upon Gaedecke's studies. Niemann isolated the same four- to six-sided, needle-like crystals from coca leaf. And, like Gaedecke, Niemann also noticed that when he placed the crystals on his tongue, it felt numb. The crystals were almost certainly identical to those described by Gaedecke. However, Niemann's discovery attracted a great deal more attention than the work of Gaedecke, perhaps because Niemann was working in the laboratory of Carl Wöhler, one of the world's foremost chemists. Niemann's observations, at least those that had to do with the isolation and purification of cocaine, were taken quite seriously, particularly by a chemical manufacturer called Merck of Darmstadt. At the time, Merck was operating out of one, rather small, factory in Darmstadt, Germany. Merck chemists quickly adopted Niemann's purification techniques and, in 1862, began producing small amounts (less than 50 g per year) of purified cocaine (5). Niemann's confirmation of Gaedecke's observation on the anesthetic effects of cocaine was ignored.

A succession of other researchers repeated Gaedecke's and Niemann's experiments, but none of them ever received much recognition either. In 1862, Frederick Schroff of Vienna tried cocaine on himself. He noticed that, at first, cocaine caused feelings of cheerfulness, but soon those feelings quickly wore off. After the drug-induced cheerfulness wore off, Schroff became thoroughly depressed (6). He also noted that cocaine made his tongue numb, and reported the findings of his cocaine experiments in a paper he read before the Viennese Medical Society. He advised others not to use cocaine because of the severe depression he had experienced. In spite of Schroff's warning, other researchers continued to experiment with cocaine.

In 1868, little notice was taken of a monograph published by Tomés Moreno y Maiz, the former surgeon of the Peruvian Army. Both Moreno and another Peruvian, Alfredo Bignon, had been students of José Casimiro Ulloa, a native of Peru who had trained in Paris during the early 1800s. Ulloa had founded the local medical society in Lima, started a medical journal, and did everything he could to promote the adoption of European medical advances. He also fostered research on the coca plant. Probably as a result of Ulloa's encouragement, y Maiz moved to Paris in order to continue his studies.

Also, because of Ulloa's teachings, Moreno probably believed in the experimental-scientific approach advocated by Claude Bernard. As a consequence, the experimental studies conducted by Moreno were not all that different from ones that would be used today. Moreno conducted a series of experiments, and published his results in a book entitled, "Recherches Chimiques et Physiologiques sur l'Erythroxylon coca du Pérou et la Cocaine". The body of the book contained descriptions of the reactions he had observed when he injected frogs with cocaine (7). The beginning and the end of the book contain the most interesting material. In the introduction, Moreno complained about the high prices and short supply of both refined cocaine and coca leaf. He finally resorted to buying coca leaf and refining it himself, although he found Niemann's method to be both "difficult and uncertain (8)." In a footnote at the end of the book, Moreno wondered, "Could one utilize it as a local anesthetic? One cannot make a decision on the basis of such a limited number of experiments; it must be decided by the future."

At least one person believed Moreno was on the right track. Early in the 1870s, Charles Fauvel, a Parisian physician, started to use cocaine-containing solutions to relieve throat pain, and to help in the examination of the vocal cords (9). Fauvel employed a solution provided by Angelo Mariani, his cousin and the originator of the popular coca-containing wine. It was probably as a result of Fauvel's encouragement that Mariani launched his wildly successful coca-containing wine, Vin Mariani (10). At Fauvel's request, Mariani prepared a special tincture of cocaine which, when applied to the throat, effectively blocked painful sensations. Visiting American and English physicians observed Fauvel's techniques, and adopted the practice (3). In spite of the visitors' enthusiasm, Fauvel's ideas never gained general acceptance, at least not until Karl Koller publicized his discovery in 1884.

Vassili von Anrep (1852-1925) received as little recognition as Moreno, but he did prove that Moreno's speculations were correct. He even concluded that cocaine could be recommended "as a local anesthetic as well as (a treatment) for melancholics (11)."

Unfortunately for von Anrep, his researches, like those of Moreno, went largely unnoticed. von Anrep stopped doing research and became an administrator. He returned to Russia and eventually founded the first women's medical school in that country. He also chaired the Russian Red Cross during World War I. In spite of his good works, von Anrep was imprisoned at the outbreak of the Russian Revolution and was eventually expelled from the country. He died in Paris, in 1925, without ever receiving any recognition for his discoveries (12). Freud, however, had read the works of both von Anrep and Moreno, and he quoted from both of them in his paper on cocaine.

The reason Karl Koller became famous, while most of his predecessors did not, has to do with the fact that Koller's results could be duplicated. When other researchers tried to replicate the work of von Anrep, Moreno, or Fauvel, they were unable to do so. The reason they could not conduct successful experiments had to do with the cocaine supply. The cocaine content of stored coca leaves deteriorates rapidly. Before the 1880s, coca leaves were not shipped to Europe with any regularity. And the quality of the leaves that did arrive on the wharves of London, Hamburg, and Amsterdam, was dubious at best. Not only was the quality of the raw material unreliable, but, as Moreno observed, Niemann's extraction process was difficult and "unpredictable".

Experimenters failed to obtain responses, and were unable to replicate the work of Moreno and von Anrep, because what they were experimenting with was, as often as not, not cocaine. By 1884, the year before Koller's and Freud's papers were published, Merck's annual total cocaine production was still less than one pound. Edward Squibb, the founder of what was later to become the Squibb Pharmaceutical Company (now part of Bristol Meyers Squibb), became so frustrated with the situation that he decided to stop selling coca-based products altogether. As far as Squibb was concerned, good coca leaf was unobtainable. When he analyzed the coca-containing products that were then being sold, Squibb found that none of them contained any cocaine! Squibb suggested that physicians might just as well prescribe caffeine.

Caffeine was available and cheap. Squibb believed that caffeine probably had the same effects as cocaine. He helpfully supplied a conversion table. According to Squibb's calculations — it is not entirely clear on what he based them — 180 mg of caffeine (roughly the content of three cans of today's Coca-Cola™) exerted the same effects on the body as 2700 mg of cocaine (in today's parlance, the equivalent of 50 to 60 lines of cocaine). Of course, Squibb's notions of equivalency were absurd. But cocaine and caffeine are related alkaloids, and caffeine was, at the time, much simpler to purify than cocaine, and much cheaper. By the time Squibb's paper was first published, consensus was emerging that many of cocaine's effects could also be produced by caffeine (13). Squibb's paper was published just two weeks before reports of Koller's discovery of cocaine's anesthetic properties became known in New York City (14). Subsequent events in 1884 forced Squibb to reconsider his position on cocaine.

In the spring of that year, Freud published *On Coca*, in which he recommended the use of cocaine in a number of conditions, including the treatment of morphine addiction. In the fall, Koller discovered that cocaine could be used as a local anesthetic. The reasons that Freud's paper, and Koller's discovery, were taken seriously, while those of earlier workers were not, had more to do with the existence of Merck chemists in Darmstadt, than with any novel scientific discoveries on the part of Freud or Koller.

Merck was able to supply pure, chemically active, cocaine. Given a reliable cocaine supply, it finally became possible for researchers to duplicate one another's findings. Still, things may have turned out differently if the chemistry of alkaloids had been better understood at the time. Freud, for example, might have received credit for the discovery of local anesthesia, or at least could have shared credit with Koller. Freud had suggested to Leopold Königstein, an ophthalmologist friend, that he should try to use a cocaine solution to relieve the pain of individuals with eye diseases such as trachoma. Königstein obliged, but found that not only did the cocaine solution not relieve the pain, it made things worse. Even though pure Merck cocaine had been provided, the pharmacist who had prepared the eye drops mixed the cocaine with too much acid. The mistake effectively neutralized the anesthetic effects of cocaine, and at the same time caused great irritation to the patient's eyes (5)(15).

In July of 1884, Freud published the first in a series of papers on cocaine. The first paper, *On Coca*, was the one which became the most famous (16). It recounted the history of cocaine, and what was then known about its chemistry and pharmacology. After reviewing what was known, Freud listed a series of conditions where, he thought, treatment with cocaine could be useful. Some of the suggestions were good. Several were reasonable, and several were very bad. To Freud's credit, he recommended cocaine as a local anesthetic. Unfortunately, he also recommended cocaine as a treatment for morphine addiction. The latter suggestion was immediately adopted, but Freud's suggestion that cocaine might have some anesthetic value was generally ignored. Except by Karl Koller.

Freud was not the first to suggest this approach. In light of medical thinking at the time, it was, in fact, quite a reasonable suggestion. By the time Freud sat down to write *On Coca*, American physicians had already published several papers describing how coca extracts, if not cocaine itself, had proven effective in the treatment of morphine addiction. The idea that stimulants, such as cocaine and caffeine, could be used to antagonize narcotics like opium and morphine, was widely accepted (17)(18). Freud had based his suggestion on the existing literature, but, as Albert Erlenmeyer pointed out, it was an idea "expounded by individuals without any truly scientific experience (1)." Had Freud been more experienced, he may have realized that several of the American papers he quoted in his paper were actually little more than paid advertisements for Parke, Davis & Company.

Traditionally, Freud's critics have attributed his morphine misadventures to his need for money and his desire to become famous (19). Such suggestions probably contain an element of truth, but do not explain how Freud was taken in by the cocaine endorsements contained in the *Therapeutic Gazette*, nor do they explain why his recommendations that cocaine could be used as an anesthetic, were so halfhearted. The truth will never be known with certainty, but these particular errors of judgment can be easily explained by Freud's lack of training, and his lack of clinical experience. Freud was only 28 years old, and barely out of medical school, when he published *On Coca*.

Medical training in the 1870s was far different than what it is today, and Freud's training was somewhat unusual even for his time. Then, lecturing was the only means of instruction; there was no bedside teaching. Students could graduate from medical school, as Freud did, without ever having examined a patient. In 1873, during his third year of training, Freud became a student in the laboratory of Ernst Wilhelm Ritter von Brücke. He spent six years as a researcher in von Brücke's laboratory, where he learned microscopic techniques and studied the comparative neuroanatomy of developing animals. The work addressed no clinical issues and involved no patient contact.

Freud made time to attend the occasional lecture at the medical school, which was enough to allow him to sit for his examinations and get his medical degree. While training with von Brücke, Freud became close friends with one of von Brücke's assistants, a pathologist named Fleischl-Marxow. Fleischl-Marxow had become addicted to morphine after having surgery to amputate his thumb. It was Freud's personal knowledge of Fleischl-Marxow's problems that aroused his interest in treating morphine addiction. In 1882, after Freud met his fiancee, Martha Bernays, he decided to abandon research in favor of clinical medicine. He left the research laboratory and began what today would be called a "rotating internship", at Vienna General Hospital.

Freud spent two months on the surgical service of Christian Billroth (1829-1894), the first surgeon to perform gastric surgery and have patients survive. Freud's surgical rotation was followed by nine months in general medicine. In May 1883, Freud transferred to the neurology and psychiatry service, where much of his time was spent, again, performing microscopic neuroanatomy. Freud published several papers on neuroanatomic research. He was working part time in the research laboratory when he wrote *On Coca* in the summer of 1884. The following year he was given a teaching appointment at the hospital. *On Coca*, which discussed possible clinical applications for cocaine, was written by Freud when he had less than one year of general clinical experience, and no experience, whatsoever, with addiction, except for that of his poor addicted friend, Fleischl-Marxow.

Freud had located the papers he quoted in *On Coca* by consulting a copy of the Index Catalog of the Library of the Surgeon-General's Office (known as the Surgeon General's List), the predecessor of today's "Index Medicus", a comprehensive list of published scientific papers. Freud's paper would be described as an editorial review: a paper describing the researches of others, weighing their importance, and making recommendations for treatment. Freud's paper was composed of mostly unsubstantiated and anecdotal material. A paper like Freud's would never be published today because no reputable modern journal would accept a paper that was based on anecdotal reports, written by a physician with no experience in the field.

Even before Freud consulted the Surgeon General's List, he had read Theodore Aschenbrandt's article which claimed that cocaine could be used to increase the endurance of soldiers (20). On April 21, 1884, Freud wrote to Martha and told her he had decided to do a study on cocaine. He told her about Aschenbrandt's paper, and that he had decided to order some cocaine and try it himself: "Perhaps others are working at it; perhaps nothing will come of it. But I shall certainly try it, and you know that when one perseveres, sooner or later one succeeds. We do not need more than one such lucky hit to be able to think of setting up house (21)."

The records of Merck Pharmaceuticals show that on April 24, 1884, C. Haubner's "Angel's Pharmacy", which served Vienna General Hospital and the area where Freud lived, received a carton containing 15 g of hydrochloride of cocaine, and 5 g of cocaine free base (5). (Note: Today, that amount would be equivalent to approximately 150 "lines" of snorted cocaine, or 50 "rocks" of smokable crack cocaine.) Freud's initial purchase was only 1 g, which was all he could afford. One gram cost him one-tenth of his monthly salary.

The following week, Freud tried cocaine on himself. He must have been favorably impressed. He decided to expand on the work done by Aschenbrandt, and by a group of enthusiastic, if uncritical, American doctors. When Freud reviewed the Surgeon General's List for papers on cocaine, he came upon references from the *Therapeutic Gazette*, edited by George Davis, one of the owners of Parke, Davis & Company, based in Detroit. During the 1870s, Parke, Davis manufactured a fluid extract of coca. During the 1880s, Parke, Davis started to manufacture refined cocaine, and ultimately challenged Merck for leadership of the market. In the early 1880s, Davis published an article by W.H. Bentley of Valley Oaks, Kentucky. Since the *Therapeutic Gazette* was written for advertising purposes, it is likely that Bentley was paid for his submission. Bentley claimed to have been successfully treating opium and alcohol addiction since 1872. The secret to Bentley's success was coca extract. Bentley singled out the Parke, Davis extract for mention in the article (22).

In addition to discussing his theory of addiction, Bentley offered opinions on some other diseases. Before condemning Freud too roundly for suggesting that cocaine could be used to treat morphine addiction, critics would be well advised to consider the state of medical thinking in the late 1870s. It is clearly reflected by Bentley's proposed etiology of tuberculosis: "I think the brain and the nerves become enervated from various causes, and from whatever cause, digestion and assimilation become impaired; next the blood, by losing some of its healthy constituent becomes too thin and watery, and the circulation thereby languid and sluggish. Then, as it passes through the lungs, a spongy tissue, it parts with a portion of its fibrin, which, being semivitalized, organizes in the form of a tubercle." The best that can be said is that Bentley's thinking about addiction was no more, and no less, magical than his thinking about infectious diseases! The worst that can be said is that Freud read this paper and actually took it seriously!

Another paper, also written for the *Therapeutic Gazette* and also quoted by Freud, was somewhat less theoretical. Dr. Edward Huse of Rockford, Illinois, described a 30-year-old Swedish man with a history of rheumatic fever. The man had been taking laudanum (a solution of opium taken orally) for over two years and had become addicted. According to Huse, the man's cravings disappeared over the course of two months of treatment. By the end of that time, the man had gained 17 pounds, and claimed he had never felt so well in his life. His only treatment was "half an ounce of Parke, Davis & Company's fluid extract of coca, night and morning — no other medicine (23)."

Freud also cited the papers of a Dr. Palmer from Louisville, Kentucky, the very same Dr. Palmer who came to the aid of a lady "pedestrianist" in distress in Chapter 2. Palmer claimed to have achieved near miraculous cures using coca elixir. Palmer managed to insert not just the name of Parke, Davis & Company in his paper, but also the advertisement on the back label of their fluid extract of coca. According to Parke, Davis & Company, this drug "produces a gently excitant effect; is asserted to support the strength for a considerable time without food; in large doses produces a general excitation of the circulatory and nervous systems, imparting increased vigor to the muscles as well as to the intellect, with an indescribable feeling of satisfaction amounting altogether sometimes to a species of delirium, not followed by feelings of languor or depression...(24)." All seven papers cited by Freud in his discussion of opium addiction were from *Therapeutic Gazette*, published by Parke, Davis & Company, a firm that sold coca products.

Freud told Fleischl-Marxow that he had been reading about a subject that should have been of more than a little interest to him, since he was a morphine addict. It also must have been of some interest to Freud's fiancee. On June 2, 1884, while working on *On Coca*, Freud wrote to Martha, "Woe to you my Princess, when I come. I will kiss you quite red and feed you till you are plump. And if you are forward, you shall see who is the stronger, a gentle little girl who doesn't eat enough or a big wild man who has cocaine in his body. In my last severe depression I took coca again, and a small dose lifted me to the heights in a wonderful fashion. I am just now busy collecting the literature for a song of praise to this magical substance (25) (26)."

One month later, at the end of May, the Physiology Institute where Freud had trained, and where Fleischl-Marxow still worked, placed its first order for cocaine. The Institute purchased 10 g of cocaine at

Haubner's "Angel's Pharmacy", the same place where Freud had made his purchases. However, because the Institute placed a larger order, for 10 g, it received a reduced price of five marks per gram (5).

Fleischl-Marxow almost certainly was the one who placed the order for the Institute, and he soon became just as addicted to cocaine as he was to morphine. He began to order large quantities of cocaine from Merck, and the purchases immediately came to the attention of Merck administrators. From the time that Merck first started to make cocaine in 1862, until the time that Freud placed his first order in April of 1884, buyers for Merck cocaine had been notably absent. Officials at Merck wondered what Fleischl-Marxow and the Physiology Institute were doing with such a large amount cocaine.

That summer, Merck officials wrote to Fleischl-Marxow inquiring about his research. Fleischl-Marxow did not mention his own addiction. Instead, he wrote back to Merck, and described Freud's experiments in some detail. He also discussed the possible use of cocaine in the treatment of morphine addiction. In October, Freud sent his own letter to Merck, outlining his research successes. Freud's correspondence with Merck was not entirely motivated by the desire to spread scientific knowledge. As will be discussed in Chapter 6, Freud sought, and established, financial arrangements with both Merck and Parke, Davis.

Emanuel Merck recognized the possible promotional opportunities: if Freud's theories were accepted, Merck's cocaine sales could only increase. So Merck summarized the information from both reports and published several papers on the advances in cocaine research (27-29). Because Merck had been lead to believe that Fleischl-Marxow was Freud's collaborator, Merck's papers attributed the advances to both men.

Freud completed the final draft of *On Coca* in June 1884 (16). He managed to get his paper published the following month. Freud began the paper by summarizing what had previously been written about the history and effects of coca and cocaine. He concluded it by recommending seven conditions where cocaine treatment might prove useful: (1) as a mental stimulant, (2) as a possible treatment for digestive disorders, (3) as an appetite stimulant in cases of wasting diseases, (4) in the treatment of morphine and alcohol addiction, (5) as a treatment for asthma, (6) as an aphrodisiac, and (7) as a local anesthetic.

Freud's paper was widely read and, at least initially, well received. Physicians, in large numbers, began to prescribe cocaine to morphine addicts. Within a few months, clinics in Europe and the United States were packed with morphine addicts who were also addicted to cocaine. Less than six months after Freud's paper first appeared, Albert Erlenmeyer published a paper criticizing the practice (30). In his textbook on the treatment of morphine addiction published in 1887, Erlenmeyer wrote:

This therapeutic procedure (treatment of addiction with cocaine) has lately been publicly trumpeted and praised as a veritable salvation. But the greater the fuss made about this 'absolutely precious' and 'totally indispensable' route to health, the less efficacious it proved to be. These claims were made not only in medical journals but also in the popular press, a current practice which, at the risk of offending our profession, I must condemn. It was simply a question of propaganda expounded by individuals without any truly scientific experience, as objective analysis of the question easily demonstrated. But they persisted despite the warnings and ended up with the sorry and frightening result that use turned into abuse. The genies that they summoned up to help them turned into furies bearing misfortune and disaster (1).

Erlenmeyer was not the only one who had problems with the concept. As more and more bad results were reported, Freud came under some pressure to defend himself in print. In 1887, he published another paper, which made the somewhat feeble argument that addiction was a risk only in people who were already morphine addicts (31). But, Freud also made the point, which has generally been ignored or derided (32), that morphine addicts were getting into trouble because they were injecting themselves with cocaine, instead of taking cocaine orally as he had recommended. The distinction is, in fact, vitally important.

From the time that coca leaf was first introduced into Europe, probably in the late 1600s, until the 1860s, cocaine was only taken orally. Practical hypodermic syringes were not yet commercially available, and no one realized that cocaine could be "snorted". Commercial production of hypodermic syringes only began about the time of the American Civil War, circa 1855. Refined cocaine was not available in significant quantities until 1885. When cocaine finally did become available in amounts large enough to abuse, it was mostly swallowed in solution. [Note: Absorption of cocaine from the stomach is very efficient, but when taken by mouth, much of the cocaine is metabolized and inactivated by the liver, long before it ever reaches the brain. Peak blood levels are reached more slowly, and are much lower than would be if the same amount of cocaine had been "snorted" or injected. Lower blood levels translate to reduced addiction potential. When taken by subcutaneous injection, however, higher blood levels are achieved, more cocaine reaches the brain more quickly, and the addiction potential is increased (33)(34).]

Freud, of course, knew absolutely nothing about what happened to cocaine once it entered the body, but his observations were, nonetheless, valid. Injected cocaine is more addictive than cocaine taken orally, and smoked cocaine ("crack") is more addictive than injected cocaine (34). The difference is explained by the speed with which the cocaine gets to the brain; the faster that process occurs, the higher the "high", and the greater the addiction potential. The evidence suggests that no one thought about snorting cocaine until 1905 or 1906. Frequent bouts of cocaine snorting corrode the nasal septum, but the process takes several years to develop. No cases of perforated nasal septum were described in the medical literature until 1910 (35).

Freud's pronouncements on the use of cocaine as a local anesthetic were, and to some extent still are, the cause of much contention. Freudians cite his recommendations in *On Coca* as evidence that Freud really had thought of using cocaine as a local anesthetic before Koller. Detractors argue that Freud never pursued the idea, never did experiments himself, and was just quoting from von Anrep and Moreno (36). Whatever the merits of the arguments, one thing is clear. Freud almost certainly had not read all of the research that he quoted in *On Coca*.

Freud wrote, "Cocaine and its salts have a marked anesthetizing effect when brought in contact with the skin and mucous membranes..." However, that certainly is not the case, and the authors cited by Freud never claimed any such thing. Cocaine solutions do produce anesthesia when painted on mucous membranes, such as the lining of the nose or throat, but they have no effect, whatsoever, on intact skin, because the solution cannot penetrate to the nerves that carry nerve impulses back to the brain. In order to anesthetize the skin with cocaine, cocaine-containing solutions must be directly injected into the skin so that the underlying nerve fibers come directly in contact with cocaine molecules. Both von Anrep and Moreno realized that in order to be an effective anesthetic, cocaine would have to be injected into the skin (36).

Nowhere in *On Coca* does Freud ever mention that cocaine would have to be injected to produce an anesthetic effect. The omission raises the question of whether or not Freud had actually read the papers by von Anrep and Moreno. Physicians began injecting cocaine only after Koller's paper appeared. Freud was certainly not the first writer who did not bother to read the reference he was citing. The practice still occurs today, and is especially common when review papers are written by authors not well acquainted with their subject. That seems to be an accurate description of Freud when he was writing *On Coca*.

Doctors in training at the Allgemeine Krankenhaus (Vienna General Hospital) shared living space at the hospital. It was in the hospital's dormitory where Karl Koller first met Sigmund Freud. Letters discovered after Koller's death reveal that the two became close friends. Freud shared his aspirations with Koller, and he even shared his cocaine. During the summer of 1884, Koller helped Freud with some of his studies. They both took cocaine (orally), and then used various measuring devices to see if the drug could increase muscle strength (37).

Freud was so very impressed with this experimental approach that, in January 1885, he published another cocaine paper, this one devoted to cocaine's effects on muscle strength (38). He used a "dynamometer" for the experiments. The device consisted of a spring-metal clip which, "upon being pressed together moves a pointer connected to it along a graduate scale". Freud would take cocaine, squeeze the clamp, and compare the results with measurements made without cocaine. Freud was already convinced that cocaine was a wonder drug, so it is hardly surprising that he observed increases in his own strength. It is somewhat more surprising that he observed that the effects persisted for a number of hours, at a time when we now know that cocaine would have been cleared from his bloodstream. These experiments were, of course, uncontrolled, unblinded, statistically insignificant, and totally unacceptable by today's standards. At the time they passed as real science.

In September, Freud left town to visit Martha, no doubt with the intention of making her "quite red". Koller continued on with the cocaine studies. During one of these experimental sessions, Koller gave some cocaine to another intern, a Dr. Engel. Engel licked some cocaine from the tip of his pen knife and remarked that the cocaine made his tongue numb. Koller wrote that "... in that moment it flashed upon me that I was carrying in my pocket the local anesthetic for which I had searched for some years earlier. I went straight to the laboratory, asked the assistant for a guinea pig for the experiment, made a solution of cocaine from the powder which I carried in my pocketbook, and instilled this into the eye of the animal."

When Koller put the cocaine drops into the guinea pig's eyes, they became insensible to pain. Koller and his laboratory assistant, a Dr. Gaertner, then put cocaine into each other's eyes and found that neither could feel anything. Freud's official biographer, Ernest Jones, recounts the story somewhat differently, but Koller's account was confirmed by Dr. Gaertner. Gaertner went on to become a successful physician and the editor of a medical newspaper. On the 35th anniversary of Koller's discovery, Gaertner published an editorial recalling the events (39). The contents of the editorial match exactly the description given in Koller's diaries.

Prior to the discovery that made Koller famous, he and his family were hardly on speaking terms. Afterwards, Koller was warmly embraced by his stepmother and his wealthy grandparents. However, when Koller first made his discovery, just a few weeks before the Heidelberg Ophthalmological Society was due to hold its annual meeting, Koller did not have enough money to get to Heidelberg. He convinced a friend, Joseph Brettauer of Trieste, to go to the meeting and present a paper in Koller's name. Brettauer presented Koller's paper on

September 19, 1884. At the conference, Brettauer also conducted a demonstration on a patient from the eye clinic.

In attendance at the Heidelberg conference was an American, Dr. Henry Noyes from New York City. Noyes mailed an account of the discovery back to the editors of the *New York Medical Record* (40). It was published on October 11, 1884, not quite one month after the meeting, and one week before Koller himself was able to present the same material on October 17, at the meeting of the Viennese Medical Society.

By the end of September 1884, E. R. Squibb had given up on the idea of making refined cocaine, but Noyes' report changed Squibb's way of thinking. Within six weeks of the publication of Noyes' report, Squibb had received 300 orders for cocaine. In fact, the day after Noyes letter was published, there was a rush to buy cocaine. At the time, only one druggist in New York City had any cocaine in stock, and he had less than 1 g. As demand increased, so did cocaine's price. During the first week or so after Noyes' report was published, a 2% cocaine solution sold for $0.04 per gram (41). The price of cocaine in New York City rose, from $1 per gram to $2.50 per gram to $7.50 per gram (42). In 1996 dollars, the price was four times as high as current wholesale prices on the black market! By the end of 1884, less than two months after Koller's paper had been read at Heidelberg, and less than five months after the publication of *On Coca*, cocaine production at Merck increased from three quarters of a pound in 1883 to 3179 pounds in 1884, and to 158,352 pounds in 1886 (5)!

One of the first Americans to experiment with cocaine was Dr. William Stewart Halsted, a young surgeon, then chief of Roosevelt Hospital's Outpatient Department, and a visiting surgeon at Bellevue Hospital in New York City. Within one week of hearing about Koller's discovery, Halsted and his associates, Richard Hall and Frank Hartley, had experimented on themselves, on their surgical colleagues, and on students, not to mention the occasional patient. It became apparent to Halsted, and to his group, that cocaine could do much more than just make the eye insensible to pain. If cocaine was injected directly into nerves, they observed it would block the nerve and prevent pain in the area supplied by that nerve. The group's first paper, which described nerve blocks performed by Halsted and Hall, was published six weeks after they read Noyes' account of the Heidelberg Congress (43). One of the cases described by Hall was his own, where Halsted injected Hall's inferior dental nerve. Anyone who has ever had a cavity filled in a lower tooth is familiar with the procedure first devised by Hall and Halsted.

In the 1800s, doctors thought nothing of experimenting on themselves. Herman Knapp, editor of the *Archives of Ophthalmology*, also had read the Noyes' report, and set to work testing Koller's claims. He experimented on himself, his patients, and his 15-year-old son. Knapp described the results in an article he wrote for the October 25, 1884, issue of *Medical Record*. He stated that he had placed cocaine drops in his own eyes, ears, nose, mouth, throat, urethra, and rectum. He then applied silver nitrate to his eye and to the end of his penis. Silver nitrate is used to cauterize bleeding from small blood vessels; its application is normally very painful. Knapp found that when cocaine was applied to his eye and his urethra, the silver nitrate produced no pain whatsoever. Perhaps his enthusiasm had waned by the time he got around to checking his rectum because he applied no silver nitrate there, believing it sufficient to observe that he experienced a feeling of numbness (44).

Within one year, William Halsted's group had used nerve blocks on more than 1000 patients (45), allowing the physicians to carry out surgical procedures that had never previously been thought practical. In 1885, Halsted traveled to Europe, visited Vienna General Hospital, and taught Christian Billroth's assistant, Adolph Wölfer, how to produce anesthesia by injecting cocaine directly into nerves. Wölfer had already experimented with giving cocaine anesthetics, but without much success. Wölfer had declared the whole business a waste of time. After Halsted showed Wölfer the proper techniques, Wölfer became a convert and began publishing his own papers on cocaine anesthesia (46).

Another Viennese surgeon, Carl Ludwig Schleich, took Wölfer's work one step further, finding ways to avoid cocaine's side effects by using highly diluted cocaine solutions ("infiltration anesthesia") (47). One of Halsted's students, Leonard Corning, is credited with the discovery of spinal anesthesia, again using cocaine (48). As was the case with Freud and Koller, a dispute arose over whether Halsted or Corning had discovered spinal anesthesia. Like the dispute between Freud and Koller, the question is now one of only academic interest.

Not surprisingly, Halsted, Hall, and several of Halsted's assistants became addicted. Hall retired from academics and moved to California, where he founded the Santa Barbara County Medical Society. He became the first surgeon at Santa Barbara Cottage Hospital. Unfortunately, it appears that Hall remained addicted (49), as Halsted certainly did. Halsted's friend, William Welch, a pathologist at Bellevue Hospital, tried to break Halsted's cocaine habit by chartering a schooner with a crew of three, and sailing Halsted around the Caribbean. When that did not work, Halsted checked into Butler Hospital in Providence, Rhode Island, where the staff at Butler cured him of his cocaine addiction, but only by addicting him to morphine. After a second admission to Butler in 1887, Halsted was pronounced "cured" of his morphine problem (50). Halsted went on to become the first professor of Surgery at Johns Hopkins School of Medicine, where he spent the rest of his career. After Halsted's death, his friend William Osler, the first professor of Medicine at Johns Hopkins, confirmed that Halsted had never been cured of his addiction, and that Halsted was still using morphine at the time of his death (51).

History has shown these early pioneers in drug discoveries did not receive the accolades due them. Had all of these researchers been working with a mold or some bacteria that they had found in an Egyptian tomb, the question of a mummy's curse would surely have arisen. von Anrep was imprisoned by Russian revolutionaries and died an exile in Paris. Niemann died prematurely, but the cause remains unknown. Moreno disappeared from public life almost as soon as his paper was published, and no one knows what happened to him. Freud lived into his 80s, but died a lingering and painful death from cancer of the mouth. Halsted spent the rest of his life addicted to cocaine and/or morphine. Several of Halsted's colleagues were said to have died of drug abuse. Schleich was nearly laughed out of the meeting hall at the German Surgical Society Congress in Berlin in 1892 when he suggested, quite appropriately at the time, that local anesthesia might be much safer than general anesthesia. No one in Germany ever took Schleich seriously afterward (47). Koller was challenged to a duel by an anti-Semitic junior surgeon working for Christian Billroth. Contrary to Freud's account that Koller had had only one dueling lesson, Koller was actually a reserve army officer and an experienced fencer (12). Koller won the duel, but realized that his possibilities for advancement in Vienna were, to say the least, limited. He emigrated to New York where he died in 1944. He was never eligible for the Nobel Prize because it was not created until after his discovery. The only physician to profit from cocaine during this epoch was Arthur Conan Doyle. Doyle was never very successful as an ophthalmologist, but he did attend lectures at Vienna General Hospital, and he learned all about cocaine. Doyle's knowledge of cocaine and its side effects may explain why Sherlock Holmes made such a convincing addict (52).

Europeans had known about the coca plant for several hundred years, but interest in the plant remained desultory until a legitimate medical use was found for cocaine. By today's standards, cocaine is only a moderately good local anesthetic, but in 1884 it was the only local anesthetic, and the medical community became fascinated with its possibilities. During the following two years, hundreds of clinical reports, mostly singing the praises of cocaine, were published. Reports of toxicity started to appear at almost the same time. At first, they were not taken very seriously, and drug companies could not keep up with the demand for cocaine. Drugmakers' eyes turned to South America, but some visionaries looked towards Southeast Asia.

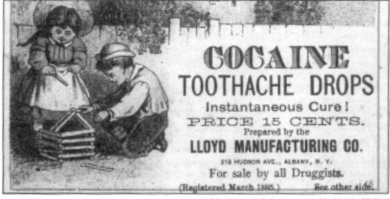

Cocaine toothdrops: The cocaine content of the first coca wines was very low, which probably explains why there were no toxic reactions. The only way to increase the cocaine content was to add more leaves, but that made the wine taste bitter. When large quantities of purified cocaine finally became available, snake oil and quack medicine makers began adding larger quantities of cocaine to their remedies. Reports of medical complications occurred not long after. These consisted mainly of seizures, heart attacks, and strokes which occurred when doctors gave too much cocaine at one time. Using cocaine to treat toothache was a real temptation, and more than a few fatalities resulted. From the National Library of Medicine, circa 1900.

Chapter 5

Therapeutic Bouquets and Brickbats

Cucaine is being used in this country for nearly everything; but we have already found out that this sweet rose of our therapeutic bouquet has its bitter thorn...

From an American correspondent to the *British Medical Journal* for January 2, 1886 (1)

Just weeks after Koller's discovery of local anesthesia was announced, articles about cocaine were prominently featured in most of the important medical journals. Not all of the publicity was good. For every article touting the effectiveness of cocaine, there was another describing dangerous, sometimes life threatening, side effects. The dangerous side effects should have surprised no one. Even the earliest Amazon explorers had raised the possibility that coca's positive actions might be outweighed by its dangerous side effects. Concerns had been raised as early as 1817, when von Spix and von Martius reported on what they had seen during the three years they spent exploring the Amazon.

von Martius, like most of the other explorers, was impressed with the way the Indians appeared to be able to subsist on maize, flour, and water, as long as they had a supply of coca. But, he also observed that "use of the plant had become an abuse amongst them, as opium-smoking in China. Its effect is to deaden sensation and produce even madness; it has morally, a most pernicious influence on those who take it in excess" (2). von Martius was just the first of many researchers and explorers to express concern that not all of the properties of the coca leaf were miraculous or desirable. However, no one except the explorers had any direct experience with coca. Physicians, and the public at large, believed what they wanted to hear and discounted most of the bad news. That was certainly how Freud dealt with Edward Poeppig, another German naturalist and explorer, who had spent five years on the Amazon. Poeppig authored several books about his experiences and observations. Portions of one, *Travels in Chile, through Peru and Down the Amazon*, were translated into English by Sir William Hooker, the director of the Royal Botanical Gardens at Kew.

Hooker edited a periodical called *Companion to the Botanical Magazine*. In 1835, Hooker published a special issue that included some excerpts from Poeppig's book, along with Hooker's own drawings of the coca plant. These were the first drawings of a coca plant to appear in an English publication (3). Poeppig, like von Martius, believed that coca abusers were like opium eaters. Poeppig warned, in no uncertain terms, against the immoderate use of coca. Sigmund Freud read these warnings, but when he wrote *On Coca*, he dismissed Poeppig's observations as unrepresentative and inaccurate (4).

Another naturalist with negative views about coca was Hughes-Algernon Weddell, an English botanist who moved to France sometime in the early 1800s. Weddell was the botanist attached to a French scientific expedition that visited Bolivia in 1843. Weddell wrote a book, *Voyage dans le nord de la Bolivie*, about his Bolivian experiences. Portions of Weddell's book were later translated and published in English and American medical journals (5). Weddell disagreed with much of what Poeppig had to say, but he did not give coca a completely clean bill of health. According to Weddell, coca chewing "does sometimes produce evil consequences among Europeans who have not accustomed themselves to it..." He also observed that chewing too much coca could result in a "peculiar aberration of the intellectual facilities indicated by hallucinations."

Johan von Tschudi and Weddell were both exploring in Peru at the same time, but it appears their paths never crossed. von Tschudi's book, *Travels in Peru*, was first published in 1847, and translated into English in 1854 (6). Freud quotes a section of von Tschudi's book in *On Coca*. The section he chose was the one describing the previously reported exploits of the Indian laborer Hataum Humang, who worked at excavating a foundation for five days and nights, slept only two hours a night, and took nothing by mouth except coca. Freud, like many other Europeans, seized on the story as confirmation of coca's miraculous powers. But a blanket endorsement of coca was hardly what von Tschudi intended. He was concerned about coca's undesirable side effects. He was also worried that Europeans could be even more at risk than natives who had grown up chewing coca.

According to von Tschudi,

> *He who indulges for a time in the use of coca finds it difficult, indeed almost impossible to relinquish it...They give themselves*

*up for days together, to the passionate enjoyment of the leaves.
Then their excited imaginations conjure up the most wonderful
visions...I have never yet been able to ascertain correctly the
conditions the Coquero (coca chewer) passes through on
returning to his ordinary state; it, however, appears that it is
not so much want of sleep, or the absence of food, as the want
of Coca that puts an end to the debauch.*

The "wonderful visions" reported by von Tschudi were experienced first hand by Paolo Mantegazza (1831-1910), an Italian physician, who worked in Northern Argentina during the 1850s. He agreed with the American physicians who believed that "the very strong digestive power of this leaf eliminates the most uncomfortable complications of alcoholic overindulgence (7)." Mantegazza, like Freud, also believed in self-experimentation, and he treated himself with prodigious quantities of coca extract. He experienced what appears to have been coca-related hallucinations on a number of occasions, and wrote vivid descriptions about his experiences. One description of his hallucinatory experiences is still widely quoted, probably because the prose was so overheated:

*...I sneered at the poor mortals condemned to live in this valley
of tears while I, carried on the wings of two leaves of coca, went
flying through the spaces of 77,438 words, each more splendid
than the one before...An hour later I was sufficiently calm to
write these words in a steady hand: God is unjust because he
made man incapable of sustaining the effect of coca all life long.
I would rather have a life span of ten years with coca than one
of 10000000...(and here I had inserted a line of zeros) centuries
without coca (8).*

Mantegazza's accounts and von Tschudi's writings both provide clinically accurate descriptions of a chronic cocaine user on a "binge". Mantegazza's accounts were equally valid, although it appears that he had little insight into what he was doing to himself. Under appropriate circumstances, cocaine users will continue to use cocaine until they have exhausted their supply. The situation can readily be reproduced in the laboratory; animals connected to a source of morphine will give themselves injections on a regular basis, but not to the exclusion of all other activities. Animals instrumented to self-inject cocaine will continue doing so until they die. No other drug, with the possible exception of methamphetamine, possesses that property.

Freud acknowledged Poeppig's and Weddell's concerns about toxicity, but he either ignored, or possibly never read, the negative comments of von Martius and von Tschudi. Freud dismissed the warnings of Poeppig and Weddell by pointing out that most "experts" disagreed with their assessments. And even though Mantegazza's writings had inspired "but little confidence", Freud stated that he had "come across so many correct observations in Mantegazza's publications that I am inclined to accept his allegations...(4)". In his paper, Freud summarized expert opinion with the statement that "other observers affirm that the use of coca in moderation is more likely to promote health than to impair it."

Freud's summary is almost certainly correct. In the modern era, few medical complications have ever been demonstrated in coca leaf-chewing Indians. In Spanish colonial days, the first Spanish writers and historians were mainly mute on the subject. It was only some years later, after large scale coca production had been initiated, that the Church began to condemn the evils of the practice. And even then, it is difficult to separate the evil effects of coca from the evil effects of rampant Chagas' disease (a parasite which beset the indigenous population when they were forced to work in low lying areas), and the effects of working in silver and mercury mines located at elevations of over 13,000 feet.

The big mistake made by Freud was that he confused coca with cocaine. The two terms are far from synonymous. Of course, coca leaf contains cocaine, but it contains very small amounts of cocaine, usually much less than 1% (9)(10). Comparing coca leaf and cocaine is like comparing fire hoses with flame throwers. While there have been reports describing sores in the mouths of leaf chewers, similar to those seen in people who chew tobacco, reports of vascular disease and sudden death in coca leaf-chewers are uncommon.

The apparent absence of vascular toxicity in the Andes' natives is explained by the relatively small amount of cocaine in their blood (11); their blood levels never get high enough to put them at risk. Even though experienced coca-leaf chewers can achieve fairly high blood concentrations, these concentrations still only amount to a fraction of those seen after cocaine is smoked or injected intravenously. Today, young people in South America do smoke cocaine paste (which is like crack), and toxicity among the South American paste smokers has become a significant public health issue.

It would take an enormous amount of leaf, and a great deal of chewing, to extract enough cocaine from the coca to produce a toxic reaction. As Freud found out, the use of purified cocaine is an entirely different matter. Even when taken orally, purified cocaine is more toxic than chewed leaf just because more cocaine is introduced into the body (12). Both the amount of cocaine used, and the way it is taken, are codeterminants of toxicity and addiction. In a very real sense, the history of cocaine toxicity is determined by technology. First, there had to be ample supplies of purified cocaine, then there had to be more efficient ways to get the cocaine from outside of the body into the brain.

Certain features of cocaine toxicity and cocaine addiction are now well understood. The chances of becoming addicted are determined by the amount of cocaine that gets to the brain, and the speed with which it gets there. Pure cocaine taken orally is certainly more potent than cocaine from chewing leaves, but even so, it is unlikely to produce much in the way of toxicity, nor will it cause much of a "high", at least not compared to cocaine taken by injection under the skin, or into a vein. The explanation has to do with the considerable time lag between the moment when cocaine moves out of the stomach and into the bloodstream, the time it takes for the cocaine to arrive in the brain, and the amount of cocaine that reaches the brain.

Because cocaine in the stomach enters the bloodstream much more slowly than cocaine injected into a muscle or vein, blood levels after using a given amount of cocaine never get as high as after injection, and the result is a less intense "high". The possibility of toxicity is also reduced. Not only does injecting produce a more intense high, it also increases the risks of addiction and toxicity (13)(14). Smoked cocaine produces blood levels approximately the same as those seen in intravenous users, but smoked cocaine ("free base" or "crack") produces the most intense stimulation, the greatest risk of addiction, and the greatest risk of toxicity (12).

Until Freud and Koller published their observations, hardly anyone in Europe or the United States had ever heard of cocaine, and physicians certainly had no experience with the problems of cocaine toxicity. The medical community gradually learned, but the full picture of the disease took more than 20 years to emerge. The reason that it took so long had as much to do with the way cocaine was being used as with its availability.

During the 1870s, large amounts of cocaine were consumed in Europe, but it was all in the form of coca wine. No one had thought to inject cocaine and, besides, there were few syringes around with which to inject it. Freud took his cocaine by mouth and so did his friends, at least until Fleischl-Marxow started to give himself subcutaneous injections, and until surgeons started injecting cocaine anesthetics into their patients. In fact, initial reports describing cocaine toxicity all had to do with cocaine being injected for medical purposes. Decades passed before there were large numbers of addicted abusers with medical problems.

Snorting cocaine only became a common practice at the turn of the century. Although not nearly as efficient a way to get cocaine into the bloodstream as injecting, snorted cocaine does enter the blood much more quickly than cocaine that is swallowed. The enhanced absorption translates into increased potential for addiction and toxicity. In addition, chronic cocaine snorting produces a characteristic pattern of changes in the tissues that line the nasal cavity. Cocaine causes all blood vessels to contract, sometimes so intensely that no blood can pass through them. When the blood vessels in the septum contract, the cartilage in the middle of the nose will be temporarily deprived of its normal blood supply. Blood flow only returns to normal as the cocaine effects wear off.

Two things happen as a consequence: (1) the tissue swells when the blood supply is restored, which explains why cocaine users tend to have stuffy, runny noses, and (2) the tissue is eventually weakened and destroyed. The process is not unique to cocaine users. It also occurs in people who become addicted to nose drops (15). It can also occur in certain disease states. Syphilis is one, and a mysterious disorder, known was Wegner's Granulomatosis, is another. In both cases, disease of the underlying blood vessels is thought to be a component of the disorder. More than a few chronic cocaine users have presented with what, for all intents and purposes, looked like Wegner's disease.

Regardless of the drug causing the problem, it takes years to develop a perforated nasal septum; the first perforated nasal septum was not reported until 1910. That suggests that the practice of snorting cocaine could not have begun much before 1905 (16). But not all the consequences of cocaine-induced vasoconstriction are bad. Because cocaine causes the vessels in the nose to go into spasm, it delays its own absorption. With some of the blood vessels closed down, absorption of cocaine is also slowed down, blood levels do not rise quite so rapidly, and toxicity is less than when cocaine is injected. Detectable quantities of snorted cocaine may remain present on the nasal septum for some time. At autopsy, if cocaine was used, nasal swabs can usually disclose its presence, even if several days have elapsed.

Of course, injecting cocaine is more efficient than snorting it, and the intravenous route is much more effective than injection into skin or muscle — the route chosen by Freud's friend, Fleischl-Marxow. But there is nothing in the literature to suggest that cocaine was being taken intravenously until a few years before World War I. Stranger still, there is no evidence that anyone thought to smoke cocaine until the 1980s. Smoked cocaine goes directly into the bloodstream, and its absorption is not impeded by vasoconstriction. Absorption is nearly instantaneous. After 1884, in the post-Koller, post-Freud era, when people started injecting cocaine, the results were almost predictable. As cocaine dosages escalated, so did the number of reported medical problems.

News about Koller's anesthetic discovery spread like wildfire. American doctors first learned about it when they read the October 11, 1884 issue of the *Medical Record*, published just five weeks after the

Heidelberg Ophthalmology Congress, where Koller's announcement had first been made (17)(18).

Some physicians learned about Koller's discovery sooner than others. The contents of the *Medical Record* article were leaked before they appeared in print, and Herman Knapp, editor of *Archives of Ophthalmology*, knew about the discovery even before the *Medical Record* article was published. Hundreds of letters and reports followed on the subject. All of the reports were anecdotal: one doctor describing the experiences he had had treating one or two patients.

Physicians in Europe and America used cocaine to treat a host of unrelated conditions. Enthusiasm often got the better of common sense, and cocaine was not infrequently prescribed for conditions that today are not even recognized as diseases. Cocaine was touted as the cure for almost every conceivable disorder, from prostate enlargement (19) to nymphomania (20), asthma, sea sickness, hemorrhoids (21), and hay fever (20).

Some of the indications for cocaine made more sense than others. Cocaine raises blood epinephrine levels, and epinephrine-like drugs are a recognized treatment for asthma. On the other hand, using cocaine to treat nymphomania was probably not a very good choice. Cocaine is a potent sexual stimulant for many users, increasing libido and decreasing inhibition at the same time. Many addiction specialists believe that cocaine-related compulsive sexuality actually contributes to treatment failure and chronic relapse to drug use. More importantly, the phenomena of sex-for-drugs is now recognized as an important factor in HIV transmission. One hundred years ago, sex-for-drugs may well have been a contributing factor in the transmission of syphilis.

Cocaine was mainly used as a local anesthetic, and it was vastly more effective than anything else that had ever come before. Koller had shown that cocaine drops applied to the membranes of the eye made the eye insensible to pain. The next logical step, then, was to apply cocaine solutions to other surfaces in the body. Cocaine solutions applied to other membranes, such as the urethra, bladder, rectum, and vagina worked well, at least in terms of preventing pain, but cocaine injected into body tissues worked even better.

When cocaine solutions are applied to body membranes, the solutions are very rapidly absorbed into the body. Even when only a few drops of dilute cocaine solution are placed in the eye, detectable concentrations of cocaine appear in the bloodstream a few seconds later. Most of the early eye surgeons used relatively small amounts of solution, so complications were uncommon. But when larger doses were used, or when the cocaine was injected into the lining of the eye, complications occurred.

In the fall of 1885, less than a year after the announcement of Koller's discovery, Dr. Anton Ziem, an eye surgeon in Danzig, Germany, reviewed 17 cases where cocaine anesthesia had caused potentially serious side effects, usually seizures (22). Similar reports from other eye surgeons soon followed (23), as did reports of eye infections in patients given cocaine anesthetics(24). It was the problem of eye infections, rather than the risk of seizures, that did much to dampen initial enthusiasm about cocaine.

Fortunately for the eye surgeons, and for their patients, humans have relatively small eyes, and instilling large volumes of cocaine-containing solutions is difficult, though not impossible. The eye surgeons, and their patients, were also fortunate in that cocaine is only a moderately good local anesthetic. As a general rule, the more potent and long lasting a local anesthetic is, the more toxic it will be. Local anesthetics used today are, in some respects, considerably more toxic than cocaine. But, as the ophthalmologists soon found out, large doses of local anesthetics can cause seizures which, if prolonged, are followed by coma and death. With so many physicians prescribing cocaine to treat so many disorders, complications were inevitable. Deaths from cocaine anesthesia were not rare, although they were certainly not an every day occurrence either.

The first cocaine-related death, at least to be described by the international medical journals, occurred in 1886. The death was a result of cocaine administered during rectal surgery. Gonorrhea and syphilis were rampant in the late 1800s. Victims of either disease, and sometimes even patients with tuberculosis, were prone to inflammation, scarring, and occasionally, ulceration of the rectum, urethra, and bladder. Filling the urethra and bladder with cocaine-containing solutions allowed the painless passage of instruments into the bladder and also effectively anesthetized the bladder wall. However, the bladder walls provide a tremendous surface area for the absorption of cocaine, especially if the wall was already inflamed. The same danger existed during surgery of the rectum and vagina. Attempts at genitourinary surgery, using cocaine anesthesia, often lead to disastrous results (25-27).

The first known cocaine-anesthetic-related death in the United States occurred in New York City, in 1892. Benjamin M. Noe, a 42-year-old tailor went to Bellevue Hospital for hand surgery. Noe's hand was injected with a 4% cocaine solution. According to an account in the *New York Times*, Noe developed uncontrollable convulsions and was dead within five minutes of being injected. An autopsy was performed, and a coroner's inquest was held. The autopsy disclosed "congestion" of the major organs and fluid in the lungs. The findings of the inquest read:

It is supposed that this intense congestion was caused by the cocaine, but as there has been no other death after the administration of cocaine in this city, the medical profession is not familiar with the effects of the drug.

The inquest panel ruled that death was caused by the cocaine injection, but decided that the surgeon had exercised proper judgment. The panel felt that death was in some way due to "a peculiar, unknown existing idiosyncrasy"(28).

It was only a matter of chance that no cocaine-associated deaths were reported in New York until 1892. The first cocaine death in London had occurred three years earlier in January 1889. Charles Sidney Fletcher was admitted to the University College Hospital of London where he was scheduled to have surgery on his tuberculosis-scarred bladder. However, a medication error proved fatal for Fletcher. A concentrated cocaine solution, containing 1200 mg of cocaine, was to have been injected into Fletcher's bladder. Instead, it was given him to drink. Had the cocaine been instilled into his bladder, much of it would have stayed there until drained out by the surgeon. When swallowed, all of the cocaine was absorbed from his stomach. The resultant uncontrolled convulsions proved fatal. Although it was not recognized at the time, Fletcher's autopsy revealed, in addition to extensive tuberculosis, the typical findings seen in cocaine-associated deaths: a swollen brain and fluid-filled lungs (29).

The most famous of the anesthetic disasters occurred in 1887, and involved not only the death of a young woman, but of her surgeon as well. The suicide of Professor Sergei Petrovich Kolomnin was widely reported. Kolomnin was treating a young woman who had an open sore on the inside of her rectum, presumed to be a complication of tuberculosis. Kolomnin decided to scrape and cauterize the lesion, using cocaine as an anesthetic. He had never used cocaine as an anesthetic in rectal surgery, but he reviewed the literature and found reports from other physicians who claimed great success. One in particular, from France, described using cocaine in an operation exactly like the one that Kolomnin was planning. To be on the safe side, Kolomnin injected the patient with only 1380 mg of cocaine, half as much as the French surgeon had recommended, but still a very large amount (equivalent to approximately 20 to 30 "lines" of cocaine). The surgery itself was uneventful. Kolomnin scraped the ulcer, packed it with gauze to prevent bleeding, and sent the woman back to her room. He was called to her side half an hour later. Her pulse was weak, her face was blue, and she was barely breathing. Kolomnin tried everything he could think of, including, "Faradization (electric shocks), artificial respiration, hypo-dermatic injection of ether, administration of ammonia, tracheotomy for the inhalation of oxygen, (and) stimulating and nutrient enemata," but the woman could not be revived.

Analysis of the ulcer scrapings taken at surgery revealed that the woman was not, after all, suffering from tuberculosis, and surgery was almost certainly not necessary. Shortly afterwards, Kolomnin committed suicide, telling friends that, "I cannot help feeling at times that I killed her (30)." Cocaine is no longer used for rectal or vaginal surgery, though application of cocaine to the rectum and vagina, as an exercise in eroticism, is still widely practiced. Whether the intent is erotic or surgical, the result can be equally disastrous. Deaths associated with genital cocaine application are still fairly common (31-33).

Dentistry was another problem area. The general level of dental hygiene during the "Gay 90s" was not good, and before the availability of cocaine, dental procedures were extremely painful. Injecting small amounts of cocaine into the nerves supplying the jaw, as first described by Halsted (34), was a safe and effective procedure, much the same as it is today. However, injecting cocaine directly into the gums surrounding a tooth produces a reasonably absolute level of anesthesia, and requires a good deal less skill than locating and injecting the nerve to the lower jaw. In the 1890s, that was the approach most commonly used by dentists. Unfortunately, most of the cocaine injected into the gums goes directly into the bloodstream, and results in dangerously high blood levels. Seizures, occasionally fatal, were a regular occurrence in dentist's offices(35)(26).

A goodly number of the complications described at the turn of the century would have occurred, even if the unfortunate patients had been given excessive amounts of today's local anesthetics, such as lidocaine or marcaine. However, cocaine is more than a local anesthetic, and cocaine does things that other local anesthetics do not. Cocaine disrupts the metabolism and distribution of neurotransmitters [epinephrine, dopamine, and serotonin, to name but a few], the family of chemicals that allow communications between different parts of the brain. The "high" experienced by cocaine users is the result of altered dopamine metabolism, with too much dopamine accumulating in the wrong parts of the brain. The racing heart and dry mouth are the result of altered adrenaline [epinephrine and norepinephrine] metabolism. Some of the medical problems associated with cocaine use, such as heart attack and stroke, are the result of altered epinephrine and norepinephrine metabolism.

Adrenaline is instrumental in preparing the body for "fight or flight". Soldiers about to go into combat, not to mention graduating seniors sitting for their final examinations, mobilize their body resources to prepare for the event. Blood pressure and heart rate go up, hearing becomes hyperacute, and extra nutrients are released into the bloodstream. Blood is redirected away from the stomach and intestines, and sent to supply the heart, brain, arms, and legs. All of these adaptations are mediated by adrenaline, and all can be seen in cocaine users. They may feel "high", but in a very real sense their bodies are being stressed. Over the long term, the stress response extracts a heavy price. A cocaine user with high blood pressure differs little from a stressed out, non-drug using CEO with high blood pressure.

The vascular system, especially the blood vessels that supply the heart and brain, bears the brunt of the damage from long-term cocaine use. The hearts of long term cocaine users, even those without symptoms, become slightly enlarged, and that slight degree of enlargement places them at increased risk for sudden death (36). Compounding the problem is that chronic stimulant abuse, whether it is cocaine or amphetamine, seems to increase the risk of coronary artery disease. The combination is deadly because coronary artery disease rarely goes away. Cocaine abusers who stop taking the drug still may remain at risk from their blocked coronary arteries. Cocaine abusers who continue to use the drug are at increased risk because cocaine makes the heart work harder, and partially blocked arteries may not be able to supply enough blood to meet the increased oxygen demands caused by the added work. Since autopsies were rarely performed on cocaine-related fatalities at the turn of the century, there is no good way to determine how many cocaine-associated deaths were due to heart disease, but it seems likely that many were. Of course, individuals with preexisting heart disease are at even greater risk when they use cocaine.

At the turn of the century, going to the dentist was a risky proposition, even for those with normal hearts. But for those with heart disease, visiting the dentist could be fatal. The case of Jane Favish was typical. She died on January 25, 1908, in a dentist's office in Soho, London. The dentist, an illegal immigrant without a degree, injected the woman's gums with 30 mg of cocaine prior to carrying out multiple extractions. Favish died before the procedure could be completed. An autopsy disclosed that she had a badly scarred mitral valve, a consequence of rheumatic fever which she had had as a child. The dentist was charged with manslaughter (37). The death toll among those with preexisting heart disease must have been fairly high. An early case report from 1886 described the death of an 11-year-old girl. She suffered from "fainting spells". As in the case of Ms. Favish, these fainting spells were probably a consequence of childhood rheumatic fever. The child's physician decided to treat her with cocaine injections. She was dead within a few minutes of the first injection (35).

A physician named J.B. Mattison from Brooklyn, New York, Director of the Brooklyn Home for "Habitues", was the first person to systematically study the problem of cocaine toxicity. Mattison reported his findings at a meeting of the Kings County Medical Society on February 15, 1887. He had reviewed the world literature and discovered 4 reported deaths and 46 cases where serious adverse complications had occurred (35). All of the cases had occurred during the 18 months that had elapsed since the announcement of Koller's discovery. Mattison's talk was transcribed and, soon afterwards, portions of it were reprinted in England in the *Lancet* (May 23, 1887) and in newspapers in the United States.

In November of that same year, in a speech given before the American Association for the Cure of Inebriety, Mattison added three more cocaine-related deaths, and 73 instances of severe complications. Mattison's speech was reprinted in *La Tribune Medicale*, in Paris on January 1, 1888. Mattison appears to have turned crusading against cocaine into something of an industry. He gave at least one other speech on the same subject. On March 11, 1891, he spoke on the subject at a meeting of the New York Medico-Legal Society. According to Mattison, since his last accounting in 1888, there had been another six deaths, along with another 53 additional cases where patients had experienced life threatening side effects (38).

Mattison was not the only physician worried about the cocaine problem. In January 1886, Dr. George Catelet wrote to the *Medical Gazette* describing the case of Ester C., a 39-year-old mother of four children. Ester had been admitted to the State Lunatic Asylum in St. Joseph, Missouri. One year prior to admission, her behavior started to change, and she periodically threatened to kill herself and her baby. Six months of intensive treatment improved things somewhat, and her husband removed her from the hospital. She was readmitted three months later, worse than before. Because Ester had become so depressed, a decision was reached to treat her with cocaine. She was given a 60-mg injection of cocaine each morning, and another later in the afternoon. The treatment continued for two weeks.

Dr. Catelet's patient seemed to be getting stronger. She was eating more, but remained as depressed as ever. However, the injections, while they lasted, definitely made her feel better, and she constantly asked for more. After her death, a review of her chart showed that each injection increased her heart rate by 20 to 25 beats, and increased her blood pressure "considerably". On the evening of the 14th night of treatment, Ester complained of a left-sided headache, and spent a restless, sleepless, night. The following morning, her temperature and pulse were elevated, her extremities pale and cool. Her eyes were obviously swollen, more so on the right side. She lost consciousness, the swelling of her eyes became worse, and she died 30 hours after the last injection.

Ester C. had all the symptoms of cavernous sinus thrombosis, a type of stroke. It is a somewhat uncommon disorder, seen in patients who are abnormally prone to blood clot formation. Today, birth control pills are the most common cause of cavernous sinus thrombosis in young women, but there is firm evidence that cocaine also makes abnormal blood clot formation more likely.

For several decades, papers that described the dangers of cocaine use were a regular feature in medical journals. Physicians who treated themselves seemed to be particularly at risk. There were more than a few reports which described physicians who were totally incapacitated by cocaine use. Not infrequently, self-medicating doctors managed to kill themselves. The case of Daniel McIntyre was typical. He was a 27-year-old surgeon at Edinburgh University, who tried to cure his tooth-ache by applying cocaine crystals directly to the tooth. The Coroners Jury returned a verdict of "Death by misadventure (39)."

By the turn of the century, there was a glut of cocaine on the market. Cocaine could be purchased at local pharmacies, usually without a prescription. Cocaine was also sold openly on the streets. Even in cities where pharmacy sales were regulated, enforcement was lax, and there was no shortage of physicians and pharmacists willing to make money selling drugs. Patent medicines further complicated the situation. These remedies contained large amounts of cocaine, and their sales were largely unregulated. Predictably, the number of cocaine abusers grew steadily. The number of reported fatalities continued to increase as well (40). When expressed as a percentage of the population, the cocaine problem then was worse than it is today. According to a U.S. government report, the total number of heroin and cocaine fatalities in 1912 exceeded 5000. The number is slightly more than twice that today, but our population is four times what it was then.

The dawn of the new century brought new problems. During the 1890s, toxic reactions usually occurred because doctors had given their patients too much cocaine at one time. After the turn of the century, the pattern gradually changed. Anesthetic misadventures still occurred, but as physicians learned more about cocaine, they used it more sparingly. In 1924, a select panel was appointed by the American Medical Association to investigate deaths from local anesthesia. By that time, a number of other local anesthetics had come into use, but half of the 43 deaths reviewed by the committee were cocaine-related (41). The committee recommended using less cocaine, and avoiding injections of cocaine altogether. The recommendations obviously had some impact, since the number of reported fatalities rapidly declined thereafter.

In the 1900s, unsupervised, often "recreational", drug use replaced medical misadventures as the most common cause of drug-related death and disability. Cocaine-associated medical disorders were more likely to be the result of using large amounts of cocaine for too long a time, rather than from taking an enormous amount at one time. And the most striking disorders associated with using a large amount of cocaine over a long period of time, besides sudden cardiac death, are some very strange psychiatric syndromes. They result from long term alterations in brain chemistry. Freud's addicted friend, Fleischl-Marxow, was probably the first to suffer from one of these syndromes.

Freud thought he noticed decreased morphine cravings in Fleischl-Marxow when he gave cocaine to his friend. Of course, the improvement was only temporary, and Fleischl-Marxow became addicted to morphine and cocaine simultaneously. One night in June of 1885, Freud and his friends spent the evening trying to calm Fleischl-Marxow who, by then, had become quite psychotic; he was convinced that white snakes were crawling over his skin (42).

The belief that small animals are crawling out of, or through, a cocaine user's skin has come to be known as Magnon's syndrome. It was named for the French neurologist Valentine Magnon, who recognized that what Fleishl-Marxow had experienced was a unique syndrome associated with chronic cocaine abuse. In 1898, at a meeting of the French Biological Society, Magnon described three patients with symptoms almost identical to those of Freud's friend. One patient claimed to be covered with lice, that his clothes and all the objects around him were full of "microbes". He was covered with sores and abscesses resulting from his attempts at removing the vermin. Another of Magnon's patients, a 39-year-old physician, claimed he could feel cocaine crystals under his skin. He kept scraping his tongue, and scratching his hands, in attempts to remove the crystals [quoted in (43)]. Accounts of this syndrome even made their way into the popular press. The *Scientific American* of March 20, 1897 carried an article by a reformed cocaine user who described his visions: "Other dreadful hallucinations I had in thousands, all of a persecuting character, and frightening the life out of me so long as the effects of the drug lasted. You see small animals running about your body, and feel their bite...(44)."

At least victims of Magnon's syndrome were only a danger to themselves. The other important behavioral disturbance associated with cocaine abuse, "agitated delirium", can be dangerous to others as well. Agitated delirium, also known as "excited delirium", can occur as a complication of other medical disorders, but chronic cocaine abuse is the most common cause. Victims become grossly psychotic, physically agitated, often perform amazing feats of strength, and run very high temperatures. What happens next is not entirely clear, but after a few minutes, victims become quiet and die. Agitated delirium complicating cocaine use was first described in 1914 by a physician named Williams. An account of his description was displayed prominently in the Sunday Magazine section of the *New York Times* for February 8, 1914 (45).

Williams' account was so bizarre, and so mixed with racist cant and nonsense, that, today, it is difficult to take any of his claims seriously. The *New York Times* ran William's story under the headline, "Negro cocaine 'fiends' are a new southern menace". The article described a series of murders and violent crimes, allegedly committed by black people under the influence of cocaine. According to Williams, cocaine made the perpetrators crazed and resistant to bullets because they had a "temporary immunity to shock". He even described a man who had been shot through the heart, but who was able to continue fighting with police officers. Williams also claimed that cocaine enhanced the user's ability to shoot accurately, making the "fiends" all the more dangerous. He argued that the emergence of this new "menace" was attributed to the restriction of alcohol sales: as more cities closed bars and limited alcohol sales, a switch to other drugs was inevitable. During prohibition, this line of argument was frequently used by the "wets", those individuals who were opposed to limiting the sale of alcohol (46).

Historians, with more than a little justification, dismissed Williams' observations. Cocaine user or not, gunshot wounds to the heart are fatal. But some valid observations were mixed in with Williams' racist hysteria. Compare Williams' observations to descriptions of more recent cocaine-related deaths in Miami in 1985.

> *A 37-year-old white male drank some beer with a friend. A short time later he was observed in a van, racing the engine and blowing the horn. He then rammed the vehicle into the front of a residence, jumped out, and began running about the neighborhood jumping over fences and pounding on doors. He was yelling and screaming that people were after him. When the police arrived, they found him hiding in some bushes. They coaxed him out and began a "pat down", whereupon the subject began to violently fight the police. Four officers finally restrained and subdued the victim and he was handcuffed. When placed in the police vehicle he began to kick out the windows...*

Or the case of the 26-year-old man who:

> *...took off his clothes, began yelling and screaming, and ran about the apartment smashing a variety of objects. Medical rescue units were called when he punched through a window and lacerated his arm...(47).*

Both men died shortly after they reached the hospital.

These two cases were part of a seven case cluster reported in Miami in 1985. A succession of similar cases have been reported ever since, and the number of new case reports is accelerating. [Note: The strange behavior of the victims invariably attracts police attention, which means that when the victims die, they die in police custody. Allegations of police brutality inevitably result. Virtually no one recalls that the disorder was common at the turn of the century, and it is difficult to convince the public that drugs, and not the police, are usually the cause of death (48). In reality, many of these individuals die at home, without the police ever being called, and without ever having been restrained. Often, they are found dead in their bathrooms. Because of high fevers they will often be found surrounded by wet towels and clothing, and sometimes even with empty ice trays scattered about (47).]

Results of the most recent neurochemical studies suggest that the likelihood of developing this syndrome may be genetically determined. The brains of most people who use cocaine adapt, in such a way, as to protect the individuals from the effects of too much dopamine. Individuals with cocaine psychosis are unable to make these adaptations (49-50). Fortunately, only a very small percentage of the population suffers from this deficiency, which means that the incidence of this disorder can be used as a marker for cocaine use. If cases are occurring with any frequency, it could mean that a very large number of people are using cocaine. No new cases of agitated delirium were reported between 1914 and 1981. During those years, cocaine supplies were scarce, and cocaine was very expensive. In the early 1980s, as soon as the cocaine supply increased, so did the number of agitated delirium deaths. In spite of a declared "war on drugs", more cocaine is available today than ever before, and agitated delirium is now a relatively common disease.

A. <u>Coca plants growing at the Botanical Gardens at Buitenzorg</u>: In1817, the Dutch established a research station, modeled after Kew Gardens, just southeast of Jakarta. Dutch administrators were concerned that the Javanese might not be "morally strong enough to refrain from excessive use," so they vetoed an initial proposal for commercial coca production. But just to be on the safe side, seedlings were planted with the intent of raising enough coca for "chemical and physiological" studies. Courtesy of the Royal Tropical Institute, Amsterdam (633.888.16, N 14). The photograph was taken by a Professor L. Ph de Bussy. The date is unknown.

B. <u>Bringing the coca leaves to the factory of the estate at Tegallega</u>: Photograph taken by Professor de Bussy. It shows leaves being gathered after drying in the sun. The plantation was located on Java's northern coast, roughly midway between Jakarta and Surakarta. Courtesy of the Royal Tropical Institute, Amsterdam (633.888.16, N 16).

C. Initial phase of the cocaine extraction process: The hollowed logs shown here have now been replaced by plastic lined shallow pits, but otherwise little has changed in the last 100 years. In order to extract the cocaine from the leaves, the leaves must first be soaked in a dilute solution containing water and a strong alkali, such as lime. Courtesy of the Royal Tropical Institute, Amsterdam (633.888.16, N 18).

D. The Nederlandsche Cocaine Fabriek: The Dutch Colonial Development Board and coca growers in Java formed a joint venture and built a refinery to better compete with Merck and the other German cocaine manufacturers. The Nederlandsche Cocaine Fabriek (NCF) opened in Amsterdam on March 12, 1900. The Dutch plant was so successful, that a second floor was added to the factory in 1902. By 1910, NCF claimed to be the largest cocaine manufacturer in the world, producing more than 1500 kg of refined cocaine per year. This photograph is from a trade publication,"Het Pharmaceutisch Weekblad," published in 1925. Courtesy of Marcel de Kort, Netherlands Ministry of Health.

Chapter 6

COCA JAVA AND THE SOUTHEAST ASIA COCA INDUSTRY

...while its price is higher than that of any other known substance used in medicine, yet so beneficial are the results obtained from a very small amount of it that it is comparatively cheap...

The Pharmaceutical Record, 1884 (1)

Merck began producing small amounts of cocaine in 1862, but found few customers. In 1883, the year before cocaine's anesthetic properties became widely known, Merck's total output of cocaine amounted to less than half a pound. Doctors were unable to determine what, if anything, cocaine did to the body. The general opinion was that, if it had any effects at all, cocaine was probably not much different than caffeine. And caffeine was abundant and cheap.

Things changed drastically in 1884. In March of that year, Freud published *On Coca*, and in October, Koller discovered that cocaine could be used as a local anesthetic. Freud's paper generated more than a little interest, and Merck's cocaine sales finally began to pick up. After Koller's discovery, sales exploded. Before Koller, eye surgery was almost impossible, and surgery on other parts of the body was limited to procedures that could be performed in seconds. Thus, demand for cocaine was insatiable.

There was, however, very little cocaine to be had, and what little there was sold out almost overnight. Prices for cocaine rose dramatically. In December of 1884, Messrs J.W. Drysdale & Sons, an old line British pharmaceutical manufacturer, sold 6 ounces of cocaine to European buyers for the astronomical sum of £250 (2). No one complained. Attention turned to alternate sources of supply.

Until botanists from the Royal Botanical Gardens at Kew, just outside of London, established cinchona plantations in Ceylon and India, quinine was the most expensive drug in the world. Dutch agriculturists did the same in western Java, where the first cinchona trees were planted in 1852. Initial Dutch attempts were not successful, mainly because the bark of the variety chosen by the planters contained very little quinine. But within a few years, new, government-sponsored cinchona estates (using high-yielding hybrids of Cinchona Ledgeriana) had been established in the Pengalengan highlands of south-western Java (3).

Officials at Kew envisioned a similar scenario for coca leaf. Unlike coca seedlings, seeds of the coca plant are quite hardy. In the late 1880s, they were often sent via the regular mails, packed in a little moist soil (4). Kew officials sent coca seeds to the Botanical Gardens at Calcutta, to the Peradeniya Gardens in Ceylon, to the Agricultural Society of India, and to agricultural stations at Assam and Darjeeling (5). Seeds planted at the Botanical Gardens outside of Lagos, Nigeria, and in Sierra Leone (6) did very well, as opposed to those sent to Jamaica, which, for some reason, failed to flourish (7). For a time, the Blue Mountain area of Jamaica was planted with coca, but Blue Mountain coca did not grow as successfully as Blue Mountain coffee, and attempts at coca growing were abandoned after several years. Coca growers in India met with more success, particularly in the Tea Estates of Assam, where coca remained a minor cash crop for at least 20 years (8).

In 1854, a Dutch botanist named Kasskarl, who had assisted the Indian government in establishing cinchona plantations, wrote a letter to the Dutch Colonial office suggesting that coca cultivation offered nearly as many opportunities as cinchona. Kasskarl described how coca chewing imparted energy and feelings of well being, and he outlined in some detail his reasons for believing that coca plants were well adapted for growth in Java. However, his suggestions were rejected by both the chief of the Public Health Service and the head of the Department of Agriculture.

Both of the Dutch colonial officials were convinced that, once the Javanese found out how good coca could make them feel, they would not be "morally strong enough to refrain from excessive use (9)." They also argued that there was really no need to start growing another dangerous stimulant. After all, coffee already grew in Java. Why risk the "moral health" of the country just to make more money? In spite of the early decision not to pursue commercial coca development, just to be on the safe side, Fromber, the agriculture chief, decided to start a trial garden, with the intent of raising enough coca for "chemical and physiological" studies.

The Dutch government's botanical research station was modeled along the lines of Kew Gardens. The Lands Plantentuin (literally the "Government Botanical Gardens") in Buitenzorg, southeast of Jakarta, was founded in 1817. The gardens were situated at 2,600 feet above sea level, and covered an area of 135 acres. In 1868, a new director, R.C. Sheffer, shifted the focus of the garden from taxonomy to the cultivation of plants with potential economic value (10). Sheffer would have been the individual responsible for contacting Herman Linden, a Belgian seed exporter located in Ghent, who sent a new strain of coca seedlings to Buitenzorg (11). Initial experiments with the new coca plants were very encouraging, so much so that seed was provided to growers throughout Java.

Other plantations in Java and Sumatra were not nearly as successful as those at the botanical garden. Much of Java is too wet to permit coca cultivation. But seeds planted at higher elevations, and shrubs planted between existing trees, did very well. By 1883, the year before the cocaine market took fire, modest quantities of coca leaf, mostly for use in the production of coca-based wines, were being exported from Java and Sumatra for auction in Amsterdam (12).

By 1885, coca seed was in such demand that the agriculturists at Buitenzorg could not keep up with all of the requests for seeds. Many of the tea growers wanted to switch over to coca and stop growing tea entirely. They were advised not to. A colonial office agriculturist, named Van Gorkum, wrote a newspaper article advising the tea growers to only plant coca between rows of tea bushes, as a supplemental crop. Van Gorkum warned that if the growers planted too much coca, prices would go down, and coca cultivation would eventually not be worth the effort (9). Six years later, in 1889, leaf from Java finally began to appear at London's Mincing Lane auctions (12).

Java coca may have been available, but buyers for the European drug houses wanted only South American leaf. Extracting cocaine from the type of plant grown in Java was much more difficult than extracting it from South American varieties. Java coca leaves may have been difficult to process, but at least they were available. Obtaining adequate supplies of South American leaf was problematic. Coca leaves do not travel well, and they had to travel some distance from the mountainous areas where they were grown, to the ports where they were loaded onto European ships.

Packing the coca leaves was also a problem. Wooden presses were used to form leaves into bales called *cesta*. These bales were wrapped, first with banana leaves, and then with crude woolen fabric. Two cestas bound together formed a *tambore*. Pack animals could carry six tambores, with three tambores bound together and balanced on each side. Mules were the preferred pack animals since they could carry more weight than llamas. Depending on which animal was being used to bring leaves down from the mountains, the weight of the cestas was adjusted upward or downward. Cestas carried by mules weighed 25 pounds, giving an average total load per mule of 300 pounds. If llamas were used, 20 pound cestas were formed, giving a total load of 240 pounds (13).

Improperly packed leaves, if they became too damp, fermented while in transit. Leaves that were overly dry lost their potency altogether. For a time, during 1885 and 1886, soldered, tin-lined chests were used for shipping the leaves. The chests did not solve the problem of deterioration, and after a few years, the chests were abandoned by South American growers (11). Dutch growers in Java, however, continued to use tin chests for quite some time (9). Whether the point of origin was South America or Indonesia, shipping bulk leaf was an expensive, and not very satisfactory, process. Even so, exporters in Peru demanded and received $.11 per pound. In the beginning, at least, the Dutch were unable to extract such grand sums. South American coca producers got another boost when the American botanist, Henry H. Rusby, found a way to eliminate the shipping problems.

Almost as soon as Parke, Davis was incorporated in 1871, Parke and George Davis began sending out teams of explorers in hope of discovering new and exotic medications. The initial results of the expeditions were not exactly earth shaking; Parke, Davis explorers brought back guarana root, bearsfoot root, and eucalyptus, the latter being "especially recommended in malarial diseases and for its influence on the mucous membrane in croup, diphtheria, catarrh, etc..." In the early 1880s, several years before the discoveries of Freud and Koller, Parke, Davis began to market a line of products made from coca leaf extracts (14). After 1884, Parke, Davis began supplying purified cocaine for use as an anesthetic, and also expanded its product line to include a range of cocaine-containing preparations.

Like all of the other large drug houses, Parke, Davis feared it would be unable to keep up with the explosive demand resulting from Koller's discovery. Almost as soon as Davis heard of Koller's discovery, Davis approached a young chemist working in Parke, Davis's laboratories, and asked him how soon he could leave for Bolivia. The chemist was Henry H. Rusby, recent medical school graduate, with an additional degree in botany. On January 10, 1885, the Pacific Mail S.S. Acapulco sailed from the foot of Canal Street in New York with Henry Rusby aboard. Rusby had doubts about the trip almost as soon as the ship sailed out of the harbor. One of the passengers was Frederick Carl Lehman, another botanist. Lehman had spent the last 10 years exploring Colombia, Ecuador, and northern Peru. When Rusby told him that he planned to cross the continent, Lehman laughed and suggested that by the first night camping out Rusby would probably die from insect bites.

In spite of the warnings, Rusby persevered. After sailing through violent storms, which washed one of the passengers overboard and then back onto the ship, Rusby finally made land. He hiked across the Isthmus of Panama, then made his way south along the coastal roads of Colombia, Ecuador, and Peru to La Paz, Bolivia. In Bolivia he organized an expedition that included two Texans who were fleeing the law, and an Indian guide whose participation was not quite voluntary. Rusby then crossed the Andes, and traveled down the Amazon River, collecting specimens and recording his observations.

By any standard, Rusby's expedition was a success. As instructed by his employers, he identified potential new sources of coca leaves. But Rusby did something more important than just identify new sources; he solved the shipping problem. Almost as soon as he arrived in Lima, he had organized a large shipment of coca leaves back to the United States. The leaves, however, never reached their destination. A civil war in Columbia had placed an effective halt to all shipping. And, while Rusby's leaves were rotting in a Colombian warehouse, the price of cocaine fell precipitously. A Parke, Davis competitor had arranged huge shipments around Cape Horn, bypassing the war zone, and undercutting Parke, Davis' price. Rusby concluded that shipping coca leaf was a very risky proposition and he determined to find a better way. Rusby set out to devise a method for making semi-refined cocaine (15). He knew the general principles for extracting alkaloids, like cocaine and quinine, and thought he might be able to develop a simplified approach, one that could be accomplished outside of the laboratory. He used his hotel room for a laboratory.

Rusby's hotel room in La Paz had no running water. This was not surprising since, at that time, the only water in La Paz was carried in by laborers every morning. Some people might question the thinking of a trained chemist who set up an alcohol still in a room with no water, but that was exactly what Rusby did. The still was a crudely made affair of heavy tin with a copper bottom. Rusby was in the process of distilling off alcohol from a 5-gallon batch of coca leaf extract, and had placed the still directly over a charcoal fire, when a seam in the still came apart, leaking alcohol onto the open fire, and causing an explosion and a giant plume of flame. Rusby remained calm enough to throw the still out into the hotel verandah, where, instead of burning down much of La Paz, the alcohol still quietly burned itself out.

In spite of getting some blisters, Rusby carried on with his experiments. Even though he is generally given the credit for discovering the process, a Peruvian chemist, named Alfredo Bignon, had devised a similar process years before Rusby ever set foot in South America. Bignon was a contemporary of Moreno, both men trained in Paris and both studied with José Casimiro Ulloa, a Paris-trained Peruvian with an interest in coca and coca research (16). Rusby never made mention of Bignon in any of his writings, and it may be that he was unaware of Bignon's process because it was proprietary. Andes historian Jo Ann Kawell, an expert on the early years of the South American coca industry, believes there is evidence suggesting a link between Bignon and French cocaine manufacturers. It may well be that Bignon's process was kept secret in order to give the French drugmakers a competitive advantage (16).

Clandestine chemists in South America still use the same basic process developed by Rusby, except on a vastly larger scale. The initial steps are still the same. Leaves are soaked for three or four days in a dilute solution of water and alkali, usually lime. Rusby added alcohol to the mixture, but today's illegal producers use gasoline or kerosene, taking up the dissolved cocaine. The leaves are discarded, and dilute sulfuric acid is added. Lime or ammonia is used to neutralize the acid, causing the dissolved cocaine to come out of the solution and collect on the bottom of the container. The liquid is discarded and the crude cocaine allowed to dry in room air. The final product is very much like crack cocaine. Called *buzco*, it can be, and is, widely smoked in South America today.

Rusby's extract was not as pure as the refined product sold by drug houses, but it did have two important advantages over coca leaf: the semi-refined material did not lose its potency when stored, and it could be transported in a fraction of the space required to ship coca leaf. In one stroke, Rusby succeeded in converting coca from a perishable commodity to a stable commodity, like copper or silver.

Rusby never went on another expedition which, considering his penchant for risk taking, was probably just as well. Eventually, he became a Professor at the Columbia University College of Pharmacy. At some point, he must have had a change of heart about stimulant drugs. In 1905, he served as an expert witness for the prosecution when the government charged the Coca-Cola Company with violations of the Pure Food and Drug Act. At the time, Coca-Cola did, and still does, contain caffeine. Crusading government chemists decided that although caffeine was not banned under the Pure Food and Drug Act, it was, nonetheless, a toxic compound, and Coca-Cola should be held accountable. Rusby testified as a witness for the prosecution.

Converting cocaine from a perishable to a stable product changed the economics of the cocaine business. Some of the changes were unforeseen, and not always good for the cocaine growers. Nearly 100 tons of leaf were auctioned in Hamburg in 1886, the same year that the first shipments of crude cocaine came to auction. A 35-pound portion of that first consignment was shipped to England where it sold for "1 shilling 5 pence per gram (17)". Sales of coca leaf in Hamburg dropped rapidly as South American exports shifted more and more of their production into coca paste. By the end of 1887, Hamburg coca leaf sales had dropped by almost two thirds, to under 37 tons (18). At the same time, cocaine refineries in Peru were proliferating. In 1897, the British Consul reported that ten refineries had been built in Peru and more were under construction.

If the U.S. Congress had not passed the McKinley Act, exports of coca leaf might have ceased entirely. The Act set tariff rates for a range of products, but was a particular source of irritation to cocaine refiners in England and Germany. Refined cocaine came under Section 76 of the Act, along with all other "alkaloids, distilled oils, essential oils, expressed oils, rendered oils, chemical compounds and their salts." As such, refined cocaine imported into the United States from Europe, as well as semi-refined crude cocaine imported from Peru, was subject to a 25% tax. Coca leaf was not taxed. But, in 1891, after intense lobbying efforts, pharmaceutical houses in the United States were able to persuade the Board of Appraisers in Washington, D.C. to reclassify crude cocaine under Section 74 of the tariff, along with other necessary medications which were not taxed (19).

As a result of pharmaceutical company lobbying, the price of crude cocaine in the United States dropped. Total imports, however, increased and South American exporters shifted more and more of their production into making coca paste. In 1897, Peruvian leaf exports peaked at 110 tons. Assuming an average cocaine content of .6%, 110 tons of leaf would have contained .66 tons of cocaine. Exports of cocaine paste for that same year were more than twice as high (20). About the same time that American pharmaceutical houses were lobbying over cocaine tariffs in Washington, the first significant shipments of coca leaf from Java and Ceylon reached auction houses in Amsterdam and Hamburg. Their arrival was greeted with some skepticism.

The skepticism had to do with the kind of coca being grown in Java. All cultivated coca comes from two closely related New World species: *Erythroxylum coca Lamarck* and *Erythroxylum novogranatense* from New Granada, the former name of Columbia. Each of the two species has two distinct varieties. The seeds that botanists at Kew Gardens sent around the world were, almost certainly, *E. Coca novogranatense* var. *truxillense*. But the variety most commonly grown in the Amazon basin was *Erythroxylum coca Lamarck*. The first seeds of *E. Coca Novogranatense* arrived at Kew in 1870. They had been collected from the vicinity of Huanuco. Once enough plants had been germinated, Kew botanists distributed seeds to agricultural stations in British colonies around the world. Unfortunately, the seeds that the Kew botanists chose to distribute were not the ones that produced the most extractable cocaine (21).

During the late 1800s, chemists analyzing coca leaves separated their components into two categories: "crystallized" and "uncrystallized" alkaloid. "Crystallizable" alkaloid is another word for cocaine. "Uncrystallized" alkaloid is another way of referring to other molecules, closely related to cocaine, that are also contained in the coca leaf. At the turn of the century, no one had any idea of what to do with the "uncrystallized" alkaloid. Cocaine was what everyone wanted, so leaves containing the most "crystallized" and the least "uncrystallized" alkaloid were the leaves most highly valued.

The total alkaloid content of *Erythroxylum coca Lamarck*, at least at the turn of the century, was usually in the range of .5%, nearly all of it "crystallizable". The alkaloid content of *Novogranatense* varieties was between 1 and 2%, but only one third was "crystallizable". That explains why the experts at the time felt that leaf which came from Southeast Asia had no value, except to make wine and other beverages (22). The experts were partially correct. Today, Coca-Cola is still said to be flavored with a cocaine-free extract made from a strain of *Novogranatense* grown in the more arid regions of Peru. Just before the turn of the century, however, German chemists discovered how to convert "uncrystallizable" alkaloid to "crystallizable" cocaine.

In its native state, Java-grown coca leaf contained mostly "uncrystallizable" cinnamyl-cocaine, ecgonine, and other alkaloids closely related to cocaine. In 1898, Farbwerke, a German chemical manufacturer, used a patented process to convert all of the alkaloid in coca leaf into usable cocaine. The cinnamyl-cocaine was first converted to ecgonine, and the ecgonine was then mixed with benzoic acid and methanol. All of the alkaloids were thereby converted into cocaine, giving a yield much higher than could be obtained from leaves grown in South America (9). The high alkaloid content of Java coca leaf, combined with the fact that four crops could be harvested each year, made Java coca leaf a very desirable product, but only to chemists at Farbwerke, who knew how to refine it. The Farbwerke factory was located in Germany.

Bulk coca leaf still had to be shipped to Germany for processing and remained, therefore, a perishable commodity. Unfortunately for Farbwerke, there were no patent agreements between the Netherlands and Germany. The Dutch Colonial Development Board and coca growers in Java formed a joint venture and built their own refinery. The Nederlandsche Cocaine Fabriek (NCF) opened on March 12, 1900, in Amsterdam (23). Even though Java leaf still had to be shipped half way across the world, the presence of a second factory in Amsterdam broke Farbwerke's stranglehold on the Indonesian market. The Amsterdam plant was so successful that a second floor was added to the factory in 1902. By 1910, NCF claimed to be the largest cocaine manufacturer in the world, producing more than 1500 kg per year of refined cocaine. NCF moved to new, even larger premises, that same year.

In 1903, when Farbwerke's patent expired, other German chemical makers began using the same process. Privately owned Dutch plants opened and went into competition with NCF. The first of these was established in nearby Bossum by a disgruntled NCF employee. Another plant, called Brocades and Steehman, opened in Meppel. From that point forward, coca exports from Java began to increase at a steady pace. Leaf exports rose from 45 tons in 1904 to 83 tons in 1906 and to 1300 tons in 1913. Exports peaked at 1650 tons in 1920 (24)(25), but were still substantial with >740 tons in 1927 (3). Java leaf that was not shipped to Amsterdam was purchased by representatives of German and Japanese drug houses for their own cocaine refineries. Merck and other drug makers, including the Japanese, eventually bought their own plantations in Java, avoiding the brokers, and shipping coca leaf directly to their factories (26).

While the early history of the cocaine market was characterized by shortages of the raw material and attempts at finding new sources, the later history could be described as an orderly progression from excess production to market manipulation, and eventually to black market sales. The first cocaine cartels were formed in Europe, probably around 1910. A group of eight European drug manufacturers met and agreed, if not to fix prices for cocaine, then at least not to start any price wars either (27). As discussed in Chapter 7, the group was actually referred to as the Cocaine Manufacturers Syndicate, not cartel, and its existence was kept a secret. To counter the pressures exerted by the Cocaine Manufacturers Syndicate, Dutch growers in Java formed their own syndicate. But even that step was not enough to save the Dutch coca planters in Java.

The Netherlands had signed the Geneva Convention. The convention required signatories to initiate import and export controls, and to limit production to what could be justified by medical needs. This meant that growers in Java, and operators of the Nederlandsche Cocaine Fabriek (NCF) in Amsterdam, could no longer continue to produce cocaine on a massive scale, and expect to find legitimate buyers for their product. With the medical use of cocaine having already declined to negligible levels, there was simply no way to hide, or justify, the enormous amount of cocaine being produced. The magnitude of the surplus production can be gauged from the fact that during the months leading up to the implementation of import certificate regulations, more than 220 tons of stored coca leaf were shipped from warehouses in the Netherlands (28). The other event that crippled the Dutch cocaine industry had to do with Japan.

When pharmaceutical companies in Japan first began producing cocaine, it was from Indonesian coca leaf purchased through Japanese brokers. In Tokyo, there were two major companies selling Java leaf: the Sumatra Industrial Company and the Trading Corporation of Japan (Koeki Eidan). A third firm, Nonomiya and Company located in Lima, Peru, supplied coca leaf from South America. Many of the Japanese companies emulated the German cocaine producers, and acquired their own plantations in Java. During World War II, the Japanese government, through its Medicine Controlling Company, became the sole importer of coca leaf, and also took over distribution of refined cocaine (29).

As cocaine production increased, Japan's drugmakers moved to ensure their supply and reduce their costs. In 1918, Hoshi Pharmaceuticals, with approval of both the Japanese Home Ministry and Ministry of Welfare and Social Affairs in Peru, purchased a 500-acre coca plantation in Peru, and began shipping coca leaf directly to its Tokyo factory. At the same time, Hoshi began growing coca in the Kagi district of Formosa. Takeda Pharmaceutical Industries of Osaka, through one of its subsidiaries, purchased 102 acres of land on Okinawa and began growing its own supply of coca (29).

Koto Pharmaceuticals, another of the major Japanese drug houses, started its own plantations on Iwo Jima and Okinawa. Shionogi Pharmaceutical Company purchased crude cocaine from Taiwan Shoyaku Company Limited in Formosa, and from Nonomiya and Company in Lima. According to Saburo Hagiwara, manager of Shionogi's Tokyo branch, they had to stop buying from their Lima exporter because of pressure from the Japanese government "to patronize their home markets in an effort to build up their trade balance". From 1938 forward, all of Shionogi's crude cocaine came from Taiwan (29).

At an even earlier date, Japan's central government had intervened to limit the amount of coca leaf being imported from Indonesia. Beginning in 1929, they simply stopped granting import permits for Java coca, unless, of course, the leaves came from plantations owned by Japanese companies operating in Java. The Dutch Coca Producers Association was, quite understandably, upset by this move, and filed a series of complaints with the Colonial Minister's office in Amsterdam (30-33). Japan ignored the complaints. The simultaneous shrinkage of legitimate markets, coupled with Japan's refusal to use coca leaf not grown on Japanese soil, spelled the death knell for Indonesia coca growers. By 1937, Java's exports of leaf fell to 41 tons (3). Professor Van Gorkum had been correct. Coca was an unreliable cash crop.

Japanese coca growers, however, continued to progress quite nicely, although deceptively. In 1934, in response to a request from the U.S. Secretary of State, the American Consul queried the government in

Taiwan and was told that a total of 694 acres were devoted to coca cultivation (Taiwan Shoyaku 448 acres, Hoshi Pharmaceuticals 246 acres), that in 1930 a total of 179,939 kg of coca leaf had been grown for a yield of 506 kg per acre, and that 785 kg of cocaine had been produced from those leaves (34). The numbers make no sense, and the figures supplied to the American consul almost certainly were fabricated.

Refiners in Tokyo and Taiwan were accustomed to working with high alkaloid content coca leaves from Indonesia. It can be presumed that the estates in Taiwan, Iwo Jima, and Okinawa had all planted a similar, if not identical, Indonesian variety, a strain with a yield of substantially more than 1% cocaine.

Dutch agronomists at Buitenzorg had gone to the trouble of planting sample plots and measuring output quite precisely. They had found that, in Java, 1 acre of coca plants produced 285 pounds of dry leaf, containing 1.5% alkaloid, per acre. That amount of alkaloid, using the Farbwerke process, would have yielded 3.4 kg of purified cocaine. And in Java, four crops could be harvested each year (35). Thus, if only 500 acres had been under cultivation in Taiwan, the expected yield should have been closer to 6800 kg (500 acres x 3.4 kg per acre x 4 crops per year = 6800 kg, or 3.4 metric tons). The number was equal to approximately three times the reported total cocaine production for the entire world, during the mid-1930s (36).

Production in Taiwan was understated by almost 70%, and perhaps as much as 90%. In fact, so much cocaine was accumulating in Taiwan that a special meeting was held at the Foreign Office in Tokyo to decide what to do with the surplus of 2500 kg that was sitting in storage (37). But, at the same time, Japan's reports to the League of Nation's Opium Committee put total cocaine exports at less than 10 kg per year (36). With so much cocaine to sell, and so little legitimate demand, sale on the black market was inevitable. Moving so much product eventually required the active participation of Japan's Army, Navy, and Foreign Office.

Photograph of H.H. Rusby: This photograph, showing Rusby in some sort of ceremonial bonnet, is taken from Rusby's book *Jungle Memories*. Coca leaves travel poorly, losing much of their cocaine in transit. Rusby revolutionized the industry by devising a way to produce semi-refined cocaine (very much like "crack") on site. It took much less room to ship, and lost none of its cocaine content during transport. Rusby later became a Professor of Materia Medica at Columbia University. In 1909, Rusby served as an expert witness for the U.S. Government when it sued the *Coca-Cola Company* for two violations of the Pure Food and Drug Act: (1) containing caffeine, (then a legal drug), and (2) *not* containing cocaine (then illegal under the Pure Food and Drug Act).

Chapter 7

DRUGMAKERS BECOME DRUG DEALERS

...a whole new field has been opened up by the availability of Parke's cocaine, a reliable, effective, and purer cocaine. This is beautiful white powder (available at a low price)...

Herman Guttmacher, Editor, *Vienna Medical Press*, August 9, 1885 (1)

Sigmund Freud and Karl Koller achieved success, while others failed, because they had ready access to purified cocaine. Coca wines were popular in Europe long before either Freud or Koller enrolled in medical school, but the coca extracts prescribed by physicians were notoriously unreliable, both in terms of alkaloid content and effect. Before Freud and Koller published their observations, there was no demand for purified cocaine. The small quantities that were produced by reputable chemists, such as Merck, were so expensive that few could afford to purchase the drug. After Freud and Koller published their findings, South American coca leaf was scarce, the coca plantations of Southeast Asia were yet to be planted, and few drug houses had mastered the chemistry of large scale alkaloid extraction. Almost overnight, the business of selling cocaine became very profitable. Two players came to dominate the cocaine market: E. Merck and Sons of Darmstadt, Germany, and Parke, Davis & Company, of Detroit, Michigan. Both companies had financial arrangements with Sigmund Freud.

Merck had been founded more than two centuries earlier by an apothecary named Jacob Freidrich Merck. In 1654, Merck purchased the Angel Pharmacy, located near Schiller Platz in Darmstadt, Germany. When Jacob Merck died in 1678, George Fredrick Merck, a distant relative, assumed management of the pharmacy. George Fredrick died in 1715, and left the pharmacy to his twice-married son, Johan Franz Merck (1687-1741). Johan's son from his first marriage, Johan Justus

Merck took over the pharmacy in 1754. He died at the early age of 30, when his son, Johann Anton Merck was only two years old. Johann Anton, however, managed to retain ownership, and the pharmacy apparently prospered during the years the young man was away at school. Few noticeable changes occurred during the century that elapsed between the time that Jacob Fredrich Merck purchased the Angel Pharmacy and the time that Johann Anton Merck took title to it in 1769 (2)(3).

So few changes had occurred at the pharmacy because the clinical practice of medicine had changed so very little since the Middle Ages. Nonetheless, great advances had been made in mathematics and the physical sciences. During the second century of Merck ownership, apothecaries working at Angel Pharmacy watched the practice of medicine undergo a series of profound changes. The Merck family's contribution to those changes was not insubstantial. Johann Anton's son, Heinrich Emanuel, along with another famous Darmstadt resident, Justus Liebig, were important participants in that revolution. Heinrich Emanuel (1794-1855), who was born in the same year that the cotton gin was invented, and just two years before Edward Jenner popularized vaccinations for small pox, took over management of the pharmacy in 1816. The death of Angel Pharmacy's acting manager forced Heinrich Emanuel to give up his studies in Vienna and return home to manage the business. Heinrich Emanuel was 22 years old at the time.

Heinrich Emanuel Merck first become interested in alkaloid chemistry when he was a student. At the time, techniques for isolating and purifying medically useful chemicals from plants was less than 10 years old. Of course, plant extracts had been used as medicines for thousands of years, but systematic attempts at isolating the active agents in the plants were not made until the beginning of the 19th century. Sertüner isolated morphine from opium in 1803; quinine was successfully isolated from cinchona bark the following year; and a succession of other alkaloids followed (4). Because Heinrich Emanuel Merck was a gifted alkaloid chemist, and because he was also well acquainted with the principles of industrial chemistry espoused by Liebig, it was only natural that Heinrich Emanuel would be the first to build a factory designed for the mass production of pharmaceuticals.

The original Angel Pharmacy, located across from the castle in old Darmstadt, was not large enough to house a factory. So Merck bought a small house outside of town, and converted it to a factory where he began drug production in 1827. The first product made at Merck's new factory was morphine. Other alkaloids were added to the product line in rapid succession. Codeine production began in 1832, and quinine in 1833. There was such demand for Merck products that larger production facilities were built around the original house, and steam power was introduced at the factory in 1843. By 1848, the process of running both the pharmacy in town, and the factory outside of town, became too much for Heinrich Emanuel. He assigned his son, George Franz, to run the pharmacy in town.

George Franz Merck (1825-1873) had also studied chemistry with Liebig, and was an important chemist in his own right. George's two brothers, Wilhelm Ernst Merck and Carl Emanuel Merck, were also chemists. Both brothers chose cocaine as the topic for their Ph.D. dissertations. Wilhelm studied cocaine breakdown products, particularly one called benzoylecgonine(6). Benzoylecgonine is an inactive compound that the body makes when it metabolizes cocaine. Unfortunately for cocaine manufacturers, the conversion of cocaine to benzoylecgonine also occurs outside of the body. Merck found that much of the cocaine produced in coca leaves disappears after the leaves are picked. It disappears because it has been converted into benzoylecgonine. Wilhelm Merck devised a way to turn the benzoylecgonine back into cocaine. Knowledge of this conversion allowed considerably more cocaine to be extracted from coca leaf. For a time, this knowledge gave Merck a considerable advantage over other cocaine producers.

In 1862, just two years after cocaine had been isolated and purified by Albert Niemann (7), Wilhelm revamped Merck's production line to begin manufacturing cocaine. There was virtually no market for cocaine at the time, and it appears that Merck only produced the cocaine as a matter of principle; Merck was the leading maker of alkaloid drugs, and offered the most comprehensive range of alkaloid plant products. Records show that sales of cocaine remained stagnant for the next 20 years. Many of Merck's records were destroyed during World War II, but the records of Carl Scriba (1854-1929), production manager at Merck from 1908 through 1926, survived (6). Scriba's records contain summaries of production figures dating back to the beginning of cocaine production at Merck. According to Scriba, the annual production of cocaine, for the first decade, at least, amounted to less than one pound per year.

Today, of course, Merck is one of the world's premier pharmaceutical manufacturers, but in the early 1880s, it was not even one of the major employers in Darmstadt. In 1882, the chief industry in Darmstadt was carpet making, followed by the production of hats and jewelry (8). But in 1884, Merck's fortunes began to change. Merck directors were, at first, puzzled when they started receiving cocaine orders, albeit small, from Vienna. The orders were coming from Freud, and from his addict friend, Fleischl-Marxow. Freud was an unknown at the time, and so was Fleischl-Marxow, for that matter. However, Fleischl-Marxow was a pathologist at the well-known, highly respected, Vienna Physiological Institute, and he was ordering cocaine through the Institute.

When Carl Emanuel Merck saw the orders coming from the Institute, he wrote to Fleischl-Marxow inquiring about his research. Fleischl-Marxow wrote back and described Freud's experiments. He also discussed the possible use of cocaine in the treatment of morphine addiction. He did not mention that he was the addict whom Freud had been experimenting upon. In October, Freud sent his own letter to Merck, and outlined his research successes. Emanuel Merck summarized the information from both reports and, within the next few months, published two papers on the advances in cocaine research (9, 10). Because the correspondence had originated with Fleischl-Marxow, Merck credited him as being one of the researchers.

Even though Freud's paper, *On Coca*, was well received, sales of cocaine were not all that impressive, and Merck began to look at some of the other compounds contained in coca leaf, hoping that one might prove to have some commercial value. Merck observed that another compound found in coca leaves, named ecgonine, shared some chemical properties with cocaine. Merck contacted Freud and Fleischl-Marxow and inquired if they would be willing, for a fee, to study the effects of ecgonine. They were. On October 21, 1884, the factory in Darmstadt sent Freud a 100-g sample of ecgonine. He tested it on both animals and humans, and apparently on himself. Unfortunately for Merck and Freud, ecgonine is essentially devoid of stimulant, or any other clinically useful properties. In reality, ecgonine is formed when the breakdown product, benzoylecgonine, itself breaks down.

From the end of 1884 to the end of 1885, Merck imported 1.9 tons of coca leaves, from which it produced 30 kg of purified cocaine. As the local anesthetic properties of cocaine became more widely known, demand increased. In 1887, Merck, and most of the other German manufacturers stopped importing coca leaf and began importing raw, semi-refined cocaine, manufactured in Peru. Merck bought most of its raw cocaine from a German refinery, Kilz & Co., located in Lima. Boehringer in Waldhof and Knoll in Ludwigshafen were the two largest competitors. Merck ultimately produced about half of all the cocaine made in Germany (11). From 1887 until 1913, and the beginning of World War I, Merck imported 88 tons of semi-refined cocaine, and used it to manufacture 76 tons of pure cocaine, an average of nearly three tons of pure cocaine each year (6).

Merck's cocaine production figures were inconsequential by today's standards — South American production of refined cocaine in 1996 is thought to have been in excess of 750 tons (see the Afterword for a more detailed discussion of the current situation), but such quantities of refined cocaine had never been available before. The amounts being produced were wildly in excess of legitimate medical needs. During the period just before World War II, a select committee of experts working for the League of Nations estimated that medical and scientific requirements for cocaine, worldwide, amounted to less than 1 ton (11)!

In 1906, Merck began to import coca leaves from plantations it had established in Java. Between 1906 and 1918, Merck managed to extract and sell almost a ton of Javanese cocaine each year, bringing its total cocaine output to almost 4 tons a year. Merck had been charging 6 marks per gram prior to the Heidelberg Congress, but over the course of a few weeks, demand became so great that Merck was able to raise its price to 15 marks. As other competitors entered the market, including competitors from the United States, supplies increased, and prices dropped almost as rapidly as they had risen. By 1887, the cost of cocaine had decreased by almost 90%, from 15 marks to 85 pfennings per gram (6). The drop in price was largely the result of price competition from Merck's American competitor, Parke, Davis & Company.

Parke, Davis also had its start in a drug store, but it was hardly a family operation. The drug store was founded in 1862, in Detroit, by Samuel P. Duffield, a physician. Duffield had studied chemistry in Berlin, and was conversant with the modern approaches to chemistry taught by Liebig, and so successfully utilized by Merck. Duffield hoped to emulate Merck's success in America. Duffield's Pharmacy also contained a small manufacturing facility. His initial product offerings included "Ether, Sweet Spirit of Nitre, Oil of Wine, Hoffman's Anodyne, and Blue Pill Mass". For whatever reason (the names really were not that outrageous for the times), Duffield had trouble selling his products, but he persisted. By 1866, he was ready to expand. Duffield sought outside investors. Two were recruited, but within the first year, both investors dropped out. The last one to quit the enterprise, Francis Conant, sold his interest to C. Parke (14).

Parke was a successful businessman with plenty of cash. He was able to provide the funds needed to relocate Duffield's production facilities from the back of his pharmacy to a new building. Duffield was able to increase production and sales, particularly on the Atlantic coast. Unfortunately for Duffield and Parke, their success prompted a price war with other larger, and better funded, drugmakers located in New York and Philadelphia. The eastern firms launched an aggressive marketing campaign designed to cut Duffield and Parke out of the market. In 1867, Duffield and Parke concluded that they needed the help of a marketing expert. They recruited George Davis.

Like Parke, George Davis was also wealthy. He knew absolutely nothing about chemistry, but apparently was a charismatic salesman who believed in advertising. Almost as soon as Davis joined the firm, Duffield left the business and returned to the practice of medicine, leaving Parke and Davis, two businessmen, to run the company. The marketing strategy the businessmen chose emphasized the purity and reliability of their products. In the 1880s, quality control was unheard of. As a result, manufactured drugs were notoriously unreliable. Parke and Davis believed they could gain a competitive edge by selling products that produced the same effect each time they were used. They also decided to emulate Merck, and concentrate on the production of alkaloids, drugs derived from plants. In 1871, hoping to discover new products, Parke and Davis started to finance expeditions to remote areas of the globe. In 1874, the expeditions bore fruit, of a sort. Parke and Davis introduced three new products: extracts of Guarana, Bearsfoot, and Eucalyptus. All three products were well received, although they are of no known medicinal value. It is difficult today to imagine just what benefit doctors thought they were conferring when they prescribed the new Parke, Davis products.

Parke and Davis had their biggest success in 1875 when they introduced an extract made from coca leaves; the following year, their drug company finally turned a profit. The next decade was marked by nearly continuous expansion. New production facilities were built, and George Davis assembled an impressive sales organization. Not only did he personally train all of the salesmen, but he also published a series of booklets, pamphlets, and magazines targeting physicians and pharmacists. Today, these journals would be called "throw aways", an acknowledgment of the fact that individuals reading them know that they are really advertisements published by drug companies, and the information contained in them has not been "peer reviewed". In fact, the concept of "peer review" did not come into existence until the early 20th century. In the late 1880s, the line between serious medical journals and advertising tracts was not always very clear.

The flagship in George Davis' line of publications was a monthly medical newspaper called the *Therapeutic Gazette*. It contained no disclaimers, and made no mention of its relationship to Parke, Davis & Company. But not surprisingly, it often carried articles detailing therapeutic successes attributable to Parke, Davis products. George Davis' biggest success may have been a series of articles he ran in the *Gazette* which described morphine addicts who had been successfully cured after treatment with Parke, Davis coca elixir (15-17). Freud read the papers on morphine addiction that appeared in Davis' publication, and he quoted from them in *On Coca* (18). The papers quoted by Freud not only mentioned giving cocaine to morphine addicts, but they specifically recommended the Parke, Davis formulation.

There is nothing to suggest that at the time he wrote *On Coca*, Freud knew that he was quoting from paid advertisements. Rather, he treated the series of papers as if they were legitimate contributions to the medical literature. Had Freud realized he was quoting from a cocaine manufacturer's "throw away", one wonders whether he would have ever recommended cocaine as a treatment for morphine addiction. In any event, Freud's endorsement of cocaine therapy, and Koller's discovery of cocaine's local anesthetic properties, did wonders for the cocaine business. Advertising helped too. Beginning in 1885, Parke, Davis & Company promotional materials cited Freud's writing as proof that cocaine was an effective treatment for morphine addiction (19). They never once mentioned the fact that Freud first got the idea from reading Parke, Davis promotional materials!

With supplies of cocaine increasing, and wholesale prices declining, manufacturers like Parke, Davis tried to increase sales by expanding its line of cocaine-based products. These included a coca wine, a coca soft drink designed to compete with Coca-Cola, coca-containing cigarettes, a cocaine formulation designed for inhalation, an assortment of different cocaine salts, and a kit for injecting cocaine. The kit contained 300 mg of powdered cocaine divided into five capsules. It also included a solution for dissolving the cocaine, a camel brush, and a syringe for injecting the drug. The kits retailed between $2 and $3. Parke, Davis also expanded its service area. It sent sales representatives to Europe and began competing head-to-head with Merck for cocaine sales (20).

Breaking into the European market proved more difficult than George Davis had imagined. Merck had the advantage of brand name recognition in general, and for cocaine-containing products, in particular. Freud and Koller had both used Merck cocaine. In fact, Freud mentioned Merck's cocaine by name in *On Coca*, mainly, it appears, so he could complain about how expensive it was.

> *I used the hydrochloric preparation of cocaine as described by Merk [sic] in Darmstadt. This preparation may be bought in Vienna in Haubner's Engelapotheke am Hof at a price which is not much higher than Merk's [sic], but which must, nevertheless, be regarded as very high. The management of the pharmacy in question is trying, as they have been kind enough to inform me, to lower the price of the drug by establishing new sources of supply...(18)*

Inspired, no doubt, both by the successes of Mariani's wine, and by Liebig's even greater success at exploiting his meat extract, Davis knew how potent a tool the endorsement of a celebrity scientist could be. And since Freud was clearly upset by what he perceived as price gouging on the part of Merck, George Davis saw an opening he could exploit. Davis offered Freud money (60 guilders, roughly $24) if he would endorse Parke, Davis cocaine. Sometime in April 1885, Freud accepted the offer (21). The endorsement took the form of an article, written under another person's name, and published in the August 9, 1885 issue of the *Viennese Medical Press* (1).

Supposedly, the article was written by the journal's editor, Herman Guttmacher, and it may have been. But within the body of the article, Freud is quoted directly:

> *I have examined cocaine muriaticum produced by Parke, Davis...and can state that it is fully equal in effect to the Merck preparation of the same name...The only difference I can detect between the two preparations is that in their taste. The satisfactory results found with Parke cocaine are probably the result of the greater availability of coca leaves in America, and since the price is lower than European products because of lowered transportation expense, this preparation should have a great future.*

Just in case Freud's endorsement proved too subtle for the general readership, Guttmacher added his own opinion that "*a whole new field has been opened up by the availability of Parke's cocaine, a reliable, effective, and purer cocaine. This is beautiful white powder, available at a low price...*"

Needless to say, Merck and Company were not happy with the article. On October 1, 1885, Merck wrote a letter to the *Viennese Medical Press* and complained that "Under the pretense of scientific research, this material was written merely to further the interests of an American firm (22)." Merck pointed out that Parke, Davis prices were just slightly less than his own, and he argued that his company was entitled to charge more, since purchasers of Merck cocaine are guaranteed "obtaining a totally usable cocaine...For the physician, a fact not to be overlooked!" Merck's note concludes with the statement "...it remains a mystery why the author of said article directs the attention to America and forecasts the 'greatest future' for American cocaine." Whether it was really a mystery, or whether Merck knew that Freud had been paid to write the article, is impossible to say.

In 1917, the American division of Merck was seized by the United States Government, a victim of World War I. Parke, Davis survived somewhat longer, but finally lost its corporate identity when it was taken over by Warner Lambert. However, Merck and Parke, Davis were far from the only players in the cocaine business. In 1906, Merck formed a joint venture with Knoll and Boehringer, and produced cocaine under the MBK label. It took only a few years before other drugmakers, in other countries, entered the market. Several firms were located in Germany, including Boehringer and Sons near Mannheim, and Knoll Pharmaceuticals in Ludwigshafen.

In 1929, Dame Rachel Crowdy, then Chief of the League of Nations Opium Traffic and Social Issues Section, wrote to W.G. Van Wettum, then the Dutch Colonial Administrator. He was also the Netherlands representative at the League of Nations Opium Committee. Crowdy requested information about a cocaine cartel. She was planning a conference on cocaine and opium production limitation, and she had just heard about some sort of cocaine producer's syndicate. Crowdy complained that "practically no information has so far been available to the Committee regarding the organization and working of this convention (23)." One month later, Van Wettum responded with a note saying that "all correspondence regarding the Convention being confidential, the opinion of the manager of the cocaine factory at Amsterdam is that he cannot give the information off-hand and he is therefore consulting his fellow-members in the question (24)." Van Wettum promised to get back to Crowdy with more information. And he did, one month later (25).

Van Wettum informed Dame Crowdy that the Convention, or Syndicate, consisted of eight members. He identified the members as C.F. Boehringer & Söhne, G.m.b.H., Mannheim; Waldhof, C.H. Boehringer Sohn, A.G., Hamburg; F. Hoffman La Roche & Co., A.G., Berlin; F. Hoffman La Roche, & Co. A.G., Basel; Knoll, A.G., Ludwigshafen a/ Rh., E. Merck, Chem Fabriek, Darmstadt; Nederlandsche Cocainefabriek, N.V., Amsterdam; and Etablissements Rocques, S.A., Paris. Crowdy was informed that all of the European manufacturers were members of the syndicate except the factory of Buchler, Brunswick and Sico of Paris, and the British firm of May and Baker. Some factories in Russia wanted to become members, but since they were refining coca paste only, not extracting it from leaves, they were ineligible for membership (26). Not only were the American producers excluded from the cartel, but they also competed against themselves. Parke, Davis faced stiff competition from Squibb Pharmaceutical (now incorporated into Bristol Meyers Squibb) and Dhome Pharmaceuticals (which was ultimately absorbed by the American Branch of Merck, as a component of Merck Sharpe and Dhome).

Members of the cocaine manufacturers syndicate were under no obligation to limit output, and they were allowed to sell their product wherever it was legal. Syndicate members also agreed not to dump products. Any member could sell in any country as long as they met the import and export regulations of the countries involved (27). Rather than stabilizing prices, the real purpose of the organization appears to have been the maximization of profit. Not only did the producers not compete, they also conspired to force down the price of raw materials. Growers and crude cocaine refiners in South America were not as well organized as the Convention. As leaf from Java, Borneo, and Sumatra became more available, members of the Convention stopped buying crude cocaine from South American exporters. As a result, semi-refined cocaine accumulated in South American ports, and prices fell substantially. Representatives of the Convention were there to buy it at reduced prices.

Allowing for market disruptions brought about by World War I, and for the occasional, unpredictable supply disruption due to local conditions, the amount of cocaine produced by legitimate manufacturers increased steadily from 1885 until the end of World War I. The increase was surprising, only if one presumes that the increased production was intended for legitimate medical use. By the end of World War I, the medical community had largely lost interest in the drug. When cocaine was used for eye surgery, there was an increased risk of infection. When cocaine was injected as an anesthetic elsewhere in the body, the incidence of distressing, occasionally life threatening complications, was unacceptably high. And it did not take very long for the risk of addiction to become obvious to everyone in the medical community. Yet, the large drug manufacturers continued to make, and sell, prodigious amounts of cocaine. The drug companies knew very well that the cocaine was being diverted to the black market.

By the early 1930s, the United States and Germany had both been eclipsed as the world's leading suppliers of cocaine. According to the League of Nations' statistics, manufacturers in the United States produced 21.3% of the world's refined cocaine, Germany trailed with 15%, the United Kingdom with 9.9%, and France with 8.3%. Japan was the world's leading cocaine producer, accounting for 23.3% of the world's total production (28). Evidence obtained after World War II indicates that Japan produced much more cocaine than it ever reported to the League of Nations, and that all of the surplus was sold on the black market. In fact, Japanese drug dealers were able to sell much more drug than they could produce and imported cocaine was required to meet the demand. Japan had no difficulty finding European drugmakers with cocaine to sell.

German and Swiss members of the "syndicate" were happy to supply the Japanese with as much refined cocaine as they required. The League of Nations was well aware of that fact. On March 20, 1930, Dame Crowdy wrote to Dr. H. Carriére, the Director of the Swiss Federal Health Service and complained about the enormous quantities of cocaine and heroin, much of it bearing the Hoffman La Roche label, finding its way into Occupied China.

Two months later, Carriére wrote back to Crowdy saying he had checked with Hoffman La Roche, and could find no evidence that the sales she was referring to had ever occurred. Carriére did hedge his bets by pointing out that, even if such sales had occurred, they would have been legal under Swiss law. Carriére was being as diplomatic as he was disingenuous. European drug manufacturers had been exporting huge quantities of narcotics to the Far East since just after the turn of the century, and Hoffman La Roche was one of the largest exporters (29).

Hoffman La Roche did everything it could to accommodate its Far East clients. It provided buyers in Tokyo and Shanghai with secret codes, allowing them to check spot drug prices and available inventories of heroin and cocaine. All a would-be-buyer had to do was send a cable to Hoffman La Roche's offices in Bern, Switzerland. League of Nations' reports frequently singled out Hoffman La Roche for attention. In the early 1920s, their drug transactions were legal. But, after the adoption of the Hague Treaty in 1925, and the Geneva Treaty of 1931, such transactions were in violation of international law. European manufacturers were then forced to resort to subterfuge. And they were very good at it.

In 1926, the Hamburg police seized a large shipment of Hoffman La Roche heroin which had been shipped into the free port of Hamburg. The shipment was labeled, and listed on the manifest, as "harmless chemicals". It was addressed to a Herr Aisenberg. Once they arrived in the free port, the "harmless chemicals" were then repackaged into 15- to 25-kg lots, and mixed in with other shipments on their way to Darien in Manchuria, and to Shanghai. A search of customs' records disclosed that Herr Aisenberg had received at least 20 similar shipments during the preceding two years.

Herr Aisenberg was not Hoffman La Roche's only customer for "harmless chemicals". In 1924 and 1925, similar shipments were made directly to a Mr. Tanaka in Shanghai. They were also labeled as "harmless chemicals". The League of Nations estimated that, during the 1920s, hundreds of kilograms of "harmless chemicals" had been shipped to Japanese middlemen in the Far East (29).

Mislabeling shipments was a favorite method for shipping larger quantities of drugs. Smaller shipments were often sent by mail, or simply smuggled on board outbound freighters. Some drugmakers used all three methods. On March 15, 1928, customs officers in Rotterdam carried out a routine inspection on the Gemma, a Dutch steamer bound for Osaka. They found 60 kg of heroin in a crate that was supposed to contain medicines and perfumes. Markings on the container indicated the crate had originated at the Naarden Chemical Factory at Bossum, just outside of Rotterdam.

The local police were contacted and a search warrant was obtained. By the time the search party reached the factory at Bossum, most of the records and correspondence had been destroyed. But, the remaining records were revealing enough. Over the preceding two years, officials at Naarden had shipped 664 kg of morphine, 2,112 kg of heroin, and 56 kg of cocaine to Far Eastern buyers. More than half of the shipments had been mailed to Japan and Japanese possessions in the Far East, even though the owners of Naarden had never bothered to obtain the export certificates (30). Such transactions were actually legal. It seems there was a problem with the import-export regulations, and the drugmakers were quicker to spot the problem than the government.

By the late 1920s, the League of Nations had established an elaborate system of import and export controls. And, because all the major governments had a very good idea of what Japan was doing with its imported narcotics, it became increasingly difficult to get the import certificates needed for shipments to Japan. The terms of the Limitation Act of 1925 required that each country file a yearly report estimating legitimate medical needs within that country, and then limit imports to conform to that number. Because the estimated yearly morphine requirement for Japan was well under 600 kg, the Japanese government could not justify issuing certificates for multiple 1000-kg purchases. Similar considerations applied to cocaine. Enterprising drug exporters found a way to get around that problem.

The Naarden Chemical Factory was able to circumvent the law because treaty requirements for import and export certificates were not uniformly implemented by all signatories to the treaty. Not every country required both types of certificates, at least not initially. Until late in 1929, the Netherlands issued import certificates only when the exporting country requested them. Germany was one of the countries that did not ask for them (30, 31). German narcotic manufacturers, particularly C.H. Böehringer and Son of Hamburg, and C.F. Böehringer and Son of Mannheim, availed themselves of this happy circumstance and shipped their products to legitimate narcotic factories in Holland. There, the drugs were stored in bonded warehouses. A technicality in Dutch law permitted the firms owning the warehouses to withdraw drugs, repackage them, and then ship them overseas. As far as the Dutch government was concerned, the drugs were never there. They were simply in transit, and never appeared, either as imports or exports, in the Dutch statistics reported to the League of Nations.

Sandoz Pharmaceuticals and Hoffman La Roche, both located in Basel, were two of Naarden's best customers. There can be no question that the executives of the Swiss pharmaceutical houses knew that the drugs shipped through Naarden were being sent to shell companies in Shanghai, Tientsin, Darien, and Osaka. The Asian shell companies were owned by known drug smugglers who made little effort to hide that fact. Several of the companies that regularly placed large orders for drugs from Germany and Switzerland shared the same mailbox! Larger drug dealers had adjacent mailboxes. Naarden had many customers in Shanghai: the Holland Company had Naarden ship drugs to P.O. Box 1604, Boonhua & Company had Naarden ship their orders to P.O. Box 1607, Ting Long & Company received Naarden shipments at P.O. Box 1608. Multiple drug shipments were sent to these boxes, which all happened to be located at the same address as the Own Trading Company. All of the post boxes were owned by the Paul Yip Opium Syndicate, and its front operation, the Own Trading Company (30).

American producers were never able to participate in the booming Japanese market for abused drugs. By the 1920s, U.S. drug and import regulations made large scale cocaine production and diversion all but impossible. There would have been no way to import sufficient raw material. There was, however, an American connection to the Far East drug industry. The largest Japanese cocaine manufacturer, Sankyo Pharmaceutical, had close ties with Parke, Davis. In fact, the chairman of Sankyo's board, Jokichi Takamine, had worked for George Davis years before. Takamine, a trained analytic chemist, had arrived in the United States in 1890. He had isolated a starch splitting enzyme, which he called "Taka-Diastase". Takamine thought that the enzyme could be useful to distillers. He traveled to the United States with hopes of selling his invention to them.

Takamine was unsuccessful in his attempts to sell his enzyme, but he did make a favorable impression on George Davis, who hired Takamine as a consultant. Takamine remained in the United States for a number of years, working for Davis, and Parke, Davis successfully marketed "Taka-Diastase" as a digestive aid. Parke, Davis eventually was able to exploit another Takamine discovery: adrenaline. In 1894, researchers in London had discovered that, when given to animals, extracts of the adrenal gland raised blood pressure and heart rate. In 1901, Takamine and a second scientist named Thomas Aldrich, working independently, both managed to purify and isolate the compound. Takamine called it adrenaline.

Four years later, a German chemist, Friedrich Stolz (1860-1936) managed to synthesize adrenaline without using any animal extracts, and adrenaline became the first hormone to be isolated and synthesized artificially. Later, when Parke, Davis decided it would be the first company to manufacture adrenaline. Takamine was placed in charge of setting up production. Takamine's discovery is not without irony. Cocaine causes adrenaline, and a closely related compound noradrenaline (norepinephrine) to accumulate in the bloodstream. Cocaine toxicity is, at least partially, a result of excessive adrenaline and noradrenaline levels!

In his position as a supervising industrial chemist at Parke, Davis, Takamine would certainly have been well acquainted with the latest techniques used by Parke, Davis for making cocaine. And that knowledge almost certainly was of some use to Takamine when he returned to Japan, at the invitation of Matasaju Shiohara, the chairman of the Board of Sankyo & Co., Ltd. Sankyo was one of only five companies in Japan licensed to process coca and produce cocaine from leaf.

Sankyo had strong connections with the American chemical industry. It held cross-licensing agreements with a number of well-known American manufacturers, including Hooker Electrochemical, Johnson and Johnson, and Parke, Davis. At the end of World War I, when Shiohara invited Takamine back to Japan, he made him president of Sankyo, with Shiohara remaining as Managing Director (32). Partly because of the valuable training Takamine had received from America's largest cocaine producer, Sankyo was able to produce more cocaine than either Carl Emanuel Merck or George Parke would ever have imagined possible. Almost none of the cocaine was destined for use by doctors.

Vol. II.   OCTOBER, 1878.   No. 4.

New Preparations:

A QUARTERLY JOURNAL OF MEDICINE

DEVOTED TO THE INTRODUCTION OF

NEW THERAPEUTICAL AGENTS

" Remedinm non consenmutum est, donec id expertum sil."

EDITED BY

GEO. S. DAVIS

AND

C. HENRI LEONARD, M. A., M. D.

CONTENTS:

NEW PREPARATIONS, reaching many thousand readers, is the best medium in America for placing before the medical profession information relative to new remedies, or old remedies applied to a new use, and practical testimony regarding their therapeutic value.

Carefully excluding from its pages all complimentary notices of proprietary or patent medicines, its columns are open to all who have any testimony to offer regarding the origin, habitat, or medicinal properties of any new remedial agent, whether wholly unknown to the profession, or but recently discovered.

The editors aim to make this journal the recognized organ of American practitioners in this special department of therapeutics, and invite the co-operation of all who are interested in the advancement of medical knowledge.

SUBSCRIPTION PRICE FOR 1879, ONE DOLLAR.

Read Editorial (page 88), and Publishers' Notes (page 103).

GEO. S. DAVIS,

PUBLISHER,

P. O. BOX 641, DETROIT, MICHIGAN.

LONDON:

BAILLIERE, TINDALL & COX, King William Street, Strand.

Therapeutic Gazette: When Freud wrote his famous paper praising cocaine, he drew heavily on source materials from this journal. There is no evidence that Freud was aware of the fact that the *Gazette* was owned by Parke, Davis & Company, America's biggest cocaine maker. Not surprisingly, the Gazette often carried articles detailing therapeutic successes attributable to Parke, Davis products, including several which described the successful treatment of morphine addiction with Parke, Davis & Company coca elixirs. Freud quoted from these papers, using them to support his arguments. In fact, these "scientific papers" were little more than paid advertisements.

Chapter 8

QUACK DRUGS AND QUACK SCIENTISTS

...the caffeine contained in the article "Coca-Cola" is one of its regular, habitual and essential constituents, and that without its presence, that is, if it were de-caffeinized, so to speak, the product would lack one of its essential elements and fail to produce upon the consumers a characteristic if not the most characteristic effect which is obtained from its use. In short Coca-Cola without caffeine would not be Coca-Cola...

Judge Terry Sanford, District Court, Eastern District, Tennessee, April 11, 1911 (1)

We are a drug-habit Nation and alcohol is only one of the many kinds that are being used to excess. The medical profession is doing everything it can to save the Nation, but it is not doing enough. Personally, I shall be glad to see this country have universal prohibition, not only of drugs but of liquor of all forms.

Dr. Harvey Wiley, head of the Bureau of Chemistry in the U.S. Department of Agriculture, addressing the New York City Republican Club, February 18, 1911 (2)

By the 1900s, important new scientific discoveries were almost a daily occurrence. The first zeppelins were flying over Germany, quantum theory had been discovered, and the human voice had been transmitted over the radio. Exciting though these discoveries may have been, they had no real impact on the practice of medicine. A few pioneers such as Halsted, the great but addicted surgeon, and Osler, the brilliant diagnostician, were leading medicine into the modern age, but encounters with the average country doctor were still very risky business. More often than not, patients came out worse for the experience.

That sad fact partially explains why patent medicines were so popular: they were cheaper than going to the doctor, and they were, at least, as likely to be as effective as anything the doctor prescribed. Users felt better after taking most patent medicines and, if they did not die of an overdose, the experience was generally considered salutary. Gastrointestinal disorders, for example, were very common at the time; and opium was, and still is, an excellent cure for stomach upsets. The fact that cocaine and morphine really do make people feel good is, after all, a tremendous marketing advantage.

Discoveries made by innovative chemists, such as Merck and Liebig, were not immediately integrated into the medical practice. Turn of the century chemists were much more sophisticated than turn of the century physicians. They were also more effective, which partially explains some of the strange dynamics involved in the writing of American drug laws. It was much easier to make and detect chemicals than it was to figure out what those same chemicals did once they were incorporated into the human body.

If our drug policies appear convoluted today, think how they must have looked to the owners of the Coca-Cola Company just after the turn of the century. In 1911, company officials found themselves in federal court, charged with, among other things, not putting cocaine in Coca-Cola (1)! Popular histories of this period usually lump Coca-Cola with the other quack nostrums, often suggesting that the problem of cocaine abuse in America was, in some way, connected to the successes of the Coca-Cola Company. Except for the titillation factor, the idea has little else to recommend it. Even when Coca-Cola contained cocaine, the quantities were trivial; too small to produce measurable physiologic or behavioral changes. Coca-Cola was not responsible for America's cocaine problem, but government harassment of the Atlanta soft drink maker did mark an important turning point in the development of American drug policy, and is worth examining in some detail.

Government moves against Coca-Cola were orchestrated by Dr. Harvey Wiley, a zealous bureaucrat. Wiley was the first head of the Bureau of Chemistry within the Department of Agriculture, the agency responsible for enforcing the Pure Food and Drug Act of 1906. Wiley was one in a series of government officials, such as Hamilton Wright and Harry Anslinger, who made their living by campaigning against the evils of drug abuse. These anti-drug crusaders had more in common than just the desire to rid society of its drug problem; all were willing to use very bad, sometimes fraudulent, science to advance their arguments. The dual problems of "drug careerism", and the tendency to use political considerations as a means of determining scientific truth, have not gone away. However, the issues were more clearly framed at the turn of the century.

During the early 1900s, the patent medicine market was crowded and fiercely competitive. No central registry for these products ever existed, but informed estimates suggest that, at one time, more than 25,000 different patent medications were for sale in the United States (3). As is true today, the success or failure of a new product was determined by the amount of money producers could spend on advertising. Millions upon millions were spent promoting these products, and since the market was completely unregulated, even the most outrageous claims were permitted. Revenues from patent drugmakers turned publishers into lobbyists for the drugmakers. Drug producers offered long term advertising contracts, but the contracts all contained automatic cancellation clauses if, by some accident, laws were passed prohibiting sales of their product. The publishers, of course, made every effort to see that that did not occur (4) .

While some of the claims for Angelo Mariani's wine may have been overblown, there never was any doubt that the product contained wine and coca. Using only coca leaf meant there was a limit on how much cocaine Mariani could get into the wine. By the mid-1890s, however, there was a glut of cocaine on the market, and patent drugmakers were able to dump large amounts of cocaine into their products, making them very popular, but also addictive and dangerous.

The medical literature of the late 1800s contains dozens of reports describing severe, occasionally lethal, reactions to cocaine anesthesia. But, as far as anyone knows, no one ever became ill, let alone addicted, to Vin Mariani, or any other coca-based wine. Vin Mariani contained only a very small amount of cocaine, probably less than 6 mg per ounce, not enough to cause toxicity. When combined with alcohol, however, a 6- to 8-ounce serving would have been more than enough to create feelings of well being. The real secret behind Vin Mariani's success was not even known to Mariani, and was only discovered more than a century later.

In the late 1980s, the number of cocaine-related deaths in Miami, Florida, began to explode. Lee Hearn, a toxicologist with the Miami Dade County Medical Examiner office, and Deborah Mash, a neurochemist at the University of Miami, first noticed that when the deceased had been drinking alcohol and using cocaine at the same time, a new molecule, somewhat like cocaine, could be detected in their urine. These observations were confirmed by Peter Jatlow at Yale, and another group of scientists in Barcelona (5, 6). It is now clear that cocaethylene has most of the same stimulant properties as cocaine, but it lasts much longer. Even though the cocaine content of Mariani's wine was relatively low, mixing the cocaine with alcohol resulted in a much higher effective dose!

Coca-Cola contained even less cocaine than Vin Mariani. According to a formula held by the great-grandson of Frank Robinson, one of Coca-Cola's founders, 10 pounds of coca leaf were used to make 36 gallons of syrup (7). Coca leaf from South America contains very little cocaine, probably less than 0.5%, and not all of that can be extracted. Thus, Coca-Cola, as originally produced, would have contained about 100 mg of cocaine per gallon (10 lb = 22.5 kg, .5% × 22.5 kg = 112 mg), or 1.5 mg per ounce, only one-fourth the amount of cocaine found in Vin Mariani. Such minute amounts of cocaine would certainly not have been enough to produce a detectable physiologic response, and it is absurd to suggest that Coca-Cola ever had addictive properties, or that its cocaine content was responsible for its success. Coca-Cola was successful for the very same reason that Vin Mariani was successful: it was brilliantly promoted (8). Coca-Cola's managers were better salesmen than Mariani's, and Coca-Cola prospered, while Mariani gradually lost market share. Coca-Cola continued to grow and prosper long after cocaine had been dropped from the original formula. Vin Mariani was not so well promoted, and after World War I, it simply faded from existence.

The inventor of Coca-Cola was John Styth Pemberton, who was born in Knoxville, Georgia in 1831 (9). He first trained as a physician at a medical school founded by an herbalist named Samuel Thompson. Thompson relied on treatment with various combinations of exotic herbs. While not qualifying as either rational or scientific, Thompson's theories were, at least, less dangerous than other approaches fashionable at the time (such as bleeding patients in order to remove imagined toxins circulating in their systems). Pemberton also trained for a year as a pharmacist. He opened his first pharmacy in Columbus, Georgia, in 1852. In 1869, Pemberton moved to Atlanta, which was then going through a post-Civil War building and financial boom.

In 1876, Pemberton read, and was fascinated by, Sir Robert Christison's paper describing the magical properties of the coca leaf. And, of course, Angelo Mariani's advertisements for his coca-based wines were seen everywhere. Taking his inspiration from Mariani, Pemberton began to make and sell Pemberton's French Wine Coca. According to advertisements for Pemberton's concoction, it contained not only Peruvian Coca, but also an extract of African cola nuts, and "true Damiana" (a plant growing wild in the American West called *Turnera diffusaa*). Pemberton's claims for his product were primarily medical; advertisements said it would cure both mental and physical exhaustion in addition to being "a most wonderful invigorator of the sexual organs (7)."

Pemberton's wine sold fairly well, but not enough to make him rich. His fortunes should have changed in 1884, when Freud announced that cocaine could be used to treat morphine addiction (10). Sales of cocaine, and cocaine-containing products, increased in both Europe and America. Pemberton's sales should have increased as well, except the temperance movement took hold in the South, and late in 1885, Atlanta voted to outlaw alcohol. Fearing the effects of prohibition, Pemberton began to reformulate his product. Work continued during the first several months of 1886. While Pemberton was reformulating his coca wine, he took in new partners. One of the new partners, Frank Robinson, devised not only a new name for the alcohol-free product, Coca-Cola, but also the logo which is now recognized around the world. As it turned out, Pemberton need not have worried about temperance. Prohibition in Atlanta lasted only one year. During that time, Pemberton was able to continue selling his old wine-based product as a medication while, at the same time, promoting sales of the newly formulated, non-alcohol version, Coca-Cola (7).

The 1870s witnessed not only the invention of carbonated water and commercial refrigeration, but also the birth of the soda fountain. These institutions were especially popular in the South (11). Coca-Cola, like Vin Mariani, was a patent medicine, but it was also being sold as a soda fountain beverage, and that meant it had many more potential sales outlets than Vin Mariani. Robinson appears to have had much more advertising acumen than Pemberton, and he realized that soda fountain products were easier to sell than medicines. Robinson resorted to one of the favorite techniques then used by patent medicine makers; he gave away free samples (12).

Thousands of tickets, redeemable for free Coca-Cola at local soda fountains, were distributed around Atlanta. Coca-Cola was, of course, not the only soda-fountain beverage making medicinal claims, and Robinson had no shortage of role models. The makers of Hires Root Beer, first introduced in 1876, claimed that it would "purify the blood". Advertisements for Dr. Pepper, which came along a few years later, mirrored Pemberton's claims, and strongly implied that drinking Dr. Pepper would do good things for one's love life.

Pemberton filed a patent on Coca-Cola on June 6, 1887. There followed, almost immediately, a confusing period where title to both the product, and to Pemberton's company, became a matter of dispute. New partners came and went, dummy companies were formed, allegations of forgery were raised, Pemberton died of stomach cancer, and the company experienced phenomenal growth (7).

By the turn of the century, Coca-Cola had dropped its medicinal claims. Whether this was a marketing decision, or a result of a special tax passed by Congress in 1898, to pay for the Spanish-American War (medicines were taxed, soft drinks were not) is hard to say. The rest of the Coca-Cola story reads very much like a soap opera, and has been recounted in some detail by Mark Pendergrast (7). Interesting though the story may be, neither Coca-Cola's corporate history, nor its chemical composition, have any bearing on the problem of drug abuse in general, or cocaine abuse in particular. But what transpired between Coca-Cola and the federal government does. If zealous federal regulators had had their way, Coca-Cola might have disappeared from the marketplace.

Congress moved to regulate the food and drug industry in 1906. Public, if not professional, sentiment had favored some type of regulation for at least a quarter of a century before that. In 1880, Edward Robinson Squibb (1819-1900), the same Squibb who, unable to procure adequate supplies of coca leaf, had declared that there was no future for the cocaine business, managed to get the New York State legislature to pass a bill that served as the model for the one finally passed by Congress in 1906 (13). Federal attempts at regulation had begun even earlier, in the 1870s, but were rejected by both houses of Congress. In 1884, during the Forty-Seventh Congress, a Senator from New York State introduced Senate Bill (SB) 649, which was almost a word for word copy of the bill Squibb had introduced in New York State. Members of the Proprietary Association, the trade organization for the makers of patent medicines, lobbied intensely and saw to it that SB 649 never emerged from committee. Regulation would have meant added cost for the industries involved (13).

The situation was different in 1906. In that year, Congress finally passed, and President Theodore Roosevelt signed, the Pure Food and Drug Act. A Meat Inspection Amendment to the Act was passed a few months later. The 1906 Act superseded an assortment of ineffective state laws, and gave federal regulators some authority over the production, distribution, and marketing of food and drugs. This same bill also established the U.S. Pharmacopoeia as the legal standard of official preparations. Patent remedies which contained compounds not listed in the Pharmacopoeia had to list their ingredients on the label.

Popular accounts credit four men (Upton Sinclair, Harvey Wiley, Theodore Roosevelt, and Samuel Hopkins Adams) for the passage of the Pure Food and Drug Act, and the reformation of the food and drug industry in the U.S. In reality, the food and drug industries themselves had as much to do with passage of the new laws as the reformers. Socialist writer Upton Sinclair is probably the best known of the group. At the turn of the century, he was one of many "muckrakers" who wrote about abuses within the meat and drug industry. Sinclair's great grandfather had fought in the Revolutionary War and was one of the founders of the U.S. Naval Academy. But the Civil War bankrupted the Sinclair family, and Sinclair's father died of alcoholism, an event which may well have colored Sinclair's opinions about intoxicants. Sinclair began his literary career writing jokes and short stories for papers in New York City, but he eventually shifted his focus to the perceived injustices of laissez faire capitalism, and the monopolies or "trusts" that controlled so much of American commerce.

Sinclair was prompted to write his famous book, *The Jungle*, by testimony that Theodore Roosevelt gave to a Senate Committee (14). Roosevelt had told the Committee that during the Spanish-American War, the tinned beef supplied to the U.S. Army was horribly adulterated and basically inedible. After reading Roosevelt's testimony, and other accounts in the popular press, Sinclair wrote a graphic account of the unsanitary practices then common in the meat packing industry. The book was highly publicized and well received. It caused a public outcry for remedial action.

Even before Sinclair's book was published, a series of articles written for *Collier's Magazine*, in 1905, by Samuel Hopkins Adams, had focused public attention on abuses not just in meat packing, but also on the proprietary drug industry. Articles written by Adams ran under the title of "The Great American Fraud" (4, 12, 15), his code name for quack nostrums and remedies. The articles were published over the course of several months. They were so popular that they were later reprinted, in book form, by the American Medical Association (16). The *Ladies Home Journal* published a similar series of articles.

The exposes that Adams wrote about patent medicines were every bit as damning as Sinclair's treatment of the meat packing industry. And just as Sinclair's writings were often credited with initiating the push for regulating meat packers, Adam's articles are often credited with doing the same for the patent drug industry.

Actually, neither assumption is correct. Long before publication of *The Jungle*, meat industry lobbyists had begun to pressure the United States Congress for legislative reform. Most of the countries of Europe had already enacted laws regulating meat quality, and meat inspection was a part of those regulations. European producers were using these disparities in the laws to lock out American exports. German producers argued that inspection controls on imported pork should be at least as rigorous as the local controls applied within Germany. Had the U.S. government not passed comparable legislation, American meat exporters would have been out of business. The Pure Food and Drug Act greatly benefited the industries it regulated; sales improved when trust was restored in the products and producers were no longer locked out of European markets.

Proprietary drugmakers were also coming under pressure. By any rational standard, the composition of many turn of the century remedies could only be described as criminal. Combinations of alcohol and cocaine were popular, but not in as much demand as combinations of morphine, opium, and alcohol. The public had its choice between Dr. Fahrney's Teething Syrup which contained morphine, Dr. James' Soothing Syrup which contained heroin, and Dr. Moffett's Teething Powder which was made from opium. Among the cocaine-containing remedies, Cassebeer's Coca Calisaya was typical. Touted as an "agreeable and efficient tonic" capable of "sustaining the strength under extreme physical exertion", it was also very good for treating those persons "enfeebled by sickness or disability". The label indicated that Coca Calisaya contained 35% alcohol. Government chemists found 42% alcohol, combined with cocaine, quinine, and other uncharacterized alkaloids.

Coca-Bola was a cocaine-containing chewing gum sold by C.L. Mitchell, a Philadelphia-based physician. According to Mitchell, his product was designed to be chewed at "occasional intervals throughout the day". It contained 710 mg of cocaine per ounce of gum. A "line" of cocaine today contains roughly 50 to 75 mg, enough to cause a pleasurable "rush" when "snorted" by a user. Each piece of Dr. Mitchell's gum contained nearly 10 "lines" of cocaine! According to Mitchell's advertisements, "A small portion chewed occasionally acts as a powerful tonic to the muscular and nervous system, enabling the chewer to perform additional labor, and also relieves fatigue and exhaustion without evil after-effects. It contains no injurious ingredients and is perfectly harmless." Although the idea had been thoroughly rejected many years before, Coca-Bola advertisements published in 1909 still claimed that the gum could be used to treat morphine and alcohol addiction.

The most famous of the cocaine-containing nostrums was Dr. Tucker's Asthma Specific, formulated and sold by Nathan Tucker of Gilead, Ohio. Tucker's medication was applied directly to the nasal membranes. It was alleged to be a cure for "asthma, hay fever, and catarrhal disease of the respiratory tract". Analysis by government chemists confirmed a cocaine content of 420 mg per ounce, not quite in a league with Coca-Bola, but containing an extraordinary high concentration of cocaine, nonetheless. Because Tucker correctly stated the cocaine content on his product label, sales remained legal even after the passage of the Pure Food and Drug Act in 1906.

By the turn of the century, Congress also began to take a serious look at the patent medicine problem. Several different committees undertook formal investigations. Harvey Wiley was a frequent witness before these committees. Of the four people associated with food and drug reform, Wiley did the most to shape long term U.S. drug policy. Wiley, like Sinclair, was a committed activist. Raised on a farm, in 1883, he became the chief chemist at the U.S. Department of Agriculture. He held a Bachelors Degree in chemistry from Harvard University, had been a professor of chemistry at Purdue University, and eventually served as the president of the American Chemical Society, a post held in earlier years by Edward Robinson Squibb. In spite of Wiley's impressive curriculum vitae, he appears to have been a better showman than scientist.

Wiley first came to center stage because of his research on preservatives. In 1902, he began a series of experiments to determine the "character of food preservatives, coloring matters, and other substances added to food". The experiments were vague, poorly defined and, by today's standards, totally unacceptable. In some ways, his studies resembled Freud's on the treatment of morphine addiction, but with one important difference: Freud's conclusions were based on what was known at the time. Freud was, of course, wrong, but opiate receptors and neurotransmitters were yet to be discovered, and without such basic building blocks, rational theories about drug addiction could not be formulated. Wiley had no such excuse, he just interpreted the data to fit his preconceived conclusions.

Wiley's studies on benzoic acid illustrate the problem (17). Today benzoic acid is used everywhere as a food preservative. Its properties have been extensively studied by the U.S. Government, and by the World Health Organization. It is an effective preservative and, provided daily consumption is kept below 500 mg per day (enough to preserve, for example, 2.5 pounds of butter), benzoic acid possess relatively little toxicity. Even at higher levels, the most common side effect is an upset stomach.

Benzoic acid was first introduced as a preservative at the turn of this century. In spite of the total absence of any evidence to support his concerns, Wiley became convinced that benzoic acid was a dangerous compound. And he was outraged by the fact that small amounts could go undetected in the food of U.S. consumers. Wiley set out to prove that even small quantities of the compound could have deleterious effects. The strange thing about Wiley's quest was that he chose to ignore a very large body of thoroughly reputable research on the topic.

With his educational background and experience, Wiley surely would have known that benzoic acid is a naturally occurring compound found in fruits and berries, a fact that had been known for at least 150 years before Wiley started his research (18). Chemists in the 16th century had succeeded in crystallizing benzoic acid from horse urine, and a century later, Justus Liebig and Friedrich Wöhler had discovered that when benzoic acid appears in the urine, it is bound to another molecule (glycine). The two molecules, when bound together, form another compound called hippuric acid, a key compound which plays a key role in the elimination of nitrogen from the system (19).

In spite of these earlier studies, Wiley became convinced that adding benzoic acid to food was a dangerous practice, and he set out to prove that benzoic acid made people ill. He decided to study the problem by experimenting on a group of 12 men, all U.S. Department of Agriculture employees. They came to be known as "Doctor Wiley's poison squad (3)." Wiley believed that studying humans had a number of advantages, not the least of which was that they could report feelings of "malaise in incipient stages". Wiley rejected the use of animals for such studies because "the results produced on one species by a certain course of treatment might not be secured with an animal of a different species (17)," still a legitimate concern today.

Wiley's critics suggested another reason: he was not a trained animal researcher. In a series of articles attacking Wiley and his experiments, the *Scientific American* pointed out that very few of the staff in his department had any experience with animal experimentation. In truth, there are important differences between species, not just in anatomy, but in biochemical responses as well. But given the technology available to Wiley, he would not have been capable of detecting these subtle differences, and his explanations for eschewing animal research simply are not credible.

Wiley's subjects were housed together, and fed an assortment of adulterated foods. At the same time, they all continued their regular work in the department, and were "simply placed upon their honor and neither watched nor confined". Wiley's answer to objections about the design of his study was that his subjects were honorable men. They were "not likely to violate their pledge". Wiley had looked "carefully into the moral character" of the volunteers, especially "their reputation for sobriety and reliability (17)." On that basis, alcohol drinkers were excluded (Wiley was a prohibitionist), but moderate tobacco users were accepted.

One half of the subjects in Wiley's experiment were given a particular item of food obtained from one source. Their reactions were compared to the reactions of the other six subjects, who had been fed a similar food item from another source. The subjects could tell when they were being fed benzoate-containing products, and when they were not. Urine and stool samples were continuously collected; subjective and objective responses were recorded. Each of the volunteers underwent daily weighing and periodic physical examinations, with occasional general inquiries made into their mental status. No psychological testing instruments were used, and the examiners knew which drug the individual had been given. Regardless of whether or not they had been given benzoic acid, "a liberal supply of fruits was incorporated with the food supply (17)." Since fresh fruit contains benzoic acid, supplementing the diet with fruit would have guaranteed that all of the participants were receiving supplemental amounts of benzoic acid, totally invalidating the study.

An equally important defect in the design of the study was that it was "unblinded". The behavioral effects of a drug can only be reliably studied if neither the test subject nor the experimenter knows whether drug or placebo is given. Freud committed exactly the same type of error when he measured his own muscle strength before and after taking cocaine (21). The force of muscle contraction is, in large part, voluntary. Since Freud knew he was taking cocaine, and since he freely admitted that he wanted to prove that cocaine was a valuable drug, it came as no surprise when he found that cocaine increased muscle strength. Wiley did much the same thing. He gave his subjects chemicals which he was sure were harmful, and then he looked for harmful effects. It would have been surprising if he had not found any. Not surprisingly, Wiley was able to conclude, just as he had expected, that "preservatives used in foods are harmful to health (17)."

The *Scientific American* waged a solitary battle against Wiley and his Bureau of Chemistry, and the flawed nature of Wiley's methodology should have been clear to anyone who gave the subject a second thought. But in the end, the persuasiveness of Wiley's personality, and his bully pulpit as chief government chemist, proved to be more important than the believability of his science. Of course later, long after Wiley was dead, the government classified benzoic acid as a "generally...safe" compound (18).

Bogus though Wiley's experiments may have been, they struck a responsive chord and received "air time". The public loved reading about Wiley and his "poison squad". Even so, Wiley's conclusions were not enough to prompt Congress into action. According to Wiley, "pure food measures were smugly looked upon as the work of cranks and reformers without much business sense". But Wiley's studies published less than half a year before Sinclair's *The Jungle*, helped pave the way for the government to finally take action. When President Theodore Roosevelt released a report confirming the accuracy of Sinclair's accusation about the meat packing industry, the Pure Food and Drug Act was rapidly drafted and passed by the U.S. Congress.

The law, as finally enacted, provided that substances may be added to food only if (1) they are safe for human consumption, and (2) their addition serves some useful purpose. As was the case with the meat packers, the drug industry dropped its hard line position, and no longer opposed regulation. Their position had more to do with the sales of their products than with any concerns for the public's welfare. As the public became better informed, patent medicines and nostrums became harder and harder to sell. Government regulation gave the appearance of respectability and reliability to these products.

In 1905, at a special secret meeting held in response to mounting public outrage, the trade organization of proprietary drug manufacturers passed a resolution calling on its members to tone down their more outrageous advertising claims, and to reduce the alcohol and narcotic contents of their products (22). The Coca-Cola Company actually supported reform legislation. Coca-Cola was, after all, truthfully labeled and made from pure products.

Passage of the Pure Food and Drug Act in 1906 should have led to rapid changes in the drug industry, but they were very slow to occur. Wiley toured the country giving speeches about the patent drug problem, but his heart was not really in it. He was much more interested in the problem of food adulteration. Government chemists, on the other hand, remained more concerned with the problem of truth-in-labeling, than with the hypothetical effects of the adulterants on the public health.

Wiley was repeatedly criticized for the narrowness of his focus by George McCabe, the head legal counsel of the U.S. Department of Agriculture. McCabe wrote numerous letters to Wiley asking him why he was not going after more patent drug makers (3). Wiley's response was that there were over 25,000 such products and he could not analyze them all.

The decision to focus on problems of food adulteration, rather than the effects of adulterants, was not entirely voluntary. Neither Wiley, nor his staff, had the technology to measure subtle drug effects, and they knew it. During the late 1800s, quantitative chemical analysis was a reasonably well-established discipline. The science of toxicology was not. There was no way for Wiley to detect the subtle changes that trace amounts of chemicals, such as benzoic acid, might produce in experimental animals. The technology existed so that adulterants could be detected in food, but their effects could not be accurately measured.

While the technology to detect food adulterants certainly existed in Wiley's time, the government's ability to use this technology to detect adulterants was suspect. Within the U.S. Department of Agriculture, testing for adulterants was the responsibility of the Bureau of Chemistry. The staff of the Bureau was relatively small, and many of its chemists poorly trained. In one editorial, the *Scientific American* observed that four of the department's key analysts had obtained degrees from medical schools that had been closed for failing to meet minimal educational standards (20).

Even if Wiley had been more energetic about pursuing patent drugmakers, there was not that much he could do about the problem. Nathan Tucker's Asthma Specific, and similar products, were clearly a menace, and needed to be regulated, but the Pure Food and Drug Act of 1906 did little to remedy the problem. Because of the U.S. government's narrow focus on the identification of adulterants, and not on the effects of the adulterants, the Act, when finally drafted, addressed only the issue of truth-in-labeling.

The Act only covered products where heroin and cocaine were added surreptitiously. If the drugs were listed on the label, there was nothing illegal about their sale. Actually, the situation was even worse than it sounded. In a speech given in 1911, at a Men's Club in Mount Vernon, New York, H.H. Rusby went as far as to call the Act a complete failure. Because the law was so narrowly drafted, it was easy to circumvent. For example, it was perfectly legal for the makers of banned products to ship individual ingredients across state lines where they could be blended by local manufacturers (23).

Wiley, along with other government scientists, and the politicians they advised, never understood or accepted the concept that proving a substance is a hazard requires more than just proving the substance is present. In order to prove toxicity, it is also necessary to establish a relationship between the magnitude of exposure to that substance and the probability that an adverse effect will occur. The scientists who wrote the Pure Food and Drug Act did not have the technology at the time to measure subtle effects produced by adulterants, but they could detect them. And so Wiley made a virtue of necessity. He became the first politician to espouse the policy of zero tolerance.

After the passage of the Pure Food and Drug Act, Wiley got another chance to apply his peculiar version of the scientific method: this time to the problem of caffeine. Wiley became convinced that caffeine was even more dangerous than benzoic acid. And even though caffeine was not on the list of dangerous drugs specifically regulated by the Pure Food and Drug Act, Wiley took it upon himself to stamp out its use. Unfortunately for the owners of the Coca-Cola Company, their product contained caffeine.

Executives of the Coca-Cola Company had supported the Pure Food and Drug Act. John Candler, the brother of Asa Candler, the majority shareholder in the Coca-Cola Company, even went to Washington to testify at congressional hearings in favor of the bill. Support for the proposed legislation seemed an act of self interest. Coca-Cola Company management assumed that passage of the bill would very likely lead to increased sales. When the Act passed in 1906, Coca-Cola advertisements included language to the effect that Coca-Cola was "Guaranteed under the Pure Food and Drug Act". That should have been the end of the matter for Coca-Cola. Except for saccharine, which was being added to Coca-Cola by some independent bottlers, Coca-Cola was, in fact, an entirely natural and pure product, truthfully labeled under the definitions of the 1906 Act.

For some reason, Coca-Cola's support for the Act seems to have infuriated Wiley. Given what is known about Wiley's personality, it may not be unreasonable to suppose that he thought Coca-Cola was actually mocking him with its endorsement of the Act. For whatever reason, Wiley began an organized campaign of government harassment against the Coca-Cola Company. He got the Acting Secretary of Agriculture to threaten legal action unless Coca-Cola stopped claiming it was pure! Wiley then formed an alliance with Martha Allen, head of the Women's Christian Temperance Union, and convinced the U.S. Army to ban Coca-Cola from its bases

Wiley's alliance with Allen was a marriage of convenience. In 1901, Coca-Cola had challenged an IRS ruling, a tax imposed to fund the Spanish-American War. During the IRS hearings, evidence had been introduced showing that Coca-Cola contained alcohol. Trace amounts were, in fact, required to dissolve the flavoring essences used to make the product. Wiley and Allen recycled the testimony from the former hearings and wrote to the Army's Surgeon General, claiming that Coca-Cola contained as much alcohol as beer and an "indefinite amount of cocaine". And so, for a few months in 1907, at least until the absurdity of the claims became clear, the U.S. Army banned Coca-Cola from its bases. Wiley was never reprimanded for making what he clearly knew were false claims. Instead, Wiley launched another federal investigation into Coca-Cola's bottling practices (3)(7).

Surprisingly, the new focus of Wiley's investigations of the Coca-Cola Company had little to do with cocaine. Rather, Wiley argued that putting caffeine in soft drinks was unethical, especially when the soft drink was being consumed by children. Defenders of Coca-Cola countered that Coca-Cola contained no more caffeine than coffee or tea. The finding of the trial court judge indicated that Coca-Cola had a caffeine content of 72 mg per ounce of syrup, with one ounce of syrup making one glass of carbonated beverage (1) (24). Drinking a glass of Coca-Cola was the equivalent, in terms of caffeine, of drinking a cup of coffee. The caffeine content of today's Coca-Cola is probably even less than what it was at the time of the trial (25).

In 1909, acting with the full approval of the U.S. Department of Agriculture and the Solicitor General, Wiley seized 40 barrels and 20 kegs of Coca-Cola syrup, charging that the syrup contained a poisonous ingredient which might be hazardous to health. Coca-Cola was also charged with false labeling; it contained no coca and hardly any cola. The case was tried in a federal court in Chattanooga, Tennessee, in March of 1911.

According to press accounts, Wiley himself directed much of the cross-examination, but he never appeared as a witness. One of the expert witnesses called by the prosecution was H.H. Rusby, the man who had revolutionized the cocaine industry by devising a way to produce crude, semirefined cocaine on site. At the time of the trial, Rusby had been appointed a professor of Materia Medica (pharmacology) at Columbia University, and was one of three editors of the *National Standard Dispensary*, a semi-official book on pharmacology. The other two editors testified for the defense (3).

Rusby was also a full time government employee, which later proved to be a problem for Wiley. Rusby was a much better scientist than Wiley, and he knew the latest literature. Unfortunately, in 1912, the literature on caffeine was comprised of mostly folklore and little fact. According to the *National Standard Dispensary*, caffeine was a good treatment for heart failure, and could be used to reverse the respiratory depression associated with opium overdose. Rusby was eventually asked by the prosecution to describe the toxic effects of caffeine, but he had to wait his turn.

First, the jury had to hear one prosecution expert, a Harvard Medical School professor, describe the terrible effects observed when frogs were injected with Coca-Cola syrup! Another government employee described the painful deaths experienced by rabbits when Coca-Cola syrup was poured into their lungs! Still another prosecution witness assured the jurors that drinking Coca-Cola encouraged boys to masturbate (7).

While the assault on Coca-Cola continued in Tennessee, Wiley was planning even grander pursuits. On March 20, long before the trial came to a close, a representative of the Bureau of Chemistry called a press conference. Dr. W. L. Baldwin, who was acting chief when Wiley was out of town, announced plans for a "strenuous warfare on all cooling concoctions that are alleged to contain harmful ingredients (26)." Just what was considered harmful by Bureau of Chemistry's standards was anyone's guess. But Baldwin announced that a list of "alleged harmful soft drinks" had already been prepared, and that "every soda fountain and soft drink store in Washington will be visited several times each week by government inspectors, with a view to learning if they contain cocaine, coca leaf, or caffeine".

Judge Edward Terry Sanford, who was appointed to the Supreme Court in 1923, was not impressed. He ordered a verdict in favor of the Coca-Cola Company. The fallout from the trial took years to sort out. In 1912, the Pure Food and Drug Act was amended, and caffeine was added to the list of dangerous drugs. The government lost its initial appeal, but won in the Supreme Court. In 1917, Coca-Cola settled out of court and agreed to reduce the amount of caffeine in the finished product. Under mounting pressure, Wiley left his government post shortly after the trial. Among other things, Wiley was accused of having paid Rusby too much for his expert testimony. Wiley went on to write a column for *Good Housekeeping* magazine. In one column he touted the virtues of coffee, claiming it had become "America's beverage".

The final outcome of the Coca-Cola Company case could not have been gratifying to Wiley. He had to drop his planned offensive against the soda fountains of America, and, for his efforts, all that he managed to do was run up a large legal bill for the Coca-Cola Company. The cost of the first trial alone was estimated to be more than $200,000, an enormous sum for 1911 (27). It is not clear whether publicity from the trial helped or hurt Coca-Cola sales.

Much more important than the outcome of the trial, however, were some of the precedents it set, the most important being government use of pseudoscience to further a perceived social good, and to win in court. In a reprise of his benzoic acid researches, where he had basically manufactured evidence to "prove" what he already knew, Wiley was so firmly convinced of the evils of Coca-Cola that he was not at all bothered by the quality of the data he presented in courts.

Granted, medical experiments done at the turn of the century lacked today's sophistication, but since Wiley later expounded on the virtues of coffee drinking, it is hard to suppose he could have had much faith in the evidence he, or his experts, presented at trial. The willingness to resort to pseudoscience, along with the refusal to accept the fact that the amount of drug used has something to do with the effects that a drug produces, has come to be, it appears, the hallmark of American, and International, "zero tolerance" drug policy today.

<u>Dr. H. Wiley, head of the Bureau of Chemistry, U.S. Department of Agriculture</u>: In a famous case filed in 1909, Wiley accused the Coca-Cola Company of violating the Pure Food and Drug Act because Coca-Cola contained caffeine, roughly the same amount found in a cup of coffee. Wiley was undeterred by the fact that caffeine was not prohibited by the Act. At the time, not much was known about caffeine toxicity, but Wiley did find some experts to testify against Coca-Cola. One witness described how rabbits reacted when he filled their lungs with *Coca Cola* syrup (they died). Another described the fatal outcome after intravenous injections of syrup in frogs. And still another opined that using *Coca-Cola* would surely lead to excessive masturbation. Wiley was also the first to advocate the "zero tolerance" approach to drug control. The photograph originally appeared in *The National Cyclopaedia of American Biography*, published in 1931.

Chapter 9

THE "LEGITIMATE BUSINESS OF POISONING HINDOOS"

...they (the German representatives at Geneva) don't understand action based on humanitarian motives and...would understand it still less when called on to enact legislation to restrict German traders in "the legitimate business of poisoning Hindoos and Chinese (1).

From a British representative at the Hague Conference to the Foreign Office in London.

In spite of the Opium Wars fought by Britain and China, drug control policy had never been a matter of international concern, at least not until the United States made it an issue at the turn of the century. In 1906, the United States launched a series of initiatives aimed at curtailing the illicit drug trade. These efforts were not made in response to any serious drug problems within American borders. At the time of the first initiatives, America was not an opium producer, and there were relatively few addicts within the borders of the United States. But in 1898, at the end of the Spanish-American War, the United States took possession of the Philippine Islands, and found itself in much the same position as Japan in 1905 when it acquired Taiwan; ward to a large population of addicted opium smokers.

The situation in the Philippine Islands was not nearly as bad as it was in Taiwan. When the United States took possession of the Philippines, there were probably fewer than 50,000 opium addicts, almost all Chinese. Philippine opium imports amounted to slightly over 100 tons per year. Initially, opium traffic in the Philippines remained unregulated, and the occupation government helped balance its budget by taxing opium imports.

A study commission, appointed by Congress, and headed by Episcopal Bishop Charles H. Brent, was appointed to investigate opium use in the Philippines, and to make recommendations to Congress. The commission reached essentially the same conclusions that the Japanese had come to a few years earlier: form a government monopoly, prohibit non-medical use of opiates, license opium smokers, and try to educate the public about the dangers of opium smoking (2). The commission made its report to Congress in 1905. Congress rejected the findings and recommendations of the committee and, instead, voted for an absolute prohibition of opium smoking. The prohibition went into effect in March of 1908.

Overnight, smuggling in the Philippines became a major problem. There are hundreds of islands in the Philippines, and thousands of landing sites for smugglers transporting opium from Borneo and Singapore. Policing the borders began to consume a major portion of the local constabulary's budget. Echoing a theme still heard today, the Chief of Philippine Customs wrote to Bishop Brent and complained that his department was receiving only "about one tenth of the amount necessary to enable this bureau to fully prosecute this prohibited evil (2)!"

Not long after the U.S. Congress had outlawed opium in the Philippines, the government of China passed an edict prohibiting opium cultivation in that country. That same year, Bishop Brent, frustrated by the flood of opium smuggled into the Philippines, wrote to President Theodore Roosevelt and suggested international action. Brent realized, even if Congress did not, that the United States and the Philippines could not simply make drug policy in a vacuum. Congress could pass all the absolute prohibitions it wanted. Enforcing them, without cooperation from the producing countries, was another matter (2).

Brent's suggestion was eventually implemented (3). The United States invited 14 countries, all with major financial interests in the Far East, to participate in a conference. Each of the countries invited to participate were countries that generated revenues from growing, refining, or selling opium. Thirteen of the countries agreed to send representatives to a meeting. Turkey was the only major opium producer that refused to attend. The delegation from the United States was led by Bishop Brent, but most of the proposals were written by Dr. Hamilton Wright, an American physician, who had been appointed to the U.S. negotiating team. Wright certainly was not chosen for his diplomatic skills. In fact, he had no diplomatic training, and managed to thoroughly alienate most of the European diplomats with whom he had to deal (3)(4). He was chosen, instead, because he knew the region and was, presumably, well acquainted with the problems of opium addiction (4).

It may seem surprising that Great Britain agreed to participate in such a conference. The colonial government in India was, after all, partially financed by taxes on opium sales. But Bishop Brent was not the only one concerned about the opium problem. In England, pressure was growing in Parliament to outlaw the opium trade altogether. The pressure came partly from the general public, but largely from missionary groups, frustrated with their lack of success in converting the Chinese to Christianity. Past attempts at legislative reform had been unsuccessful, but in the Parliamentary election of 1906, reform candidates handily beat the Tories, and they finally forced the government into action. Details of the parliamentary maneuvering are nicely described by H. Richard Frimans in his insightful book, *Narcodiplomacy* (20).

After considerable debate, Great Britain eventually agreed to curtail Indian exports of opium to China, provided that, at the same time, China reduced domestic production and imports from other countries as well (3). The latter condition was a recurring European theme in all drug control negotiations. England, like Germany and France, was home to an advanced pharmaceutical industry, and India, her possession, was a major opium producer. England did not plan to stop selling drugs to China only to see some other producer take its place.

After lengthy negotiations over the agenda, the Commission finally met in Shanghai in 1909, from February 1 to 28. The American representatives submitted eight resolutions. All but one of the resolutions had been drafted by Wright (5). The American proposals were not exactly what the other participants wanted to hear. Wright wanted the Commission to agree that opium should only be used for medical purposes, and that bans on opium smoking should be immediately put into effect. That position was supported only by China and Canada. Such draconian notions were far too radical for the other countries to accept; not that they could have done much to implement such proposals, even if they had agreed to them. As the head of the British delegation, Clementi Smith pointed out, such a ban would be impossible to carry out, that there were not enough soldiers in all of Britain to police an area as vast as India (3).

Instead of an outright ban on opium smoking, Wright was only able to negotiate a resolution favoring gradual reductions in opium production, coupled with agreements that opium smoking should be gradually regulated and suppressed. Another of Wright's suggestions, to impose export controls on producing countries, was accepted in such a watered-down version, so universal and so general, it made narcotic smuggling easier. What began as a proposal for strict international regulation of drug sales, became, in its final form, an agreement that drug control was a local, not an international problem. The resolutions finally adopted by the Commission were non-binding (6).

Even if there were no binding resolutions, there was general consensus that something had to be done about the drug dilemma. As one

British delegate put it, the "opium question required firmer handling (7)." Dr. Wright wrote a report which described what had transpired at the Shanghai meeting (8). The report did not exactly agree with the recollection of the other diplomats in attendance, but it certainly portrayed the actions of Dr. Wright and the American delegation, in a very good light (7). Many of the proposals put forward by the United States (essentially all written by Wright) had been rejected out-of-hand, but when the Conference proceedings were reported to Congress, instead of reporting that his proposals were rejected, Wright indicated they had been "waived for the sake of harmony". In internal memos, British diplomats confirmed that absolutely no agreement regarding the necessity of international drug regulation had been reached, or even considered. But when Wright wrote his report, he insisted that "it was recognized that such action (international regulation) was necessary...(8)." The foreign diplomatic corps, particularly the British, were not happy with Wright, or with his claims, or with the United States in general (9).

Wright spent the next two years organizing a second conference, this gathering to be held in the Hague. It appears that there was considerable foot dragging, both by the U.S. State Department and by the Foreign Office in England (10). While the foot dragging was going on, Wright had time to author 14 new proposals. These were forwarded by the State Department to the Foreign Office in London. As before, at the top of Wright's wish list were laws to control opium production and gradually limit opium smoking. There were also a host of other proposals designed to make it more difficult for drug producers to move drugs across international borders. Wright suggested that an international commission be appointed and charged with supervising drug production. None of the 14 new proposals submitted by Wright mentioned cocaine.

In correspondence with the various governments prior to the meeting in the Hague, U.S. State Department representatives claimed that their main concern was the eradication of opium smoking in China, and in the Far Eastern possessions owned by the various participating European countries. They insisted that problems associated with the use of other drugs were not to be discussed (11). British diplomats were not happy with that approach. Britain derived too much revenue from Indian opium sales and, in addition, many colonial administrators felt that the habit was not that pernicious. When the British Foreign Secretary, Sir Edward Grey, finally accepted the U.S. invitation to attend another conference in September of 1910, he pointed out that his acceptance was only provisional. Britain had no intention of attending, unless all:

> ...the other participating Powers are willing that the conference should thoroughly and completely deal with the question of

> *restricting the manufacture, sale, and distribution of*
> *morphia...and also with the allied question of cocaine. In India,*
> *in China, and in other Eastern countries the importation of*
> *morphia and cocaine from occidental countries, and the spread*
> *of morphia and the cocaine habit, is becoming an evil more*
> *serious and more deadly than opium smoking, and this evil is*
> *certain to increase...(12)*

British leaders had not been enthusiastic about holding another conference. They were even less enthusiastic when they noticed that none of Wright's proposals mentioned cocaine. Regulating one drug, but not another, seemed to make little sense. British diplomats were more concerned with regulating the manufacturing process than with cultivation. In retrospect, the British approach was somewhat surprising. At the time, Great Britain was second only to Germany in the drug refining business, but the British government was becoming increasingly embarrassed by its role of English producers in the illegal drug trade (13). Although not of the epic proportions attained prior to World War II, Japanese sales of heroin and morphine in occupied China were very substantial, and most of the drug sold was supplied by British and European drugmakers.

Britain refused to attend unless the problem of other drugs was also placed on the agenda. Eventually the British got their way. Their position could be interpreted as an exercise in cynicism, since the British diplomats knew that the other participants would all be affected financially by any controls placed on drug manufacturing. Shifting the emphasis to cocaine and morphine would mean that less attention would be devoted to Indian opium production. On the other hand, it may have been that the British were simply more realistic than Wright and his delegation. It is difficult to accept the notion that anyone, including Hamilton Wright, seriously believed that the opium problem could be solved without, at the same time, addressing the problems of morphine and cocaine production. British emphasis on the control of drug manufacture, as the key to limiting the spread of drug use, was in stark contrast to that of the United States, which was chiefly concerned with the production of raw materials. Both approaches, however, proved to be equally shortsighted.

By the time the Convention was held in the Hague in 1912, most of the U.S. proposals had been abandoned or extensively modified. Still, some agreements were reached. There was general agreement that the production and distribution of raw opium should be regulated by law, the practice of opium smoking should be gradually suppressed, the manufacture and sale of other narcotic drugs, such as heroin and cocaine, should be limited to the amount necessary to supply "legitimate" medical needs, and import and export controls should be instituted.

The conclusions were contained in six separate chapters in the Convention summary (5). The first two, regarding opium, were generally not controversial and passed easily. The third chapter of the convention had to do with manufactured drugs, and was hotly debated. This section had been largely written by the British delegation and would have had the effect of severely limiting sales of refined narcotics. The provisions were vigorously opposed by Germany, the home of Merck and Bayer, the world's largest cocaine and heroin manufacturers. Max Mueller, one of the British negotiators, a former charge' d'affaires in Peking with firsthand knowledge of the opium problem, wrote back to his superiors that the representatives of the German delegation "don't understand action based on humanitarian motives and...would understand it still less when called on to enact legislation to restrict German traders in the legitimate business of poisoning Hindoos and Chinese (1)."

Financial considerations almost guaranteed that no serious agreement would come out of the Hague conference. Drug manufacturing was a major industry in all of the participating countries, except the United States and Canada. In the unlikely event that humanitarian consideration might convince one country to get out of the drug business entirely, other manufacturers would have been more than happy to supply any shortfall. Thus, implementation of the agreement became a real problem. Short of all countries signing on the same date, producing countries that signed earlier would lose revenues, while those that signed later would reap windfall profits. Two additional conferences were convened, in 1913 and 1914, solely to find a way to actually implement the agreements reached in 1912. The meetings were unsuccessful, and negotiations were still continuing at the outbreak of World War I (3).

Ratification of the Hague treaty finally became possible at the end of World War I. Turkey and Germany lost the war. Both were major drug producing countries, and neither had been enthusiastic about the Hague treaty. American President Woodrow Wilson linked the founding of the League of Nations, the predecessor of today's United Nations to the peace treaty. Few of the allies shared his passion: France strongly objected, England offered half-hearted support, and the U.S. Congress was not as enthusiastic as England. Wilson finally had to threaten to sign a separate peace treaty with Germany if the rest of the allies did not support him on the League's formation (14)(15).

Once the League of Nations had been accepted, it was only logical that the terms of the unratified Opium Convention be included in the League of Nations' charter. Germany, the world's largest narcotics maker, and Turkey, one of the world's largest opium growers, had no choice but to become signatories, and to limit their drug sales. According to Article 23 of the League of Nations Covenant, members "entrust the League with the general supervision over agreements with regard to...the traffic in opium and other dangerous drugs."

At the first meeting of the League in 1921, the Assembly voted to create the Advisory Committee on Traffic in Opium and Other Dangerous Drugs. The Committee was charged with finding ways to implement the provisions of the 1912 Hague Convention. Many approaches to the problem were discussed, but only two were seriously considered: production controls and sales controls. Drug manufacturing countries were heavily represented on the Committee, and they effectively stonewalled any proposal to limit production. The approach ultimately chosen relied on the regulation and control of drug sales.

A system of import and export certificates was devised. Narcotic exports were only permitted if buyers could produce certificates attesting to legitimate medical need (16). There were, of course, certain problems with this approach. For instance, there was no agreement as to what constituted legitimate medical need. Per capita cocaine and opiate consumption varied widely from country to country, partly because of differences in medical practices, partly because of sloppy bookkeeping, and, in the case of countries such as Japan and Switzerland, because the government condoned fraud and deception. During the 1920s, League of Nations' experts estimated that the legitimate medical requirements for cocaine in countries with developed medical systems were not more than 7 mg per person (17). Japanese production, alone, amounted to far more than that amount.

Another problem with the chosen approach was enforcement. All the Opium Committee could do was recommend that more drugs not be sold to countries that violated the import-export system. A series of cases, such as the Naarden Chemical scandal (see Chapter 7), where the intent, if not the letter, of the law was violated, made it clear that, whatever the League of Nations was doing, was not working. According to a joint resolution approved by the U.S. Congress on March 2, 1923, the Opium Committee's approach had "utterly failed to suppress such illicit traffic". And the reason for the failure, according to the U.S. Congress, was that the League had wrongly emphasized the regulation of transport and sale. According to Congress, the failure to: "provide adequate restrictions upon production has resulted in extensive and flagrant violation of the laws (18)."

On May 10, 1923, the U.S. State Department sent a delegation headed by Stephen Porter (R-Pennsylvania), the chairman of the House Foreign Affairs Committee, to a meeting of the Opium Committee in Geneva. Bishop Brent was one of the representatives. Because of its doubts about both the League of Nations itself, and the way the League was approaching the drug problem, the U.S. Congress chose not to participate in the deliberations of the Opium Committee. Observers, such as Brent and Porter, were sent, but did not participate. When Porter went to Geneva he had been instructed to present the U.S. position as being essentially non-negotiable. The U.S. proposals had the effect of limiting production, and outlawing drug use, except for medical purposes. Porter presented his suggestions and left. His suggestions were never accepted, largely because of pressure from the narcotic manufacturing countries (3).

Another convention was held in Geneva in 1925. American suggestions were, again, largely ignored. This time Porter and his delegation went home early. But, at least, the differences between the European and American approaches were clearly drawn. Europeans continued to focus on manufacturing. The Americans felt that that approach was totally wrongheaded. In a memorandum to the President of the Conference, Porter wrote:

> There is, however, no likelihood of obtaining a complete control of all opium and coca leaf derivatives. Irrespective of the measure of control provided for manufactured drugs, it is believed that, by reason of the very small bulk, the ease of transportation with minimum risk of detection, and the large financial gains to be obtained from their illicit handling, such drugs and their derivatives can only be effectively controlled if the production of the raw opium and coca leaves from which they are obtained is strictly limited to medical and scientific purposes (19).

The Committee did not agree, and its focus remained squarely on drug sales and distribution. It is not clear from the records why the Europeans where so opposed to the U.S. emphasis on limiting raw materials, but they were certainly acting correctly when they rejected the U.S. demands. The number of acres devoted to opium and coca in the 1920s amounted to only a tiny fraction of the acres under cultivation today, even though a host of laws and treaties prohibit their cultivation of both coca and the opium poppy.

The following year, the Permanent Central Board (the title was later changed to the Permanent Central Opium Board, and then to the Permanent Central Narcotics Board) was established. Governments were required to submit annual reports on the amount of opium and coca cultivated, the quantities of drugs produced, and the amount of each drug actually consumed by its citizens. Participating governments were also required to submit quarterly reports to the Board on imports and exports. At the same time, the system of import certificates and export authorizations was formalized (6). Unlike the earlier Opium Committee, which was composed of representatives from drug-producing countries, the Permanent Central Board was comprised of eight independent experts. The eight were charged with supervising the requirements set down in the original convention.

In none of these deliberations is there any evidence that suggests that Porter, Brent, any other member of the U.S. delegation, or any of the committee members ever considered the possibility of clandestine production. They understood that extracting cocaine from coca was a relatively simple procedure, but they did not recognize the possibility of small, underground laboratories. Today, only insignificant amounts of cocaine are made by legitimate manufacturers. For reasons that are impossible to fathom today, not one participant at the League of Nations, except Japan, seemed to have considered the possibility of large scale narcotic production, occurring totally outside of government production controls. Japan recognized this opportunity for what it was, and began to finance its territorial expansion with drug sales.

Two further Conventions were held before the outbreak of World War II. The Geneva Convention of 1931 prohibited members from producing or importing more drugs then they actually needed. The Geneva Convention of 1936 called for the enactment of measures to prevent drug smuggling, and to facilitate extradition for drug offenses (5). The treaties proved to be a blessing for Japan's war chest. Japan was able to make a great deal of money while feigning support for international drug control. But, signing the treaties proved to be a mixed blessing, and eventually became a liability for Japan. Violation of the various drug treaties was cited as one justification for holding the Tokyo War Crime Trials at the end of World War II.

<u>Dr. Hamilton Wright</u>: For reasons having more to do with the balance of naval power in the Pacific, and the American trade balances with China, than with any humanitarian concerns, the United States invited 14 countries to a conference on the opium problem. All of the invited guests had major financial interests in the Far East, and most were opium producers. The conference was held in Shanghai in 1909. Hamilton Wright, an American physician, with experience in Tropical medicine, but none in diplomacy or negotiation, drafted the U.S. proposals for the 1909 and subsequent conferences. He was frequently outmaneuvered by European negotiators. This drawing appeared in *Appletons' Cyclopaedia of American Biography* (J. Homans and H. Linen, Eds.), published in 1922.

Chapter 10

JAPAN'S ADVENTURES IN THE COCAINE TRADE

How the import of raw material is to be limited without keeping an exact record of these imports transcends one's comprehension, though possibly to the statisticians in Japan it may not be so difficult.

Letter from the British Consul in Formosa to the British Ambassador in Tokyo (1)

The original Mitsukoshi Department Store in Tokyo was modeled after Selfridge's Department store in London, except that it was constructed of white bricks, instead of granite. Two bronze lions, similar to those at the base of Admiral Horatio Nelson's pillar in London, guarded its main entrance. The floors were covered with straw matting, and Japanese shoppers were required to remove their shoes before they could enter. Western tourists were issued cloth covers to put over their shoes. The building boasted a host of modern conveniences, including central heating, a sprinkler system, and elevators. A roof garden was open from June through September, and a band played daily (2).

Tourists entering the store probably would not have known that it was founded by the Mitsui Company, or that Mitsui was (and still is) the largest company in Japan, and quite possibly the world. The average tourist would have been even less likely to know that until the end of World War II, some of Mitsui's profits were generated by operating coca plantations and refineries in Taiwan, and Mitsui subsidiaries were major suppliers of cocaine and opium. They would have been incredulous if they had been told that Mitsui held a government-sanctioned franchise for opium sales in occupied China, and that the Japanese government had a financial stake in Mitsui's drug sales (3).

Nor would the visitor realize that other Japanese conglomerates, of nearly equal size, were engaged in exactly the same business of selling illegal drugs. Mitsubishi, the second largest company in Japan, along with Mitsui, shared the lucrative franchise for opium and heroin sales in occupied China. Sumitomo Bank, the third largest commercial entity in Japan, participated in a war bond offering that was guaranteed by heroin and opium sales (4)! How did these household names get into the drug business? And how did the Japanese government come to be their partner? There is no one simple answer.

Nearly every aspect of Japanese government and industry was involved, including the armed forces. The description written by a bemused British embassy officer in 1928 summed up the situation:

> *That corruption should exist in connection with the drug traffic is not surprising when it is remembered that the standards of right and wrong in this country are frequently very different to what we are taught. Scandals...in connection with drug cases...are associated with all classes, from Prime Ministers downwards (5).*

If drug dealing is viewed simply as a business, then there should be nothing surprising about the fact that, in Japan, legitimate business enterprises dominated the narcotic trade. It is somewhat more surprising to learn about the participation of the government and the military. But by the 1920s, the Japanese Army controlled the civilian government, and both needed cash.

At the close of World War II, the Allies, under General MacArthur, occupied Japan. MacArthur had a large staff of intelligence and counter-intelligence officers. But when the decision was finally made to hold War Crimes Trials, and to charge Japan with, among other things, crimes against humanity for its drug sales, there was not enough manpower to carry out all the required field investigations. One of MacArthur's aides contacted the head of the Bureau of Narcotics and asked for help. Only after resolving several disputes over pay grades, Harry Anslinger, then the Director, dispatched several of his field agents who were given temporary army appointments to MacArthur's staff. The magnitude of the drug business that these investigators were able to document surprised even Anslinger.

The boundaries between Japanese industry, the Japanese Army, and the Japanese government were often blurred, mainly as a result of events that occurred after Japan opened its doors to the West. At that time, very special relationships came to exist between the Japanese government and the great Japanese trading houses, referred to as the *zaibatsu* ("financial clique"). Japanese commerce, and, to a large extent, Japanese society, was dominated by a handful of giant trading companies. In a very real sense, the *zaibatsu* families dominated Japanese society (6)(7).

There were, of course, American ventures every bit as large as any of the *zaibatsu* enterprises in Japan. Prior to its being dissolved in 1911 by the United States Supreme Court (for violations of the Anti-trust Law of 1890), companies owned by Standard Oil of New Jersey represented an investment of over $600,000,000. Profits in 1910 were estimated at $80,000,000. The New York Central Railroad, with assets of $1,049,790,388 was even larger. Still, there were few companies, anywhere, the size of Mitsui. And the owners of Standard Oil never held the sort of power exercised by the *zaibatsu* enterprises.

Mitsui has been out of the illegal drug business since the end of World War II, but it still is the most important of the *zaibatsu* companies, and probably the largest single business enterprise in the world, with reported gross revenues in 1994 that were in excess of $171 billion dollars. It operates 742 different companies around the world. Slightly more than half of its companies are located within Japan.

Mitsui is a very old company that was founded by Takatoshi Mitsui, more than two centuries before the start of World War II. He was responsible for the introduction of modern banking techniques to Japan. The new techniques gave the firm an almost unfair advantage, and by the early 1900s, Mitsui had become the largest bank in Japan, even though banking was no longer its primary business. A mining division, which mined and/or sold nearly half the coal consumed in Japan, was almost as large as the bank. Mitsui's trading division was even larger.

The trading division was called Mitsui Bussan Kaisha, or MBK. It controlled 25% of Japan's foreign trade. MBK exported huge amounts of coal, and most of Japan's raw silk production. Even though it is difficult to visualize today, at the turn of the century, Mitsui-owned companies exported timber from Hokkaido to the United States, and rice to Europe (2). MBK imported locomotives, steamships, steel, and heavy electrical equipment. It maintained an extensive network of branch offices around the Pacific Rim, Europe, and the United States. Mitsui totally dominated commercial markets in Taiwan, Korea, and Occupied China (8).

In modern day terms, such activity is hard to conceive. Comparatively, a modern company that accounted for 25% of U.S. foreign trade today would have exports and imports of more than $30 billion per month. Current combined American exports of tobacco, chemicals, pharmaceuticals, agricultural equipment, and computers amount to less than $15 billion dollars per month. If the prewar version of Mitsui existed today, its revenues would be larger than the combined revenues of IBM, Digital Equipment, Caterpillar, John Deere, RJR Nabisco, Merck, Eli Lilly, Citibank, and Bank of America. Mitsui was a very big player. The only bigger player in Japan's illegal drug market was the Japanese government itself.

Mitsubishi was the second largest company in Japan. It also made money selling drugs. Compared to Mitsui, however, the family-held Mitsubishi Company was an upstart company, less than 70 years old when World War II began. Today, Americans associate the name Mitsubishi with automobiles and television sets, but Mitsui Bishi Goshi Kaisha was originally a steamship company. The first time the Japanese saw a modern ship was when Admiral Perry's fleet arrived in 1854. But under the leadership of Emperor Meiji, Japan rapidly became a maritime power. At first, ships were bought from other countries, then they were built in Japan by foreign contractors. By the 1920s, most of the ships were built in Japan, by the Japanese. Mitsubishi was the largest of all the Japanese shipbuilders. Its founder, Yataro Iwasaki, and his successor, Baron Yanosuké Iwasaki, became rich in the steamship business; first, by chartering vessels, then, ultimately, with vessels built by the company itself. In 1916, the Mitsubishi Company was divided into 10 separate divisions which included trade and banking, as well as mining and shipbuilding. The trading and shipping divisions were both involved in the drug trade (9).

Mitsubishi's relationship with the government is illustrative, and typically *zaibatsu*. Mitsubishi owned Japan's largest and most important steamship line, Nippon Yusen Kaisha (NYK). NYK received large Imperial subsidies, and used them to operate fast mail and passenger services around the world. During the 1920s, NYK's fleet consisted of more than 100 steamers with an aggregate capacity of over 480,000 tons. A sizable, though not controlling, number of NYK shares was held by the Imperial family. Members of the NYK Board of Directors served in the government, and government officers served on the NYK Board (2). A relationship such as this cannot be found in the United States. During the last few decades, Caspar Weinberger and George Schulz sat on the Bechtel Corporation Board of Directors, and also served in President Ronald Reagan's cabinet, but they did not hold both jobs at the same time. The Imperial family, and members of the court, however, did. As a result, the government always knew what NYK was doing because, in a very real sense, NYK and the government were one and the same.

What NYK was doing, besides delivering the mail, was delivering drugs. The relationship between NYK, the state, and the Imperial family was not at all unusual. Japan's government formed dozens of hybrid "special" companies, such as the South Manchuria Railway, and the Banks of Formosa and Korea, as well as the Yokohama Specie Bank. These companies were established by law, funded by the state, and, theoretically, were under government control. Actually, most of the money, and nearly all of the managers, came from the various *zaibatsu* families. The Imperial household usually held a financial stake. In addition to supplying start-up funds, there were tax exemptions, cheap loans, special subsidies, and guaranteed minimum dividends. Together, these incentives were sufficient to assure the success of any new venture, no matter how risky (7).

The Japanese government and industry joined hands to exploit newly conquered territories and turn substantial profits. The *zaibatsu* also had special relationships with the military. In newly occupied territories, the Japanese Army and Navy routinely turned over captured industrial and mining operations to Mitsui, Mitsubishi, or Sumitomo. Thus, Mitsubishi was "entrusted" with the Kian-Nan Shipyard and Engine Works in Shanghai, and the Shonan Shipyards and Engine Works in Singapore. Mitsui Trading, on the other hand, had an exclusive contract to sell fighter aircraft made by a smaller *zaibatsu* firm to the Japan Air Force (10). Such transactions would have been the equivalent of the U.S. Army turning over Germany's Bayer Chemical to an American company after Germany surrendered in World War II. Under Japanese law, such relationships and transactions were perfectly legal.

Japan entered the drug trade quite by chance when a unique set of circumstances made it easy to flout international law. International efforts at controlling the illicit drug trade first began in the early 1900s (11). Beginning in 1912, four separate international treaties on drug abuse had become law, and Japan had signed three of the four (The Hague International Opium Convention of 1912, The Geneva International Opium Convention of 1925, and the Convention for Limiting the Manufacture and Regulating the Distribution of Narcotic Drugs of 1931). The net effect of the three agreements was to restrict, and in some cases prohibit, the production, distribution, import, and export of commonly abused drugs.

The Convention of 1925 established a Permanent Central Board responsible for monitoring production and consumption in the participating countries. The actual monitoring process was carried out by the Opium Committee of the League of Nations. Members from each of the producing countries were appointed to the Committee which met once a year in Geneva. The Committee's policy formulations were based solely on data submitted to the Committee by participating countries. The Opium Committee did not have its own investigative branch. It only learned of violations when they were uncovered by the intelligence services of other committee members. Even when the Opium Committee had been advised of a violation, it had no effective means of enforcing any of its decisions. It could recommend that the League refuse to issue export permits for drug shipments to offending countries, but such a prospect hardly qualified as an effective deterrent.

The Opium Convention of 1912, which Japan signed on January 23 of that year, provided that parties to the agreement would enact laws controlling drug production, sales, and exports. In order to conform with the Convention, the United States Congress enacted the Harrison Narcotic Act of 1914. The Act not only restricted the non-medical use of narcotics, but it also introduced tight production controls and an elaborate tax stamp system. The law also prohibited physicians from prescribing narcotic drugs to treat addiction.

Japanese internal regulations were simpler. Japanese narcotic manufacturers were not licensed, although permission was required annually from the Welfare Minister if they intended to remain in the business of producing drugs. Manufacturers were required to report only the amount of narcotics they produced each year, and the amount of raw material used in the process. Manufacturers that produced narcotic medications which contained less than .2% narcotic had only to inform the Ministry about what they were producing. No record keeping or reporting was required. Drug wholesalers did not need to be licensed. The central government did not even keep a record of who the wholesalers were, let alone track their sales. Retailers operated under the same rules as wholesalers. The only difference was that wholesalers had more capital, could make larger purchases, and could get better prices. Doctors could buy and sell narcotics, and were required to register only once, when they first went into practice (12).

There was one other peculiarity about Japanese law that favored drug dealing. Laws that regulated Japanese possessions, such as Taiwan, applied only to opium. Heroin and cocaine production was not specifically mentioned. Production and sales of other narcotics came under the Home Office Ordinances, not the penal code. For all intents and purposes, regulations applicable to the production and sale of cocaine and heroin were no different than the regulations that applied to the production of sugar or tobacco (13).

Conviction for opium-related offenses might result in sentences of 10 years at hard labor, but cocaine and heroin dealers could not be sentenced to serve more than a 3-month term (14). In most cases, Japanese offenders were simply fined, and the fines were not very large. In essence, the market was entirely unregulated. Before placing too cynical an interpretation on Japan's laws or its intentions, it is important to remember that almost until the start of World War II, there were no Japanese drug abusers. Opium smoking was never native to Japan, and very strict laws prohibited drug taking of any kind (13). Japanese law makers can hardly be faulted for failing to address a situation that did not exist in their country.

By the 1920s, a handful of large pharmaceutical houses with close ties to the Japanese government were legally importing opium and coca by the ton, processing the raw material into cocaine, heroin, and smoking opium, and legally selling it to a network of drug wholesalers. The next level of transactions occurred on the world's black markets. More often than not, smugglers did not even bother to repackage drugs from the wholesalers. As a result, the brand names of the Japanese manufacturers, such as Hoshi, Dai Nippon, and Sankyo, were as well known in Calcutta as they were in Tokyo, even though legitimate cocaine exports to India were nil (15)(16). When black marketeers purchased cocaine from physicians, the quantities were smaller. Japanese pharmaceutical houses packaged cocaine in 1-, 5-, and 700-g containers. Drug smugglers would repackage the smaller containers purchased from physicians and then affix their own brand name, i.e., Fujitsuru (17). Although there really was no company named Fujitsuru, customs inspectors around the world were all too familiar with the Fujitsuru brand cocaine (18).

Shortly after the turn of the century, drug companies in Tokyo began refining cocaine from leaves grown in Java. However, cocaine refining did not become a major source of revenue until Japan occupied Taiwan. Even then, it took another 20 years before Japan became a major player in the illicit cocaine trade. When Japan took control of Taiwan in 1895, agriculture and forestry were the basic industries on the island. The Japanese occupation did little to change those industries (2).

By 1930, the effects of the Depression in the United States were being felt as far away as Japan and its possessions. Japanese farmers may have suffered the effects of the Depression even more than their counterparts in the United States. During the early 1930s, the average Japanese city dweller experienced a 35% decline in earnings. In the countryside, the earnings decline was closer to 60%. Peasant farmers were reduced to eating bark and selling their daughters to brothels. Starvation was a reality for many Japanese (19), in spite of a textile export boom fueled by devaluation of the yen from U.S. $.50 in November 1931 to U.S. $.21 (20). Overseas sales of sugar were particularly hard hit and slow to recover. Perhaps not coincidentally, Japan's entrance into the cocaine trade coincided with a steep decline in sugar exports.

Since sugar was almost impossible to sell, some Taiwanese growers decided to explore other possibilities. Coca production in Taiwan began in 1916. In 1916, when the medical community still used cocaine, and legitimate profits were to be made in refining and selling pharmaceutical grade cocaine. Taiwan's Governor General encouraged a plantation owner named Abe Konosuke, to try planting coca. A cocaine refinery was built, and coca seedlings were planted in different areas around the property. According to the British Consul in Taiwan, the cocaine refinery was a crude affair built a few yards away from the site of the original sugar refinery (22). Konosuke's efforts were not successful. Coca was not native to Taiwan, and had never been grown there before; the planters knew a great deal more about growing sugar than coca (23).

Konosuke lost his business in 1922, and was forced to sell out to the Ensuiko Sugar Company of Formosa. Ensuiko held the monopoly to grow sugar cane and manufacture sugar in the Kagi area, which included the village of Sinei, where Ensuiko's sugar refinery was located (21). During the early 1900s, Ensuiko was the fourth largest sugar producer on the island, processing nearly 10 tons of sugar each month. Ensuiko also owned large sugar cane plantations in Java, and regularly shipped large quantities of sugar cane back to Taiwan for refining (2). When the demand for sugar exports declined, Ensuiko's shares dropped precipitously.

Ensuiko's Chief Director, Tetsu Maki, needed a white knight to help them out of their predicament. A member of Ensuiko's Board of Directors, Norakata Takahashi, thought his father might be interested. Takahashi's father was not just any venture capitalist. He was Japan's Minister of Finance. Takahashi's father invested ¥100,000. A friend of Takahashi's, Matasakau Shiobara, invested an additional ¥150,000. After World War II, U.S. intelligence agents interviewed several sources who claimed Minister Takahashi was acting as a front man for Mitsui's trading division, Mitsui Gomei Kaisha (MGK), the same company that was supplying opium to the government monopoly (24)(25).

Regardless of the source of the money, the new investors changed the name of the company from Ensuiko to Taiwan Shoyaku. They brought in new technical experts, streamlined operations, planted coca, and reversed Ensuiko's downward slide. Takahashi, as Finance Minister for the country, was certainly in a position to steer military and government purchases towards his son's company, although no evidence for that practice was ever produced. By the fall of 1936, shares of Taiwan Shoyaku were trading at pre-depression levels. How much Taiwan Shoyaku's performance was bolstered by the Takahashi connection is difficult to say, but Matasakau Shiobara's connections probably contributed to the success of the restructured company as much as Takahashi's did.

Shiobara was the managing director of the Sankyo Company Limited of Tokyo. Sankyo was one of only five companies in Japan licensed to process coca and produce cocaine from leaf, regardless of where the leaf had been grown— Taiwan, Okinawa, Java, or imported from South America (12). Sankyo also happened to be the largest pharmaceutical company in Japan. Sankyo maintained a wholesale branch office in Formosa, with gross sales of more than ¥1 million per year (2)(26). Almost as a sideline, Sankyo, along with Dai Nippon Pharmaceutical and Hoshi Pharmaceutical, each supplied the Taiwan Monopoly Board with 1 to 2 tons of crude opium per year (14).

Shiobara started Sankyo in 1899 to import and sell a digestive aid invented by an expatriate pharmacist, Jokichi Takamine. Takamine was a skilled chemist who had worked for Parke, Davis supervising the introduction of large scale adrenaline production at the Parke, Davis factory in Michigan (27). Takamine would certainly have been familiar with the chemistry of cocaine extraction, and he would have taken that knowledge with him when he returned to Japan to become president of Sankyo.

According to the terms of a contract signed with Taiwan Shoyaku in 1928, the Sankyo factory in Tokyo was to be supplied with 22 kg of purified cocaine per month (28). Taiwan Shoyaku had other legitimate customers besides Sankyo, and its sales amounted to nearly 500 kg per month. Most of the semirefined cocaine went to drug companies in Japan, including Koto Pharmaceutical, Takeda Pharmaceutical Industries, Sankyo Company, The Shinonogi Pharmaceutical Company Limited of Osaka, and the Hoshi Pharmaceutical Company in Tokyo. During one 6-month period in 1928, shipments of purified cocaine to these companies alone amounted to nearly 1 ton (23).

The large Tokyo refiners were not, of course, totally reliant on supplies coming from Taiwan. They continued to import coca leaf from Indonesia and South America. They also began their own coca plantations on the islands of Iwo Jima and Okinawa (29). By 1929, the plantations in Japan and its colonies were producing sufficient quantities of leaf so that Japan was able to stop issuing import licenses, and thereby shut Dutch coca growers in Java out of the market. After 1929, the only coca leaf that could be imported from outside of Japan came from Taiwan, or from Japanese-owned coca plantations in Java.

Once the refined cocaine reached Tokyo, Japanese law made disposing of the cocaine an easy matter. In addition to wholesale exchanges with black marketeers, large quantities of cocaine and heroin, far beyond any conceivable medical needs, were sold to the Japanese armed forces. Onishi Takamatsu, an auditor with Sankyo until 1923, reported that when he was appointed director of Taiwan Shoyaku's Tokyo branch, he had arranged sales of semirefined cocaine to the Japanese Army and Navy. Sankyo, he said, acted as an intermediate. In 1938, Sankyo purchased 739 kg of cocaine from Taiwan Shoyaku for direct sale to the Army. From 1940 to 1942, smaller quantities were brokered through other companies for delivery to the Japanese Navy (23).

At one point, the colonial government of Taiwan took over partial control of Taiwan Shoyaku's factory and went so far as to supply special labels for the cocaine packages. During the early 1930s, packets of cocaine marked with the label "Taiwan Governor General, Central Laboratory" were regularly seized by customs agents in China and

India. The Indian government loudly complained about these irregu-
larities to the Opium Committee at the League of Nations, specifically
mentioning the "Taiwan Governor General Brand" by name (23). But
the complaints led nowhere, and for several years, "Taiwan General"
cocaine almost completely replaced the Tokyo produced "Fujitsuru" as
the most popular illegal brand of cocaine in India.

In 1918, Hoshi Pharmaceutical, with approval of both the Japanese
Home Ministry and the Ministry of Welfare and Social Affairs in Peru,
had purchased a 500-acre coca plantation in Peru. At almost the same
time, Hoshi began growing coca leaf in the Kagi district of Taiwan. The
initial plantation covered 242 acres (31). By 1944, Hoshi had 392 (some
documents put the number at 392, others as 292) acres under cultivation
in Taiwan (32). Coca grown in Taiwan had three important advantages
over the South American variety: (1) shipping costs were much less; (2)
it was easier to get import permits because the Tokyo Foreign Office did
everything in its power to convince Japanese manufacturers to buy
Japanese(33); and (3) Taiwan was a Japanese colony. But, perhaps the
most important reason for using Taiwanese coca was that more cocaine
could ultimately be extracted from it than from leaf grown in South
America (34-36).

The origin of the original seedlings grown in Taiwan and Okinawa
has never been established, but the strain of coca grown in Java contained at least a third, and sometimes 50%, more extractable cocaine
than the popular varieties grown in South America (36).

The high alkaloid content of Java leaf, combined with the fact that
four crops could be harvested every year, made Java leaf a very desirable product. Farbwerke's conversion process was tedious, but no great
secret. The Dutch Government financed a cocaine refinery in Amsterdam
using Farbwerke's technology (37), and the final draft of the 1925
Geneva Opium Convention specifically defined coca leaf as leaves from
any species "from which it may be found possible to extract cocaine
either directly or by chemical transformation (38)." Takamine would
certainly have been familiar with the process, and almost certainly
would have helped establish the cocaine production facility at Ensuiko.
Officials at Ensuiko's cocaine refinery admitted to the British consul
that the yield from their crops could be as high as 1% (1).

Japan was required, under international treaty, to file annual reports on cocaine and narcotic production with the League of Nations.
Officials at the League of Nations were apparently unaware of the
differences between Southeast Asian and South American coca, and
Japan was able to get away with understating its production figures
with impunity. Between Taiwan Shoyaku and Hoshi there were 684
acres under cultivation (31)(39)(40). The average yield for South American coca is generally approximated as .6 tons of leaf per acre per harvest

(41), with only three harvests per year. An area of 684 acres devoted to coca production in the Andes would be expected to yield 1231 tons of leaves per year (684 acres × .6 tons per acre x 3 crops per year = 1231 tons), which would give a total yield of refined cocaine that was approximately 6 tons (1231 × .5% = 6.15).

Yet, official Japanese statistics for 1927 show total Taiwanese coca leaf production at 204,640 kg (230 tons) (31). This production number is hardly believable given that coca grown in Taiwan was presumably the same strain as that grown in Java, and Javanese coca was harvested four times a year. Leaf production in Taiwan should have been 25% greater than for an equivalent area in the Andes, instead it was reported as two thirds less! And the coca leaf that was produced in Taiwan contained twice as much cocaine as leaf grown in the Andes. A general, and very rough, rule of thumb is that 400 pounds of South American leaf will yield 1 kg of cocaine. For Southeast Asian cocaine, the number would be closer to 200 pounds. Thus, 230 tons of coca leaf grown in Taiwan should have yielded at least 2.6 tons of cocaine, even if there were only three harvests per year. A realistic estimate for Taiwanese coca production, based on production experience from Java (36), would be 1500 tons of leaf per year from 684 acres; that amount of Southeast Asia leaf should have yielded nearly 7 tons of purified cocaine. Whatever the real figures were, they amounted to a great deal more than could ever be accounted for by legitimate medical use. The Health Committee of the League of Nations estimated that in countries possessing sophisticated medical care systems, the average annual cocaine requirement was 7 mg per person (42).

As testimony given at the Tokyo War Crimes Trials subsequently revealed, Japanese bureaucrats routinely "cooked the books", adjusting production figures for opium and heroin production to agree with the permissible values set by the League of Nations (43). In the case of cocaine, a somewhat different approach was used. The Japanese imported coca leaf and crude cocaine not just from Taiwan, but also from coca plantations on Iwo Jima, Okinawa, and Java. During the 1920s, imports from Java averaged more than a million pounds a year. The Ministry of Finance in Tokyo managed to hide all of these imports by lumping coca leaves together with other raw materials used to manufacture drugs. So when Japan's representative to the League of Nations Opium Committee stated that "The new policy of the Japanese Government would consist in reducing the output of cocaine," and that this reduction had been accomplished by "limiting the import of raw material," his claims were greeted with some skepticism. When asked by the Foreign Office for his opinion on Japan's statements, G.P. Patton, the British Consul in Taiwan, wrote "How the import of raw material is to be limited without keeping an exact record of these imports transcends one's comprehension, though possibly to the statisticians in Japan it may not be so difficult (1)."

In 1935, Hoshi sold off its plantation in Peru, relying entirely on its Taiwan plant for raw materials. In 1944, because of the U.S. Naval blockade, Hoshi was no longer able to get coca leaf from Taiwan to Tokyo, and had to cease production. Compared to today's clandestine cocaine manufacturers, Hoshi, at least, did its part for the environment, even if its motives were only for profit. During the 1930s, Hoshi sold the residue of its leaves, which contained large amounts of nitrogen, to farmers for fertilizer. That practice was discontinued after 10 years because the project was not profitable. The extracted leaf was then used as fuel (32).

As the years went on, and the start of World War II approached, Japan's presentations to the League of Nations became ever more fanciful. Member countries were required to file yearly reports, detailing each country's production and sales of narcotic drugs. In 1930, Japan reported that it manufactured 320 kg of cocaine in the preceding year, claiming that only 28 kg had been produced in Taiwan (31). Documents discovered after the war show Taiwan's cocaine refineries were producing more than that amount each day. Of course, the other members of the Opium Committee had a fairly good idea of what was going on in Taiwan. Criticism of Japan became even more intense until Japan's representative to the League, Yosuke Matsuoka, led Japan out of the League of Nations in 1933. Surprisingly, Japanese representatives continued to attend Opium Committee meetings for another six years, finally dropping all pretense of cooperation, and leaving the Committee, in 1939.

Finding legitimate buyers for excess Taiwanese cocaine was a problem. By the 1920s, the medical profession had pretty much abandoned the use of cocaine except for head and neck surgery, and the legitimate market for cocaine had almost disappeared. Pharmaceutical companies in Europe and the United States were not interested in purchasing cocaine from Japan. Even if they had been, it would not have solved Japan's problem. Legitimate purchasers who could get export certificates would not pay anywhere close to the amount of money that smugglers were willing to pay. In 1938, the legitimate wholesale price of cocaine was only about ¥1200 a kilogram ex factory. Bulk shipments fetched almost twice that much on the Chinese black market. At the time, 1 yen equaled roughly half a U.S. dollar.

Mitsui's trading division tried to help sell the surplus cocaine. They referred a representative of Taiwan Shoyaku to a Mitsui agent in Shanghai (24). Mitsui had a major presence in Shanghai and was already making a great deal of money supplying opium to the new Opium Monopoly. In July of 1939, Taiwan Shoyaku sent Chen Ching Po to

Shanghai with instructions to set up a branch office there. Chen Ching Po made tentative marketing arrangements with the manager of the Sino-Japanese Chung Wah Motion Picture Company, and promised to send samples of cocaine as soon as he arrived back in Taiwan. While recruiting the movie producer, Ching Po boasted that he had the backing of the Japanese authorities, and that he could arrange shipment of the cocaine to Shanghai via Japanese warships. The claim was almost certainly true (24). Evidence presented at the Tokyo War Crimes Trials revealed that not only did state-owned shipping companies carry opium and other drugs for the government, but at times the Japanese Navy also participated (44). Whether Ching Po was successful is not known, but somehow a willing buyer was found. When Allied Forces arrived in Taiwan, there was no cocaine left in the warehouse.

It would be a mistake to suppose that cocaine or heroin were important product lines for Mitsui. Compared to the enormous profits generated by its trading and mining divisions, Mitsui's dalliance in the cocaine trade was only a sideshow, best thought of as an exercise in venture capitalism, something like Intel Corporation buying a stake in a small company that uses computer chips. Even the much greater sums generated by opium sales in occupied China are dwarfed by the other Mitsui enterprises. And, compared to the current output of illegal growers in South America, estimated at a minimum of 500 tons per year (45), Taiwanese cocaine production can only be described as trivial.

A. <u>Baron Korekiyo Takahashi</u>: (1854-1936) Served as Japan's Minister of Finance during the worst years of the Depression, and did much to speed Japan's recovery. His son, Norakata Takahashi was on the board of Taiwan Shoyaku K.K. (Botanical Drug Company of Formosa, LTD), a large cocaine manufacturing company in Taiwan. While still Minister of Finance, Baron Takahashi invested ¥100,000 in the cocaine factory. After World War II, U.S. Intelligence agents interviewed several sources who claimed Minister Takahashi was acting as a front man for Mitsui's trading division, Mitsui Gomei Kaisha (MGK), the same company that was supplying opium to the government monopoly. The Baron was assassinated by right wing extremists in 1936. This photograph appeared in a 1919 yearbook on Japanese economic development (Feldwick W, Ed., Present Day Impressions of Japan. London: Globe Encyclopedia, 1919).

B. <u>Dr.Jokichi Takamine</u>: Takamine was recruited by Matasaku Shiobara, Managing Director of Sankyo Pharmaceutical, Japan's most important cocaine manufacturer, to be Chairman of its board. A trained analytic chemist, Takamine had arrived in the United States in 1890 and set up his own research laboratory. In 1901, Takamine and a British scientist named Thomas Aldrich, both working independently, managed to purify and isolate a hormone that Takamine called adrenaline. When Parke, Davis decided to mass produce adrenaline, they hired Takamine to supervise production. Since Parke, Davis was also the largest American cocaine manufacturer, Takamine would certainly have had ample opportunity to observe the process. That knowledge would have served him well when he took over at Sankyo. This photograph of Takamine appeared in a yearbook describing economic developments in Japan (Feldwick, W., Ed. Present Day Impressions of Japan. London: Globe Encyclopedia, 1919).

Date: July 14, 1938.

The following points have been agreed upon between Taiwan Shoyaku
K.K. (Botanical Drugs Co. in Formosa, Ltd.) (to be shortened
hereinafter 'Koh') and Koto Pharmaceutical Co., Ltd., Ch. Takeda
& Co., Ltd., Sankyo Pharmaceutical Co., Ltd., Shionogi Shoten,
Ltd. (shortened 'Otsu' for all the companies put together)

1. 'Koh' shall supply 'Otsu' with crude cocaine base as
   materials for medicine manufacture.
2. The amount for supply shall be seven hundred and fifty
   kilogrammes (750 kg.) and 1 per cent addition shall be
   made to cover the possible loss in weight.
3. Delivery shall be made in parts as per the annexed table.
4. Delivery shall be effected at each factory of 'Otsu'.
5. Price shall be fixed at ¥6.785 per 1 kilogramme of 1 per
   cent refined cocaine base.
6. Payment shall be made by 'Otsu' to Sankyo Pharmaceutical
   Co., Ltd., the agent of 'Koh', as temporary payment within
   ten days after receipt of the goods; and full settlement
   shall be made within thirty days following the last delivery.

In witness of the above agreement, five copies of this shall be
issued to be kept by each contracting party.

Signed by:

Korekata Takahashi
Director, President
Taiwan Shoyaku K.K.

Kenkichi Kamegawa
Executive Director
Koto Pharmaceutical Co., Ltd.

Yoshizo Takeda
Managing Director
Ch. Takeda & Co., Ltd.

Matasaku Shiobara
Managing Director
Sankyo Pharmaceutical Co., Ltd.

Gisaburo Shiono
Director
Shionogi Shoten, Ltd.

Particulars of Delivery

Month	Koto Phar. Co.	Ch. Takeda & Co.	Sankyo Phar. Co.	Shionogi	Sub-total
	kilo	kilo	kilo	kilo	kilo
July	79.333	45.787	32.413	12.467	170
August	79.334	45.787	32.413	12.467	170
September	56.000	32.320	22.880	8.800	120
October	56.000	32.320	22.880	8.800	120
November	56.000	32.320	22.880	8.800	120
December	23.333	13.466	9.534	3.667	50
Total	350.000	202.000	143.000	55.000	750

C. Contract to Sell Cocaine: Official production reports that Japan filed with the
League of Nations listed only small amounts of cocaine. Actually, very large quantities of cocaine were being produced in the Japanese colony of Taiwan. This contract was discovered by U.S. Army field investigators after World War II. It calls for
the delivery of 750 kg (roughly 1700 lb) over a 6-month period. A copy of the official
translation was found in the old records of the U.S. Bureau of Narcotics (the
predecessor of the DEA), National Archives, RG 170 - Records of the DEA, Acc #71-
A-3554, cartons #10-30.

D. The "Red Machines". American code-breakers began to read Japanese diplomatic transmissions several years before the war began, although often many days after the cables had been sent. Among other things, the content of these messages documents Japanese government involvement in drug trafficking. These intercepts can be read only at the National Archives (Record Group 456, National Security Agency / Central Security Service). They are entitled "Translations of Japanese Diplomatic Messages, 1934–1938 ('Red Machine')", boxes 1–4 1938. In 1938, the "Red Machine" was replaced when the code breakers managed to decipher the "Purple" code used by Japan throughout the war.

Contract for Underwriting the Subscription of
the Manchukuo Government's National Founding.

(original copy.)

Contract.

The Manchukuo Government (hereinafter referred to simply as A) conclude
the following contract, for the underwriting of the subscription of ¥ 30,000,00
of Japanese currency National Founding Bonds to be issued by the Manchukuo
Government, with the Industrial Bank of Japan (hereafter referred to simply
as B), which represents the Industrial Bank of Japan, Yokohama Specie Bank,
Ltd., the Bank of Chosen, Dai-Ichi Bank, Ltd., Mitsui Bank Ltd., Mitsubishi
Bank Ltd., Yasuda Bank Ltd., Kawasaki One Hundredth Bank Ltd., the Thirty-
fourth Bank Ltd., Sumitomo Bank Ltd., The Konoike Bank Ltd., the Yamaguchi
Bank Ltd., the Nagoya Bank Ltd., the Aichi Bank Ltd., the Mitsui Trust Co.
Ltd., the Mitsubishi Trust Co. Ltd., the Yasuda Trust Co. Ltd., and the
Sumitomo Trust Co. Ltd.

Article 1.

A shall issue in Japan, in accordance with the following essential points
the total value of ¥ 30,000,000 of the National Founding Bonds, based on the
regulations for the National Founding Bonds regulation promulgated on November
16, 1932; and B shall underwrite the subscriptions of their whole amount.

(1) Total amount of issue; ¥ 30,000,000 in Japanese currency.
(2) Kinds of bonds; in five denominations of ¥ 10,000.00, ¥ 5,000.00,
     ¥ 1,000.00, ¥ 500.00, and ¥ 100.00 in unregistered form with coupons
     attached.
(3) Interest rate; 6% per annum.
(4) Issue price; ¥ 96.50 against face value of ¥ 100.00.
(5) Method and period of redemption; The repayment of the principals shall
     be deferred until Nov. 10, 1935. Thereafter they shall be redeemed
     during the periods and in amounts mentioned below, and the redemption of
     the remainder shall be completed by Nov. 10, 1940.

Period of redemption.	Amount of redemption
From Jan. 11, 1935 to Jan. 10, 1936;	more than ¥ 2,000,000.00
From Jan. 11, 1936 to Jan. 10, 1937;	more than ¥ 4,000,000.00
From Jan. 11, 1937 to Jan. 10, 1938	more than ¥ 6,000,000.00
From Jan. 11, 1938 to Jan. 10, 1939;	more than ¥ 8,000,000.00
From Jan. 11, 1939 to Jan. 10, 1940;	all of the remainder.

The partial redemption of these bonds shall be made by drawings. The
bonds may be purchased at any time for the purpose of amortization.

(6) The method and periods of paying interests.
     The interests shall be calculated from the day following the issue to the
     day of redemption and shall be paid on June 1 and Dec. 1 of each year
     for the previous six months period in exchange for coupons.

E. Japanese War Bonds: Japan needed cash to occupy and administrate Manchukuo, the puppet state it had established in Manchuria. The bonds, which paid 5% per annum, were underwritten by all of the major Japanese banks. According to Article #4 of the offering, the bonds were to be "secured by the profits of the opium monopoly" with interest to be paid "preferentially from the monopoly profits". The bonds were issued on November 19, 1932. Profits from the monopoly were mainly from the sale of heroin, making these the first revenue bonds ever backed by narcotic sales. The illustration here is from the official translation introduced as evidence at the Tokyo War Crimes Trials (International Military Tribunal for the Far East, Exhibit #375, September 3, 1946).

In case the period is less than six months at the time of issue and redemption, a daily rate calculation shall be applied. However, the interest for the first period shall be paid at the rate of ¥ 1.9595 for every ¥ 100.00 face value.

No interest shall be paid for the period after the date of redemption.

(7) The place paying the principal and interest.
The head office and branch offices of the Industrial Bank of Japan, Ltd.
(8) The period of application for subscription.
From Dec. 1 to Dec. 3 of 1932. However, the time of application may be closed even during this period.
(9) Guarantee money for application for subscription.
¥ 5.00 for every ¥ 100.00 face value when the allotments are made, the amount shall be applied to subscription payment.
(10) The method of floating the bonds.
If the subscriptions exceed the amount floated, a suitable allotment shall be made.
(11) The time and method of making subscription payments.
The first time; ¥ 5.00 for every ¥ 100.00 face value.
(Guarantee money shall be applied to this payment on Dec. 20, 1932.)
The second time; ¥ 91.50 for every ¥ 100.00 face value shall be paid in on January 10, 1933.

Article 2.

B shall deliver to A the first payment on Dec. 26, 1932 and the second payment on January 16, 1933.

The time for paying the amounts which B is not able to collect by the dates mentioned in the preceding paragraph shall be agreed upon separately.

Article 3.

A shall deliver to B on January 16, 1933, ¥ 1.00 for every ¥ 100.00 face value as commission for the issuance of those loans.

Article 4.

These bonds shall be secured by the profits of the opium monopoly office and the Kirin-Heilung-Kiang Transport Toll Office. The principal and interest shall be paid preferentially from the monopoly profits.

Article 5.

The cost of printing the bonds shall be borne by A, while the costs of giving public notices and other expenses required in floating the bonds shall be borne by B.

Article 6.

In case A desires to redeem the principal of these bonds, the amounts, terms and other necessary items shall be published beforehand in more than two newspapers published each in Tokyo and Osaka.

In case A desires to purchase the bonds for amortization, it shall be unnecessary to publish such notice.

Article 7.

The payment of principal and interest of these bonds shall be made at the head office and branch offices of the Industrial Bank of Japan, Ltd. However, handling procedure and commissions shall be determined separately.

Article 8.

In regard to all business matters relating to these bonds, the Industrial Bank of Japan shall represent the aforesaid fourteen banks and four trust companies.

Article 9.

In regard to those bonds, the Regulations of the Manchukuo National Founding Bonds promulgated on November 16, 1932 and the Ordinance of Manchukuo State Affairs Board promulgated on Nov. 19, 1932 also shall be applied in addition to the preceding articles.

In witness of this contract, this document has been drawn up in duplicate in the Japanese language and duly signed by the representatives of A and B. The original copy is held by B and the duplicate copy by A.

Date: November 19, 1932.

The Representatives of the Manchukuo Government.
    Director of General Affairs of the Finance Department.
        Naoki HOSHINO (signed)
    The Vice-Governor of the Central Bank of Manchou
        Kyokoku YAMANARI (signed)

The Industrial Bank of Japan, Ltd.
The Yokohama Specie Bank, Ltd.
The Bank of Chosen
The Dai-Ichi Bank, Ltd.
The Mitsui Bank, Ltd.
The Mitsubishi Bank, Ltd.

The Yasuda Bank, Ltd.
The Kawasaki One Hundredth Bank, Ltd.
The Thirty-fourth Bank, Ltd
The Sumitomo Bank, Ltd.
The Konoike Bank, Ltd.
The Yamaguchi Bank, Ltd.
The Nagoya Bank, Ltd.
The Aichi Bank, Ltd.
The Mitsui Trust Co., Ltd.
The Mitsubishi Trust Co., Ltd.
The Yasuda Trust Co., Ltd.
The Sumitomo Trust Co., Ltd.

The representative of aforesaid banks and trust companies.

    Industrial Bank of Japan, Ltd.
    Governor Toyotaro YUKI (signed)

F. <u>Label from Hoshi Pharmaceutical's Cocaine, circa 1935</u>: Japanese pharmaceutical houses packaged cocaine in 1-, 5-, and 700-g containers. Even when cocaine was widely used as an anesthetic, a 700 gram container would have supplied several hospitals for several years. Such large packages were clearly intended for the black market. Smugglers legally acquired the cocaine from wholesalers and sold it on the black market with the original labels intact. As a result, the names of Sankyo and Hoshi were as well known in India as Japan, even though legitimate cocaine exports to India were nil. When smugglers could only obtain the smaller 1- and 5-g containers, they would repackage them and then affix their own fictitious brand name, usually, Fujitsuru. Even though there really was no company named Fujitsuru, customs inspectors around the world were all too familiar with the Fujitsuru brand cocaine. (From the National Archives, RG 170 - Records of the DEA, Acc #71-A-3554, cartons #10-30.)

Chapter 11

GOVERNMENT-SPONSORED DRUG DEALING

I received instructions through military channels to provide opium for the Chinese people by establishing an opium suppression board.

Harada Kumakichi, Japanese Military Attaché at Shanghai from 1937 to 1939 (1)

Japan took possession of Taiwan in 1895, and occupied Korea 10 years later, during a period when Japan was still governed by civilians. By 1936, however, Japan was effectively being governed by its Army. An Imperial Ordinance, signed by the Emperor in 1936, provided that neither the Minister of War nor the Minister of the Navy could be civilians. Both had to be active duty officers, holding at least the rank of Lieutenant General or Vice-Admiral (1). The same ordinance also provided that, no matter which party formed a Cabinet, membership in the Cabinet was subject to approval by the Ministers of War and Navy. What that meant, of course, was that no Cabinet could hope to survive unless the Army and Navy agreed with its policies. Strictly speaking, Japan was governed by a civilian government. In reality, Japan was a military dictatorship.

The goal of this military dictatorship was territorial expansion. A sizable proportion of the military, and large segments of the civilian population, believed Japan had a divine mission to rule the world. One of the most radical proponents of this belief was Shumei Okawa. In a book written in 1924 *(Kiyokawa Hachiro / Okawa Shumei cho)*, Okawa argued that because Japan was the first state to be created (a popular belief in Japan at the time), it was Japan's divine mission to rule all the nations of the world (1). Okawa did everything within his power to foster this outlook, including helping to assassinate politicians who were less than convinced of Japan's manifest destiny (3). Okawa had many followers in the Army, and they took his injunctions to heart.

In August 1931, Japanese troops blew up a portion of the Southern Manchurian Railway (which they owned). They blamed Chinese troops for the explosion, and used the unrest as a pretext for occupying the northeastern provinces of China. In 1932, Japan attacked Shanghai. In 1934, Japan installed Henry Pu Yi (the "last emperor") as the leader of a new puppet regime in Manchuria. Japan renamed the region Manchukuo. On July 7, 1937, the Kwangtung army invaded China south of the Great Wall. The Cabinet, back in Tokyo, which had not even been consulted, voted to express its support for the incursion. Two months later, Japan bombed Canton and Nanking, and concentrated on civilian targets. Japanese troops entered Nanking in mid-December, slaughtered thousands of innocent civilians, and committed a series of atrocities. Japan was later tried for these criminal acts at the Tokyo War Crimes Tribunal (1).

Occupying China was not like occupying Taiwan or Korea. Japanese advances were stiffly opposed by a variegated Chinese resistance movement. When they were not fighting with each other, both the Guomandang (the GMP), led by Chiang Kai Shek, and the communists (the CCP), led eventually by Mao Zedong, fought a protracted guerrilla war against the Japanese. Japan found itself busy on the one hand fighting a guerrilla war, and on the other trying to administer newly acquired territory. The process was very expensive. The evidence is overwhelming that Japan sold drugs to help pay for the war with China. Japanese drug dealers sold whatever drugs they could get their hands on, but mostly they sold heroin and opium. No doubt they would have sold cocaine as well, but the available amount of raw material was limited, and as the war progressed, getting it from Taiwan to Tokyo to China proved increasingly problematic.

The kinds of drugs sold, however, are much less relevant than what the Japanese government did to promote and nurture the drug business. Led by the military, all of the branches of the Japanese government, along with Japan's largest business concerns, actively participated in the sale of drugs. And they did so long before war was ever declared with the Allies or the United States, and in spite of their repeated protestations that Japan deplored drug use. What the Japanese drug dealers did 50 years ago is almost exactly what South American drug dealers are doing today; supplying whatever drug is in demand. Where once there were separate suppliers and distribution channels for cocaine and heroin, today's drug dealers offer both drugs through the same dealers. The idea of "one stop" drug shopping is neither new nor novel.

At the 29th Meeting of the League of Nation's Opium Committee held in Geneva in May of 1939, China formally accused Japan of "promoting the abuse of drugs in China (4)." Hoo Chi-tsai had been sent by

Chang Kai Shek to address the committee. Hoo Chi-tsai listed the ways Japan promoted drug sales. He also accused Japan of failing to implement any significant laws to curtail drug abuse, of selectively enforcing the few laws that were on the books, and of never prosecuting Japanese drug dealers. Further, Chi-tsai accused Japan of encouraging opium cultivation in areas where it had been previously suppressed, permitting the illegal importation and manufacture of drugs, and demanding that kickbacks be paid to the government and Army. According to Hoo Chi-tsai, Japan used its Consulates in China as drug distribution centers. He also claimed that Army trucks and Navy warships were used to transport narcotics disguised as war materials. These allegations were supported by the United States Representative, Stuart Fuller. Fuller read into the record detailed reports from the U.S. Military Intelligence. The reports supported almost all of the charges made by the Chinese (4).

Many of the accusations first made by China were later repeated at the Tokyo War Crimes Trials. Section 4, Appendix A, of the Indictment stated that:

> *successive Japanese governments, through their military and naval commanders and civilian agents in China and other territories which they had occupied or designed to occupy, pursued a systematic policy of weakening the native inhabitants...by directly and indirectly encouraging increased production and importation of opium and other narcotics and by promoting the sale and consumption of such drugs among such people...profits from the government-sponsored traffic in opium and other narcotics and other trading areas...were used by agents of the Japanese government...At the same time, the Japanese government was actively participating in the proceedings of the League of Nations Committee on Traffic in Opium and Other Dangerous Drugs and, despite her secret activities above-mentioned, professed to the world to be cooperating fully with other member Nations in the enforcement of treaties governing traffic in opium and other narcotics to which she was party (5).*

Newly declassified material, including Japanese Foreign Office cable intercepts which finally became available in 1992, and documents from the old Bureau of Narcotics (now the Drug Enforcement Agency, DEA) which first came to light in 1995, are even more damning than prosecutors at the tribunal had ever imagined. Specifics of the Japanese drug trade, and the charges leveled by the Chinese are worth recounting in some detail. Modern drug traffickers have copied many of the schemes first introduced by Japan and, given the opportunity, are likely to adopt others in the near future. A recounting of the legal, administrative, and diplomatic framework of Japanese drug trafficking is also worthwhile, if only as a cautionary tale.

Japan was signatory to every major international treaty on drug prohibition. Representatives from Japan continued to attend meetings of the Opium Committee at the League of Nations long after Japan had quit the League itself. Bureaucrats in Japan filed every report and completed every drug control form required by international law. However, it turned out that most of the information on drug production supplied by Japan was fabricated. Japan told the League whatever it wanted to hear, and then went about the business of selling drugs.

Medicinal opium products had been produced in Japan long before the first Westerner ever arrived, but the Japanese themselves had no direct experience with opium smokers. Opium smoking was unheard of under the old Tokugawa feudal system, and after diplomatic relations were established with the West, Japanese leaders took great pains to ensure that opium smoking never gained a foothold. In 1858, 10 years before the Meiji Restoration and the end of feudal law, Japan signed treaties with the United States (Treaty of Amity and Commerce), and England (*Regulations under which British trade is to be conducted in Japan*) which specifically prohibited opium importation, and imposed strict punishment on offenders (6).

After the Restoration, controls on drug use were tightened even further. In April 1868, Japan passed a new law which carried heavy penalties for opium users and sellers. In 1870, other laws controlling the medical use of opium were also passed, and even stricter sanctions were added to the Criminal Code in 1882 (6). There simply were no Japanese opium smokers, at least none living in Japan. Not only was opium smoking unheard of, the use of heroin and other narcotics was unthinkable, which, perhaps, explains a very peculiar anomaly in Japanese law: the criminal code only dealt with opium smoking. The sale and use of drugs such as heroin and cocaine was regulated, if at all, by civil law. Criminal penalties were rarely involved (7).

When Japan took control of Taiwan, Japanese administrators inherited a large population of native opium smokers. Japan's Governor General of Formosa, Count Kodama, initiated a model plan designed to gradually eliminate the practice of opium smoking from the newly acquired territory. The first step was the establishment of an Opium Monopoly. The Monopoly Bureau purchased raw opium, usually through the trading branch of Mitsui (MKB), refined it, and packaged it in 5- and 15-g tubes. These tubes were sold to wholesalers, who in turn sold them to licensed retailers. Markups at every level were controlled by the government. Opium addicts were required to register with the government and to be examined by a doctor who determined their daily ration of opium. To purchase opium, addicts were required to produce a license and coupon book listing the amount of their daily ration. Purchases were for cash only. Most of the addicts received a ration of 3.75 g per day (7).

During the first year of the program, 160,064 addicts, slightly more than 6% of Taiwan's total population, were licensed. The original plan was to issue no new licenses. New opium smokers would be discouraged, and when the last of the licensed smokers died, the problem would be gone. The plan, however, ran into problems. The number of real opium smokers, as opposed to the number of admitted opium smokers, was well in excess of initial estimates, so new smokers were constantly being added to the system. Another problem with the plan was cash flow. In the early 1900s, Tokyo began cutting subsidies to Taiwan, and opium revenues came to constitute an important part of the Governor's budget. The net profit of the Opium Monopoly Bureau in 1906 was ¥3,371,759 (at the time, the yen and U.S. dollar were of nearly equal value) (8). While not sufficient to balance Taiwan's budget, the sum was not insignificant either. By 1926, the number of officially registered addicts had dropped to under 35,000, but the British Consul in Taiwan claimed that that number represented "only a small fraction" of the actual number (9). As far as the British counsel in Taiwan was concerned, "the revenue derived from these drugs is the first consideration...the financial factor outweighs by far any moral influences that may be at work (2)."

Administrators in Tokyo were quick to appreciate the potential profits of selling opium to addicts. State run "Hygienic Laboratories" were opened in Tokyo and Osaka, and the Opium Monopoly was no longer allowed to buy directly from importers. To buy opium for its addicts, the Opium Monopoly now had to deal with the state-owned Hygienic Laboratories. Testimony given after World War II indicates that revenues of the Opium Monopoly were far greater than ever indicated by the official record, and that not all of the revenues went to either the Monopoly or the central government.

Processed opium sold to smokers was supposed to contain 6% morphine, but according to the production manager of Japan's largest opium processor, addicts were more likely to get opium which contained only 4% morphine. In 1945, at the end of World War II, William Bransky, a Bureau of Narcotics investigator assigned to General Douglas MacArthur's staff, interviewed a chemist, Shiro Sagawa. Sagawa was the chemist who had directed narcotic production at Hoshi Pharmaceutical's Tokyo plant for the previous 20 years. Hoshi had had a long and stormy relationship with Taiwan's Opium Monopoly. During the 1920s, Hoshi held the contract to refine raw opium imported by the Monopoly.

According to Sagawa, Hoshi had been shortchanging the Monopoly. Hoshi facilities produced refined opium with a very low morphine content, returned poor quality opium to the Monopoly, and sold the rest of the morphine, which had been removed during the refining process, in China. There very likely was some substance to Sagawa's charges, since, in 1926, Hoshi officials were tried for illegally "owning, possessing, and selling raw opium." They were eventually acquitted (9)(10). Whatever their alleged infractions, by the 1930s, Hoshi was apparently forgiven, and was doing business again with the Monopoly.

Sagawa claimed that at a 1936 meeting between the representatives of Formosa Opium Monopoly Bureau, the Home Ministry, and officials from Hoshi, Hoshi was authorized to buy and process additional opium from Formosa. The residue, to contain no less than 4% morphine, was to be shipped back to Formosa, made into smoking opium, and sold by the Formosan Monopoly Bureau to addicts in Formosa. The Home Minister in Tokyo, Eiichi Baba, specifically instructed Hoshi officials that "Extreme secrecy is to be maintained concerning these productions and storages (11)." Baba's concerns for secrecy are not hard to understand. International Treaties required Japan to report their total opium production to the League's Opium Committee, but Hoshi's output was never reported.

Sagawa also claimed that the morphine content of raw opium shipped to Hoshi by the Hygienic Laboratories was consistently greater than 12%. If the Formosa opium was even close to that quality, and presumably it was, then the Monopoly in Formosa was generating enormous quantities of surplus morphine. Out of every 100 kg of raw opium purchased and refined by the Monopoly, 4 kg of morphine would have been sold to registered opium smokers, but more than twice as much, 8.2 kg of morphine, would have been retained by the Monopoly. There was no great secret about what the Monopoly was doing.

In 1928, a report written by the second secretary at the British Embassy in Tokyo drew attention to the discrepancies between official import statistics, declared Monopoly sales, and the number of addicts on the island (12). According to import figures for 1925, the average Taiwanese opium smoker was consuming 4.5 pounds of opium a year, a very substantial quantity. In reality, the morphine content of Monopoly opium was so low that there was a thriving trade in high grade opium smuggled into Taiwan (13). Presumably, the morphine that did not end up in the addicts' opium pipes went directly to the world's black markets.

Whether or not the Opium Monopoly in Taiwan ever really worked will never be known. The decreased number of registered addicts certainly made for good public relations, but the numbers were subject to manipulation. Foreign diplomats on the scene expressed great skepticism (2). In any event, the financial, if not the therapeutic, success of the Opium Monopoly in Taiwan led Japan to introduce much the same system into the Kwangtung Leased Territory (Northern China), Korea, and Manchukuo, the puppet state in Manchuria. The situation in Manchukuo differed from that in Taiwan in two important respects; Manchukuo was a major opium-producing region in its own right, and it had hundreds of thousands of addicts long before the Japanese arrived. In terms of reducing drug demand, the Monopoly system in Manchuko could hardly be called a success. By the late 1930s, there were millions of newly addicted Chinese, though the actual number was probably far less than the 13 million addicts alleged by Western experts (14). Prosecutors at the Tokyo War Crimes Trials argued that the monopoly system was never intended as a way to treat addiction.

In fact, Japan's military used the Manchukuo Monopoly as a source of funding to support its occupation forces. At the same time, Japan's central government used the fiction of an independent Manchuko as a smoke screen for its international drug transactions. Using official trade relations with Manchuko as an excuse, Japan proceeded to manufacture prodigious amounts of heroin and opium under the guise of supplying the Manchuko Monopoly. The Monopoly, in turn, created whatever figures were needed to account for the production figures reported to the League of Nations by the Japanese central government. The League of Nations recognized the deception for the fraud that it was. Ultimately, however, so many people in Manchuko became addicted to opium, and then heroin, that the government in Tokyo had all it could do to keep Manchuko supplied.

The Manchuko Monopoly operated on a grand scale. Nearly 1000 government employees, about half of them Japanese, were employed in the project. They operated 10 district branch offices, 80 dispensaries, and contracted with 30 agents to buy raw opium. In spite of protestations to the contrary, opium cultivation in Manchuria was promoted by the Japanese government. A report filed by the secretary of the Belgian legation in Mongolia described Japan's approach. Opium growing was never made mandatory, but financial realities left the farmers little choice. The Monopoly offered high fixed prices for opium as well as cash advances and tax subsidies (15). By 1934, more than 720,000 hectares of opium were under cultivation. The raw opium was shipped back to Monopoly offices in Mukden. By 1935, U.S. Treasury Department officials stationed in Shanghai had identified nine different Japanese owned and operated narcotic refineries in Mukden. These refineries were under the protection of the Japanese Army and police. Most of their product was sold to opium dens which were licensed by the Monopoly (16).

The Opium Monopoly administrators were increasingly hard-pressed to keep up with the demand for heroin, and had to look outside their own boundaries for supplies. In addition to the heroin that was secretly imported from Tokyo, output in Korea was also increased. In fact, it appears that the main function of the Korean Monopoly Bureau was to supply Manchuko with heroin. It did supply local Korean addicts with opium, but there were far too few of those to justify an operation the size of the Korean Monopoly Bureau. By the mid-1930s, the Bureau was producing more than 50 tons of opium a year, converting most of it to heroin, and shipping it by train, under police escort, to Manchuko (17). None of the heroin produced in Korea, and none of the exports sent to Manchuko, were ever reported to the League of Nations (18), even though Japan had agreed to do just that in the treaties it had signed.

Even with the illicit imports, the Manchuko Monopoly could not keep up with the rising demands. In 1935, the Monopoly decided to build its own narcotic refinery. The exact date of construction is not clear. Photographs of the refinery were taken after World War II. Unfortunately, much of the refinery had been bombed by the Chinese in the winter of 1944. The photographs suggest that construction occurred in stages, probably beginning in 1937 or 1938. What is clear, however, is that the Manchuko Monopoly constructed the largest narcotics refinery the world had ever seen, before or since.

Rumors of a giant heroin refinery circulated for years, but when a medical relief worker visited the site in Mukden in 1948, he was so astonished by what he saw that he took new photographs of the refinery and sent them to Harry Anslinger, then U.S. Commissioner of Narcotics. Anslinger did not quite know what to make of the photographs and what they showed, but knew someone who did know: A. H. Homeyer, the production manager at Malincrodt Chemical Works in St. Louis, Missouri.

Malincrodt Chemical was one of the few licensed narcotics producers in the United States. The Malincrodt facility, however, was dwarfed by the size of the factory in Mukden (19). Homeyer, who was never able to visit the plant, had trouble interpreting the Mukden photographs because "the plant is so much larger the one with which I am familiar." The plant included an administration building, garage, transformer shed, steam generating power plant, and at least six other buildings used for the storage of raw materials, containers, and packaging. Homeyer thought the best indication of the plant's capacity was the equipment located in one of the three manufacturing buildings.

This building alone contained two 4 x 9 foot stills, and eleven 100-gallon capacity jacketed (heated) kettles, pressure tanks, and pressure kettles. Homeyer concluded that "working 24 hours per day, its capacity might be 400,000 kilos of opium per year. This might yield 50,000 kilo of morphine alkaloid." Once the opium was converted to heroin, the yield would have been close to 50,000 kg or 56.3 tons of heroin per year.

At the end of the war, U.S. Army staff investigators obtained sworn deposition from Monopoly Bureau employees and chemists who actually worked at the factory. They gave conflicting estimates of the plant's total output. One employee, Syachi Baba, put legitimate production at 32 tons per year, but Baba later went on to add that illicit production was many times greater than recorded in the official figures (20). A somewhat lower estimate was offered by the head of the Takeda Pharmaceuticals manufacturing facility in Mukden. Unlike the Monopoly plants, Takeda was actually manufacturing drugs for pharmaceutical use, converting semirefined opium it had purchased from the Monopoly Bureau into medicinal codeine and morphine. The Takeda executive thought that the Monopoly plant was processing more than half a ton of raw opium per day, equivalent to an output of 140 tons of refined opium per year, or roughly 16 tons of heroin. Homeyer's estimates, based on the known capacity of the equipment in the plant, were somewhat higher than those of the eyewitnesses, but none of the witnesses were actually in charge of production, and none had any documentation to support their claims. Syachi Baba also insisted that similar factories, though not quite as large, were located in Jakarta, Singapore, Bangkok, Saigon, Canton, Hong Kong, and Shanghai. Baba's assertion, however, was never verified.

Whatever the actual output of the plant was, once it reached full operating capacity, there were surpluses. The best way to put these heroin statistics in perspective is to compare the estimated output from Mukden with the U.S. Drug Enforcement Agency (DEA) estimates for heroin production in 1995 (the most recent year for which complete national and international statistics are available). In that year, just over 1 ton of heroin was seized in the United States, and 23 tons seized internationally (21). Today, total maximum heroin production, worldwide, is thought to be between 175 and 212 tons (22).

Even the huge number of addicts in Manchuria could not consume all the heroin that the Japanese produced, so local production began to spill over onto the world market. An intercepted cable from Mitsui's Shanghai office to its Berlin office described negotiations to deliver 10 tons of refined opium (enough to make a ton of heroin) to a German wholesaler (23). Mitsui officials were upset because the Germans were refusing to pay previously agreed to prices established in a treaty between Manchuko and the German government.

Before Japan signed the Geneva International Opium Convention of 1925 (October 10, 1928), the central authority for Japanese drug policy-making resided with the Medical Section of the Public Health Bureau in the Ministry of Welfare. In order to conform with the requirements of the new drug convention, Imperial Ordinance No. 38 was issued on April 1, 1931 (24). The ordinance created an Advisory Opium Committee, which was chaired by the Minister of Welfare. The Committee itself was composed of ministers and department heads from the Foreign Affairs, Interior, Justice, Finance, and Colonial Ministries. Other members of the Committee included representatives of the various opium monopolies in Korea, Formosa, and occupied China. At one point, the Committee was chaired for several months by Marquis Koichi Kido. Kido later become Lord Keeper of the Privy Seal, a sort of liaison between the emperor and his ministers. Kido was, in fact, a close advisor to the emperor. In 1946 he was tried and convicted as a war criminal (25).

The military was not officially represented on the Advisory Opium Committee, but ultimately, all of the Committee's decisions were filtered through, and implemented by, the Japanese Army-controlled China Development Board. The Board was better known as the Ko-A-In Bureau. At the Tokyo trials, Oikawa Genshichi, the Director of Political Affairs for the Ko-A-In branch in Shanghai, explained how his organization worked. The Ko-A-In was established in December of 1938. Its head office was in Tokyo, with major branches located in Shanghai, Peking, Amoy, and Kalgan, with two smaller branches in Canton and Tsingtao. The Tokyo office had four divisions: political, economic, cultural, and technical. Branch offices were structured similar to the Tokyo office, except they had no technical component. The president of the Ko-A-In Bureau was the Prime Minister, and he was assisted by four vice-presidents: the Minister of the Army, Navy, Finance, and Foreign Affairs.

Decisions made at the Tokyo office were passed through the local branch offices in China. These decisions were coordinated with the local Japanese military authorities. The Army's Special Services Organ was specifically tasked with Ko-A-In liaison, a reasonable decision given that Special Services agents had already established a thriving trade in opium before Ko-A-In ever arrived on the scene. The stated purpose of the Ko-A-In was to improve conditions in occupied China. But its main tasks were really to make money and supply Tokyo with the resources necessary to wage war. One of the tasks of the Ko-A-In's Economic division was to study "the needs of opium in different parts of China and arrange for distribution of the opium from Mongolia to North China, Central China and South China (26)."

Shortly after Japan occupied Shanghai, the Ko-A-In established a General Opium Suppression Bureau, but its purpose was the promulgation of drug use, not suppression. A Japanese military attaché who served at Shanghai testified that "...I received instructions through military channels to provide opium for the Chinese people by establishing an opium suppression board (1)." Hajime Satomi, who worked as an opium trader for the Special Services office in Shanghai, confirmed Oikawa's account of the real administrative structure, and explained that as Ko-A-In became more firmly established, opium sales came under the direct control of the Bureau, with profits going directly back to Bureau offices in Tokyo. Satomi was subpoenaed by the prosecution at the Tokyo Trials. His testimony gives some indication as to just how much opium the Ko-A-In was able to sell:

> Q: *How much Mongolian opium did you sell?*
> A: *Although it would be a very rough figure, the amount that was in my charge during my six years there was around ten million liang (27).*

A liang is a subdivision of another Chinese unit of measure known as a "catty". A catty is roughly equal to 1.1 pounds. Ten million liang would translated into 343 tons of opium, enough to produce as much as 34 tons of heroin. Hajime Satomi was selling the equivalent of 5 tons of heroin a year, and he was only in charge of drug transactions in the Ko-A-In Shanghai office!

The Convention for Limiting the Manufacture and Regulating the Distribution of Narcotic Drugs of 1931, required participating countries to submit annual reports on imports and exports of all drugs covered by the convention. It also required statistics on opium and coca production, stocks of drug on hand, the number of opium smokers, and the drugs confiscated. These reports were prepared by the Medical Affairs section of the Ministry of Welfare, but were ultimately the responsibility of the Advisory Opium Committee.

In a deposition taken on September 15, 1946, Yoshisuke Yasumi, a technical expert in the Drug Affairs Section of the Welfare Ministry, described how figures for the League of Nations report were prepared. In 1936, Yasumi, along with Ajii Ako, Director of the Medical Affairs Department, and another technician were assigned the task of tabulating heroin production figures for the preceding year. According to Yasumi, "we were told that...(heroin production) should not be reported as it was...and that we ought to show we were trying to reduce the production and ought to make up some proper figures." Unsure as to just what constituted a "proper" figure, Yasumi sought clarification from Ako, his immediate supervisor. Ako suggested that, since "morphine (production) was not restricted, and since the methods of reporting of morphine was so indefinite," the best thing to do would be for Yasumi to bury the heroin production within the figures for crude morphine production. The goal was to get production figures down to a low enough point to match projected figures for medical use within Japan (28).

The precedent for such creative bookkeeping had been set much earlier. In 1932, when the Manchuria Monopoly was unable to meet the increasing demand for heroin, the Advisory Opium Committee issued special licenses to three pharmaceutical companies, Dai Nippon, Sankyo, and Hoshi Pharmaceuticals. The companies were to manufacture heroin from some of the crude morphine that had been accumulated by the Formosa Monopoly. They were then to ship the refined heroin to the Manchurian Monopoly. Several tons of heroin were produced and sent to Manchuria, but these sales were never reported to the League of Nations. According to Yasumi, "these figures are not included in our production list because it was not a supply to our country and also because the raw material was supplied by the Manchurian government (28)." Yasumi's explanation was technically correct because Japan considered occupied Manchuria as a separate, independent state. The problem was that no one, least of all the League of Nations, believed Japan.

Other than the Axis powers, the only other entities willing to recognize Manchuko as an independent country were Japan's banks. Late in 1932, the Industrial Bank of Japan, acting as the lead bank for a consortium of other banks, concluded negotiations with the Manchuko government, to underwrite "National Founding" bonds. The total issue was ¥30 million, to be repaid at a rate of 5% per annum. Article 4 of the agreement stated that, "These bonds shall be secured by the profits of the Opium Monopoly Office...the principal and interest shall be paid preferentially from the Monopoly profits." These were the first, and presumably only, bonds guaranteed by narcotic sales. Other banks participating in the underwriting scheme included Mitsui Bank Ltd., Mitsubishi Bank, Ltd., Yasuda Bank, Ltd., and Sumitomo Trust Company, Ltd. (29).

The Japanese Ministry of Welfare was not the only government office involved in the drug business. The Foreign Office played a prominent role. It is not clear if Japan's consular offices were used as drug warehouses, as the Chinese claimed, but there is ample evidence that the diplomatic corps certainly helped to arrange drug deals. If the consular officials were ever physically involved, no evidence remains today. The translation below is from a Foreign Office Cable #2824 sent on September 8, 1938, from Shanghai to Tokyo. It concerns the transfer of surplus Taiwanese opium to Shanghai, where it was to be sold to Chinese opium tongs.

...About the middle of August the staff of the Formosan Army asked the Special Affairs Section in this city to take charge of the matter. The latter, however, think that they should not willingly accept responsibility for such a drug which is likely to cause international trouble. However, since it is an article that will become important when the opium control as of my #2733* will be put into practice, they have replied that they will comply with the request provided that (A) those in Formosa would be responsible for the shipment to this city, and (B) the payment to be made in installments convenient to the Central China authorities. We gave our agreement to this, believing it to be the desires of those in China. In carrying out the proposal, I think it necessary to think carefully how the shipment is to be made (I suppose there is no other way to handle it as we would war materials), how much of it is to be shipped, and how the Central China authorities are to secretly supervise the transaction. If the proposal meets with the approval of the authorities in Tokyo, please give definite instructions to officials in China so that there may be nothing happening later that will prove regrettable (30).

Since their representatives sat on the Advisory Opium Committee, the Foreign Office must have known about heroin and opium shipments to Manchuko. But when the League of Nations delegates began to complain about obvious narcotics abuses in Manchuko, Tokyo told its ambassador in Geneva to deny all accusations. In an intercepted cable dated October 20, 1938, the Japanese Foreign Minister wrote to the Ambassador in Geneva,

Tell the Central Commission that as before it is untrue that this opium was imported into Japanese Territory. You had better stop at that, but if they press you there is no objection to your saying that Manchuko imported just that amount of opium this year (31).

In 1937, the Foreign Office tried to sort out a trade dispute between Japan's two largest opium importers: Mitsui and Mitsubishi (8)(17). An argument arose between Mitsui and Mitsubishi over who would get exclusive rights to purchase raw opium from the Iranian State Monopoly. The Japanese charge d'affaires in Teheran, at the behest of the Foreign Office in Tokyo, stepped in and tried to mediate. For years, Mitsui and Mitsubishi made large profits by supplying Japan's Hygienic Laboratories with raw opium from India and Iran. The market for Iranian opium, which had originally been developed by Mitsubishi's trading branch, was hotly contested by Mitsui.

Iran wanted to barter opium for finished Japanese cotton. Would-be opium purchasers had to deal with the Iranian Cotton Cloth Import Monopoly Company, another name for the Iranian government. In November, 1935, Mitsubishi negotiated a contract with Iran for the delivery of 1000 cases of opium in early 1937. When it came time to renew the contract, Mitsui, which had recently opened a Teheran branch of its own, approached the Cotton Monopoly and made a better offer. The offer was rebuffed, at least initially, but soon an intense bidding war was underway. Because monopolies owned by the Japanese government ultimately had to pay for the imported opium, and since it was unlikely that either Mitsui or Mitsubishi would absorb the added costs that would result if the two companies tried to outbid each other, the Japanese Foreign Office entered the fray. According to one report, "It seemed to be a matter of vital importance to make the head offices of Mitsui and Mitsubishi conclude a concrete agreement." The Foreign Office wanted the two trading companies to present a united front. The idea was to create a third company, owned by Mitsubishi and Mitsui, which would deal with the Iranians, and offer them the lowest possible price. Once the opium had been purchased by this shell company, it would be divided up by Mitsui and Mitsubishi, who would then deliver it to the various state-owned monopolies.

Selling the plan to Mitsui and Mitsubishi proved a difficult undertaking. At first, Foreign Office officials were rebuffed by both sides. The diplomats went so far as to approach officials on the Army General Staff, and the Ministries of Finance, Commerce and Industry, and asked them to place pressure on Mitsui and Mitsubishi. Both companies ignored the pressure and continued to negotiate their own separate deals. The Foreign Ministry, however, eventually prevailed. An interim agreement was reached in early 1938 which gave Mitsubishi the franchise for sales in Japan and Manchuko. Mitsui received the sole rights for Central and Southern China. Any sales in Northern China were to be shared by both companies. On October 30, 1938, the Iranian Opium Purchasing Association was established. The "Association" consisted of only two members: Mitsui and Mitsubishi. Under government charter, the Association was to purchase, transport, and deliver, "all the opium required by Monopolies in China, Manchuria, and Japan. Purchases shall be decided each year and notified to the Association by the government officials of Japan, Manchuria, and China, after ascertaining the actual amount of opium collected in Korea, Manchuko, and the demand and supply in China (32)."

The complicity of the Japanese Foreign Office was also apparent in the case of the Singapore Maru. In 1937, Mitsui informed the government that it had placed an order for 428 chests of opium. A chest of opium weighed 160 pounds; thus, the Mitsui order amounted to more than 34 tons (enough to make more than 3 tons of heroin). The opium was shipped on the Singapore Maru, which sailed from Bushire (now called Büsheher at the head of the Persian Gulf) on March 14, 1938. The provisions of several international treaties required the issuance of both import and export certificates for such transactions. Japan complied with the letter of the law in the treaties. Just two days before the Singapore Maru sailed, an individual claiming to be an agent of the "North China Provisional Government" issued an import certificate to Isamu Fugita. Fugita was the Mitsui agent in Macao. The Iranian Embassy, of course, automatically issued an export certificate to Mitsui when Fugita presented his permit.

The import certificate scheme had been contrived by the Japanese Foreign Office. Instructions on how to proceed had been sent from Shanghai in a cable transmitted April 13, 1938, marked "Strictly Secret":

> As stated in my captioned message, even if the Provisional government's permit (which has already been issued for unloading at Tientsin) could be used, since it is impossible to make the notification due to the policy of prohibiting Japanese from importing opium into China, we could use a suitable fictitious Chinese name for import purposes and have Mitsui make the notification of the shipment. The only other way out is for us to give tacit consent and not to make any notification at all. Wire me back what you think. Furthermore, the ship has already left but the notification has been prepared. For your information (33).

A second cable, sent the next day, supplies further documentation: Red Intercept #1785;

> Have MITSUI make a report on the shipment as if it were imported by a Chinese, and send me a copy of the report. Furthermore, always explain (both to foreigners and Japanese) the constitutionality of this comes under the secret order of WANG KEH MING's Administration. I do not want the form of the secret order to be included in the above report (34).

When the Singapore Maru arrived at Tangku, it was flying a Japanese flag, and was met by Japanese Army officials who took possession of the opium. They later delivered it to Monopoly refineries in Shanghai and Tientsin. Using similar methods, Mitsui eventually delivered an additional 3972 chests (635,520 pounds) of opium from the beginning of 1939 until the end of 1941.

Japan's judicial system also played a key role in the drug trade, especially in the occupied territories, such as the Kwangtung Peninsula in North China. These territories came under permanent Japanese control in 1905. The region had originally been leased to Russia by China, but after the War of 1904-1905, the lease was transferred to Japan. During the 1930s, the area had a population of 1.2 million Chinese. Because it was a Japanese colony, the peninsula automatically came under the 1925 Geneva Opium Convention. On September 28, 1927, in order to conform to the Geneva Opium Convention requirements, the Kwangtung government issued Order No. 54, which regulated and controlled narcotic sales and use. Under this law, the only drugs classified as narcotics were morphine, cocaine, and "their salts and derivatives and articles containing them." For whatever reason, the words "salts and derivatives" were omitted from the final published law. In order to correct the omission, an "errata" notification was published in the Kwangtung Government Gazette. The text of the notice also carried some supplementary clauses. The third clause stated that *"the importation of narcotics other than morphine and cocaine which have been contracted for prior to the promulgation of these regulations, with this fact duly certified, and are in transit, will be permitted...without applying for or obtaining an import permit from the Governor."* The results were predictable.

Two enterprising druggists in Darien, the capital of Kwangtung Province, were among the first to realize the possibilities. They immediately ordered 3300 kg (7425 pounds) of benzoylmorphine; half of the order was placed with Hoffman La Roche in Basel, and half with Heesch-Henrichsen in Hamburg. The druggists then went to the Japanese consulate and obtained certificates stating that all of the material had been ordered before October 1, 1927, the date that Order No. 54 became effective. The drugs were shipped in small lots via parcel post, arriving in Darien between May 12 and June 21, 1928. The net profit to the two enterprising pharmacists was said to have been $500,000 (35).

Heesch-Henrichsen also used the mails to fill a second order, although this second shipment went to an ex-member of the Japanese Diet, T. Shirakawa. A friend of Shirakawa, who also happened to be the Director of the Japanese Stock Exchange, heard about the Clause 3 windfall. He bankrolled Shirakawa who, with a friend, went to Germany and arranged to buy 2400 kg of benzoylmorphine and 600 kg of heroin. The pharmacists then submitted forged purchase orders to the Kwangtung authorities and received permits which allowed the drugs to be imported. Shirakawa netted more than $600,000, even after bribing another Diet member who had threatened to expose the transaction.

Not to be outdone, Ishio Hiramatsu, who managed the Darien Branch of an Osaka-based bank, arranged a loan for himself, went to Germany, and purchased another 1850 kg of benzoylmorphine. Hiramatsu also enjoyed a substantial profit. As a result of these three transactions alone, almost 10 tons of heroin and morphine were diverted to illegal drug traffickers. All of the players were Japanese nationals living in Kwangtung. All of them, including Shirakawa, were eventually arrested and tried in the Darien courts before a Japanese magistrate, Chief Judge Morimoto. Shirakawa and his associated were brought to trial on July 30, 1931. The Chinese prosecutor subpoenaed a government clerk who testified that he had noticed the "omission" long before Order No. 54 was published, but his superiors wanted it published just the way it was. The defense, of course, argued that Order No. 54 did not mention either benzoylmorphine or heroin, and the published correction did not have the force of law. All of the accused, except for Shirakawa, were acquitted. Shirakawa was fined $300.

Even with imports from Iran, and native production in Mongolia, supplying the monopolies became an increasingly difficult undertaking. Some of the drug manufacturers were forced to resort to the black market. Japan's state-run Hygienic Laboratories obtained most of their raw opium from legitimate importers such as Mitsui and Mitsubishi. But, there was also a black market for raw opium. Court records from Delhi indicate that Indian opium was often bartered for Japanese cocaine. Court records also indicate that many of the smuggling techniques that are popular today have, in fact, a very long history. Opium from Upper and Central India was smuggled to Calcutta, usually hidden in shipments of fruit. Specially constructed cars with hidden compartments were common. Drug "mules" transported drugs hidden on their bodies. (There is even evidence that the current practice of "body packing", swallowing cocaine or heroin filled condoms, was known and utilized at that time.)

European and Eurasian drug couriers were preferred for smuggling activities because they attracted less attention. Members of one gang liked to dress couriers in military uniforms, and then accompany them dressed as servants. Once the opium arrived in Calcutta it was transferred onto Chinese ships. Payment was often made in cocaine. In order to avoid detection by customs officers in Calcutta, the cocaine was packed in watertight tins and thrown into the water just before the ships entered port. Most of the tins contained the "Fujitusuru" brand cocaine. The tins were then plucked from the water by fishermen in the employ of the drug smugglers. On several occasions, however, rubberized containers filled with cocaine appear to have been packaged directly by Sankyo. These transactions were carried out, of course, with the assistance of low level customs officials who were carried on the smugglers' payrolls. Even the police participated; one consignment of cocaine was accidentally hauled in by fishermen and the police had to be dispatched to recover the smugglers' cocaine (36)!

Japan's Army and Navy were sometimes used to protect Monopoly drug shipments, and they profited handsomely from drug sales. The relationship between the *zaibatsu* companies, the military, and the Japanese Foreign Office are clearly evident in a cable sent from Tientsin to Tokyo on March 22, 1938:

> *Circular #426, Intercept #1598, translated 4/7/38. From Shanghaito Tientsin. Forwarded to Tokyo as #942 in response to #412. "I have conferred with the local military and they say that they have been planning all along for an opium Monopoly under the control of the North China Army. This opium in North China will be handled by Mitsui and will be imported by an official permit of the Provisional government of North China. The local military (Shanghai) have a strong desire to cause the Central China regime to form another opium Monopoly but have no opium on hand, so they desire to have some of the North China imports packed and shipped to us here in case of a Monopoly...(37)".*

In Southern China, Army involvement in the drug trade was apparent from the very beginning. As soon as the Japanese Army entered Shanghai, it began to charge local opium dealers "protection money". It then imposed a tax on retail opium sales. Shortly afterwards, orders were placed with Mitsui for Iranian opium at the wholesale price of $5 per ounce. By the end of 1938, the Japanese Army Special Forces were importing more than 80 tons of raw opium a month into the Shanghai area alone. Once the opium arrived in Shanghai, it was stored in a secret warehouse in Hangkow, not far from Shanghai, and then sold to local Chinese opium dealers. No permits or licenses were required, but the minimum purchase was 1.6 tons. To place orders, opium dealers had to pay in advance at the local branch of the Bank of Taiwan, which issued a receipt of payment. To arrange for delivery, dealers took the receipt to the Special Services branch in Hangkow. The Special Forces guaranteed delivery anywhere within a reasonable distance of the city. The opium was transported on military trucks under military escort (38).

Army participation was not confined to the "Special Services" division. In 1943, according to a report from General Douglas MacArthur's Office of Counter-intelligence, the Japanese Supreme Command assigned Lt. General Nemoto, Commander-in-Chief of Japanese Mongolia, the task of organizing and streamlining the production and distribution of opium in Mongolia. According to the directive, the profits were to be used to support the espionage services of the Army. The Inner-Mongolian government encouraged farmers to grow poppies and purchased all of their production. The opium was then given to the Japanese Army who turned it over to Japanese processors, some in Mukden, and some in Korea. The plan was successful, until the Japanese Army found itself in direct conflict with the Japanese Navy which controlled production in Jehol and the neighboring provinces of Southern Manchuria.

The Japanese Navy played a vital role in providing raw materials to the drug dealers, especially after the war in Europe intensified. Even though hundreds of thousands of acres of poppies were being grown in Northern China, the quality of the Chinese opium was not nearly as good as Iranian opium. Even if it had been of comparable quality, Chinese opium was not available in sufficient quantity to meet the growing demand. Outside sources were required. After allowing for the costs of shipping, the Iranian opium was still cheaper than the home grown Chinese variety.

But getting the opium from Iran to China was no easy matter. Documents introduced at the War Crimes Trial recount one episode in which two destroyers of the Imperial Navy were dispatched to Ceylon to escort a tramp steamer laden with 80 tons of Iranian opium. The captain of the steamer was concerned about German submarines, and refused to proceed any further without an escort (39). Naval concerns about the safety of the ship's cargo were understandable; at wholesale prices alone, the shipment was worth more than $30 million dollars!

The Japanese military continued to remain involved in the drug trade after World War II ended. Just prior to their surrender in 1945, Japanese officials in the Korean Monopoly released 9 tons of refined heroin to the Japanese Navy and, after the surrender, an additional 9.4 tons to the officers of the Japanese Army. The transactions were discovered by United States Army investigators who recovered about half of the heroin released to the Japanese Army, and almost all that had been taken by the Japanese Navy. Seventy five Japanese civilians were arrested, tried, and sentenced, but it appears that none of the officers were ever apprehended (17).

In the first half of the 20th century, League of Nation efforts at international narcotics control relied on the cooperation and good will of its member nations. It was presumed that all member nations would recognize drug abuse as a threat to all peoples, and that all the members would act for the common good to control the problem. There was hardly anything unique about the notion. Similar presumptions underlay modern arms control treaties, and international agreements to control the use of biological weapons, or to prevent nuclear weapon proliferation. The League's system, however, failed miserably because Japan did not share any of these perceptions. Drug abuse was unheard of in Japan, and Japanese leaders did not perceive drug abuse as a threat to their own people.

Japan also did not share the League's perceptions of the common good, and was desperately in need of cash to finance its war effort, so it is not surprising that Japan went into the drug business. In fact, there is no evidence to support the Allies' contention that Japan "pursued a systematic policy of weakening the native inhabitants" through drug sales. Such a policy is never once articulated in any of the records surviving the war. The constant refrain, in intercepted cables, in the records of Japan's Army and Foreign Ministry, and in the depositions taken after the war is always the same: the government needed cash.

Japanese authorities at every level of government did what they could to help the war machine. And so did opportunists from around the world. Manufacturers in Germany, England, and Switzerland had no qualms about shipping tons of illegal drugs to Japan, and to recognized Japanese agents, knowing full well that the drugs had no conceivable medical use. Money and greed preempted concern for human welfare. The current state of affairs suggests we have made little progress since World War II.

AFTERWORD

In 1910, Sir Edward Grey, the British Foreign Minister, wrote to the American Ambassador in London, and warned that the "spread of morphia and the cocaine habit, is becoming an evil more serious and more deadly than opium smoking, and this evil is certain to increase...(1)." Grey's warning was certainly prophetic, though it is unlikely that even Grey could have predicted just how much worse the situation would become.

In 1930, the total population of Europe was less than 360 million, with only 122 million living in Northern and Western Europe, areas where cocaine was widely used. At the same time, 135 million people were living in North America, and another 75 million in South America. The population of Southeast Asia was approximately the same as Europe (2). Thus, the total number of people who could potentially have used cocaine during these years was less than 500 million.

League of Nations' experts estimated that during the years 1934 to 1937, the average total world cocaine production amounted to less than 5 tons per year (3). Allowing for Japanese clandestine production, the total output could not have been more than 10 tons a year for 500 million potential users, about 20 mg per year for every man, woman, and child in Western Europe, the Americas, and Southeast Asia. That figure agrees surprisingly well with League of Nations' estimates. The League maintained that legitimate medical cocaine use amounted to 7 mg per year (4).

The situation has changed drastically since the end of World War II. The cocaine content of South American coca leaf has increased substantially. Leaves grown in Bolivia now contain, on average, nearly .75% cocaine. Given current refining techniques, half of the cocaine contained in the leaves can eventually be converted to cocaine (5). Leaves grown today in South America now contain nearly as much cocaine as the old Java leaves. Not only has the cocaine content of the leaves increased, but much more land is devoted to coca cultivation. Before World War II, coca plantations were measured in hundreds of acres. Today, hundreds of thousands of acres are devoted to coca production.

The total amount of cocaine produced today is not known with any certainty. In the 1920s, the League of Nations could make reasonably accurate production estimates. The process was simple, because all production was legal and in the open. There was no clandestine industry. Today, virtually all cocaine production is clandestine, and production estimates are a matter of guesswork. Several variables, each very difficult to quantitate, are involved. Infrared satellite mapping can be used to estimate the number of acres under cultivations, but yield per acre is another matter entirely. Yield depends on the strain and age of the plants, the rainfall, and the cocaine content of the leaves. All of these factors vary from region to region, and can only be established by direct inspection, on the ground. The chemical process used to extract the cocaine is also important, but unpredictable. The percentage of cocaine finally extracted depends on the skill of the chemists, and the availability of appropriate chemicals. The only way to assess any of these variables is by inspecting the laboratories, or at least inspecting samples taken directly from the laboratories.

The Drug Enforcement Agency's (DEA) production estimates for Bolivia, which were based on direct observations and measurements, illustrate how widely divergent these figures may be. For example, the average annual yield in the Chapare region of Bolivia is 2.7 tons of leaves per hectare, while the yield in Yungas, the other prime Bolivian growing area, is only 1.8 tons (5). If the Chapare figures were used as a basis for estimating total South American production, values would be overstated by at least one third. If the Yungas yield was used as the standard, the opposite would be true. Then, of course, there is the inherent bias of the estimators. A number of authors have noted that because U.S. foreign aid to coca-producing countries is often keyed to production levels, U.S. Government officials tend to underestimate coca production at the same time that Bolivian officials are overestimating it (6)(7).

In 1993, U.S. Drug Enforcement Agency analysts placed Bolivian production at 193 metric tons, a decrease of nearly 100 tons from previous estimates. The potential output in Colombia is estimated between 60 and 80 tons, although some South American experts think that actual output is much higher (8). At least 200,000 acres are devoted to coca growing in Peru, which could, conceivably yield 500 to 700 tons of refined cocaine per year. DEA analysts believe that number is much lower. Production is now expanding into Central America, with several hundred acres of coca having been seized and destroyed in Panama in 1995.

Using the most conservative estimates, South American cocaine production probably amounts to more than 500 tons of refined cocaine per year. Using less conservative assumptions, the number could well amount to more than 1000 tons per year (9). A case could be made for the less conservative scenario because in 1994, the United States government confiscated more than 220 tons of refined cocaine (10). Not even the most optimistic experts suggest that anything close to one half of the drugs smuggled into the United States are ever detected.

The population of the United States and Europe is nearly twice what it was at the start of World War II. The population of Southeast Asia has increased by even more. Assuming that 1.5 billion people now live in those same areas, and the total refined cocaine output is 1000 tons, then at least 300 mg of cocaine are produced each year for every man, woman, and child in Western Europe, America, and Southeast Asia. The 20 mg available in the 1930s would not have been a large enough quantity to produce any measurable physiologic changes, but the 300 mg available today could. In some situations, it would be sufficient to cause toxicity. This increase has occurred in spite of four different international treaties, and the expenditures of countless billions of dollars on interdiction and policing. If Sir Edward Gray, the British Foreign Secretary, thought a worldwide production of less than 10 tons was a threat to public health, how would he have reacted to a worldwide supply of 1000 tons?

There is no evidence today that coca is now being grown in Southeast Asia. If production were to resume there, however, the total world supply could easily double, and probably triple. But a worse scenario can be envisioned. Cocaine is a relatively small molecule (m.w = 303.4). It should not be that difficult to decipher the DNA codes for its production, manufacture copies of the DNA instructions, and insert them in some innocuous plant such as corn or soybeans. The genetic manipulations necessary to produce spoilage resistant tomatoes were probably more difficult. And corn grows nearly everywhere.

Japan entered the drug trade because the time and circumstances were right. There were plenty of well-heeled investors with few moral qualms, there was a xenophobic government with few scruples, and the army had a pressing need for cash. As the millennia approaches, xenophobic governments with few scruples are not in short supply. Some may consider drug dealing an attractive option.

REFERENCES

CHAPTER 1

General Sources: Joseph Gagliano has written an excellent text, based on original documents produced during the Spanish colonial administration (*Coca prohibition in Peru*). The account presented here draws extensively on the material unearthed by Gagliano. For the general reader, the standard histories by Cespedes and Haring are highly readable and authoritative.

1. Cieza de Leon, The Incas. Translated by Harriet de Onis. University of Oklahoma Press (1959). The Civilization of the American Indian series; v. 53.
2. Office of Technical Assessment. Alternative coca reduction strategies in the Andean Region, OTA-F-556. Washington, D.C.: U.S. Government Printing Office, 1993.
3. Acosta J. Historia natural y moral de las Indias, 1588; English translation by C.R. Markham, Hakluyt Society, London, 1880.
4. Guerra F. The pre-Columbian mind. A study into the aberrant nature of sexual drives, drugs affecting behavior and the attitude towards life and death, with a survey of psycho-therapy, in pre-Columbian America. London: Seminar Press, 1971.
5. Gagliano J. Coca production in Peru, the historical debates. Tucson & London: University of Arizona Press, 1994.
6. Cespedes G. Latin America: the early years. Rice E, ed. Studies in world civilization. New York: Alfred A. Knopf, 1974.
7. Haring C. The Spanish empire in America. New York and Burlingame: Harcourt, Brace & World, Inc., 1947.
8. Brading D, Cross H. Colonial silver mining: Mexico and Peru. In: Bakewell P, Johnson J, Dodge M, eds. Readings in Latin American history. Volume 1. The formative centuries. Durham: Duke University Press, 1985.
9. Stern S. Peru's Indian peoples and the challenge of Spanish conquest. Huyamanga to 1640. (2nd Edition ed.) Madison, Wisconsin: University of Wisconsin Press, 1982.
10. Antonil. Mama coca. London: Hassle Free Press, 1978.
11. Stein S. International diplomacy, state administrators and narcotics control. The origins of a social problem. London: London School of Economics and Gower Publishing Company, 1985.
12. Beals C. Fire in the Andes. Philadelphia: J.B. Lippincott,1934.

13. Clayton L. Trade and navigation in the Seventeenth-Century Viceroyalty of Peru. In: Bakewell P, Johnson J, Dodge M, eds. Readings in Latin American history. Volume I: The formative centuries, 1985.

14. Guerra F. Sex and drugs in the 16th Century. Br J Addict 1974;69:269-290.

15. Williamson E. The Penguin history of Latin America. London: Penguin Press, 1992.

16. Whitehead P. A portrait of Dutch 17th century Brazil: animals, plants, and people by the artists of Johan Maurits of Nassau, Amsterdam and New York: North-Holland Pub. Co., 1989 Verhandelingen der Koninklijke Nederlandsche Akademie van Wetenschappen, Afdeeling Natuurkunde. Tweede sectie;d. 87.

17. Lindeboom G. Herman Boerhaave: the man and his work, with a foreword by E. Ashworth Underwood. London: Methuen & Co Ltd, 1968.

18. Jovet P, Mallet J. Charles De L'Écluse (Clasius). Dictionary of scientific biography. New York: Scribner's Sons, 1973.

19. Monardes N. Joyfulle newes out of the newe founde worlde, written in Spanish by Nicholas Monardes. English translation by John Frampton, with an introduction by Stephen Gaselee, 1925. London: Constable and Company Ltd., 1596. The Tudor translations. 2d ser.IX.

20. Calhoun T. Abraham Cowley. In: Hester M, ed. Dictionary of literary biography. Seventeenth-century British nondramatic poets, Third series. Detroit, Washington, D.C., London: Bruccoli Clark Layman, 1993:vol 131.

21. Boerhaave H. Institutiones medicae in usus annuae exercitationis domesticos digestae Ed. 3. prioribus longe auctior. Amsterdam: Isaacum Severinum, 1730.

22. Boerhaave H. Boerhaave's Materia medica, or, The druggist's guide and the physician and apothecary's table-book: being a complete account of all drugs, in alphabetical order. Transcribed from the author's lectures in London: Printed for the author and sold by J. Hodges, 1755.

23. La Condamine CM. Abridged narrative of travels through the interior of South America from the shores of the Pacific Ocean to the coasts of Brazil and Guyana, descending the river of Amazons; as read by Mr. de La Condamine. In: Pinkerton J, ed. A general collection of voyages and travels. London, 1808.

24. von Hagen V. South America called them, explorations of the great naturalists: La Condamine, Humboldt, Darwin, Spruce. New York: A.A. Knopf, 1945.

25. Weddell H. On the leaves of the coca of Peru (Erythroxylon Coca, Lamarck). Am J Pharm;27:33-38, 1855.

26. Sharp G. Coca and cocaine studied historically. Pharm J (January 9):28-30, 1909.

27. Mortimer W. History of coca. "The Divine Plant" of the Incas. New York, 1901. Reissued by And/Or Press, Fitz Hugh Ludlow Memorial Library Edition, San Francisco, 1974.

28. Anon. The cultivation of coca. Chemist and Druggist (January 26):122-124, 1899.

CHAPTER 2

General Sources: Except for the standard histories and biographies of Kew Gardens and the famous botanists, most of the information came from the medical journals of the 1860s and 1870s; *The Lancet, The*

British Medical Journal, and Pharmaceutical Journal Transactions all contain fascinating material. von Hagen's book, South America Called Them, gives a wonderful, highly readable, account of the adventurers of the early Amazon explorers.

1. Monardes N. Joyfulle newes out of the newe founde worlde, written in Spanish by Nicholas Monardes. English translation by John Frampton, with an introduction by Stephen Gaselee, 1925. London: Constable and Company Ltd., 1596. The Tudor translations. 2d ser.IX.

3. Turrill W. The Royal Botanic Gardens Kew. London: Herbert Jenkins, 1859.

4. Allan M. The Hookers of Kew, 1785-1911. London: Michael Joseph, 1967.

5. Boxer CR. Two pioneers of tropical medicine: Garcia d'Orta and Nicolas Monardes. London: London, Hispanic & Luso-Brazilian Councils, 1963. Diamante.

6. Guerra F. Sex and drugs in the 16th Century. Br J Addict;69:269-290, 1974.

7. Dowdeswell G. The coca leaf. Observations on the properties and action of the leaf of the coca plant (Erythroxylon Coca) made in the physiology laboratory of University College. Lancet (April29):631-633, 1876.

8. Poeppig E. Travels in Chile, Peru, and on the Amazon during the years 1827-1832 (translated and extracted by William Hooker) In Companion to the Botanical Magazine I:161-175, 1835.

9. Anon. Erythroxylon Coca. Bulletin of miscellaneous information, Royal Botanical Gardens, Kew:72-73, 1892.

10. Anon. Cultivation of medicinal plants in India. Chemist and Druggist; (April 17, 1886):324-324, 1886.

11. Anon. Ceylon Coca leaves. Bulletin of miscellaneous information, Royal Botanical Gardens, Kew :152-153, 1890.

12. Holland J. The useful plants of Nigeria. Bulletin of miscellaneous information, Royal Botanical Gardens, Kew; Additional Series, IX:116-121, 1909.

13. McNair J. Botanical Station at Lagos. Bulletin of miscellaneous information, Royal Botanical Gardens, Kew:162-162, 1890.

14. Anon. Transactions of the Pharmaceutical Society. The commercial varieties of coca leaves. Pharm J Trans 1892 (April 23):874-875, 1891.

15. Rusby H. The botanical origin of coca leaves. Druggists Circular & Chem Gaz; (November):222-223, 1900.

16. Reens E. La coca de Java. Monographie historique, botanique, chimique et pharmacoligique (pour l'obtention du diplome de Docteur de l'Universite de Paris, Pharmacie): Ecole Superieure de Pharmacie, 1919.

17. Anon. The coca plants in cultivation. Pharm J Trans (April 2); 817-819, 1892.

18. von Tschudi J. Travels in Peru during the years 1838-1842. New York: Wiley & Putnam, 1847.

19. Torretti C. Cocaine. Am Druggist 1886; June:106-106.

20. Niemann A. Über eine neue organische Base in Cocablättern. Reprinted in Am J Pharmacy, 33 (third series, #9), 123-127, 1861: Göttingen: E.A. Huth, Inaug.-diss., 1860.

21. Farber E. Great chemists. New York: Interscience Publishers, 1961.

22. Scherzer K, ritter von. Narrative of the circumnavigation of the globe by the Austrian frigate Novara, (Commodore B. vonWullerstorf-Urbair) undertaken by order of the imperial government in the years 1857, 1858, & 1859. London: Saunders, Otley, 1863.

23. Schlesinger H. Topics in the chemistry of cocaine. Bull Narc 1985; 37:63-78.

24. Bennett A. An experimental inquiry into the physiological actions of caffeine, theine, guaranine, cocaine and theobromine. Edinburgh Med J;19:323-341, 1873.
25. Hirschmüller A. E. Merck und das Kokain: zu Sigmund Freuds kokainstudien und ihren Beziehungen zu der Darmstädter Firma. Gesnerus;52:116-132, 1995.
26. Anon. Special Correspondence, Paris, the coca leaf. Br Med J (April 15):486-486, 1876.
27. Finlay M. Quackery and cookery: Justus von Liebig's extract of meat and the theory of nutrition in the Victorian age. Bull Hist Med;66:404-418, 1992.
28. von Liebig J. Uber die Bestandtheile der Flüssigkeiten des Fleisches. Ann Chemie und Pharm;72:257-269, 1847.
29. Mortimer W. History of coca. "The Divine Plant" of the Incas. New York, 1901. Reissued by And/Or Press, Fitz Hugh Ludlow Memorial Library Edition, San Francisco, 1974.
30. Pavy F. The effect of prolonged muscular exercise on the system. Lancet (February 26):319-320, 1876.
31. Pavy F. The effect of prolonged muscular exercise on the system. Lancet (March 18):429-430, 1876.
32. Weston E. Mr. Weston on the use of coca leaves. Lancet (March 18):447-447, 1876.
33. Palmer E. Coca in fatigue. Am Practitioner; 31:69-74, 1875.
34. Christison R. Observations of cuca, or coca, the leaves of Erythroxylon Coca. Br Med J(April 29):527-531, 1876.
35. Leebody J. The action of cuca. Br Med J(June 17):750-751, 1876.
36. Sieveking E. Coca: its therapeutic use. Br Med J (February 21):234-234, 1874.
37. Moore SA. The use of coca. Br Med J (February 28):289-289, 1874.
38. Leared A. The use of coca. Br Med J 1874 (February 28):272-272, 1874.
39. Bennett A. The physiological action of coca. Br Med J (April 18):510-510, 1874.
40. Hamilton A. Erythroxylon Coca. Br Med J 1876 (June 17)752-753, 1876.

CHAPTER 3

General Sources: Based on our experience doing the research for this book, there are no helpful books. For those who would like to learn more about this period, the best reference is a review paper by Holmstedt and Fredga. It was published in the *Journal of Ethnopharmacology*, nearly 20 years ago, but contains a wealth of information about some of the more obscure players. Otherwise, everything is to be found in the medical journals of the time.

1. Brown J. Concerning cocaine. Druggist Circular Chem Gazette; (December) 250-250, 1886.
2. Anon. Opinion of coca leaf? Druggist Circular Chem Gazette (September):157-157, 1876.
3. Julien P. Angelo Mariani et son Vin de coca: mécénat et publcité. In: Sarmiento F, ed. Farmacia e industrializacion. Libro homenaje al Doctor Guillermo Folch Jou. Madrid: Sociedad Española de Historia de la Farmcaia, 1985.
4. Brun P. Albert Robida (1848-1926) sa vie, son oeuvre, suivi d'une bibliographie compléte des ses écrits et dessins. Paris: Promodis, 1984.

5. Mariani A. Advertisement. Med Surg Report;1-1, 1889.

6. Andrews G, Solomon D, eds. The coca leaf and cocaine papers. New York and London: Harcourt Brace Jovanovich, 1975.

7. Anon. Wine of coca. Druggists Circular Chem Gaz, (May):92-92, 1885.

8. Anon. Coca wine or vin Mariani. Pharm J; (June 15):1159-1159, 1895.

9. Mitchell C. Coca wines of the market. Druggist Circular Chem Gaz (February):82-82, 1886.

10. Barclay J. Coca-wine of commerce. Notes on a speech given before the Midland Chemists' Assistants' Association, (April 7) Chemist and Druggist 1897 (April 17, 1897):618-618, 1897.

11. Anon. Medicated-wine essences. Chemist and Druggist (January 3):198-198, 1897.

12. Pendergrast M. For God, country, and Coca-Cola. The unauthorized history of the great American soft drink and the company that makes it. New York: Collier Books, 1993.

13. Anon. Advertisement for Metcalf's Coca Wine. Med Surg Reporter; 15: 188-188, 1897.

14. Karch S. The Pathology of Drug Abuse. (2nd edition ed.) Boca Raton, Fl: CRC Press, CRC Forensics Series, 1996.

15. Farre M, de la Torre R, Llorente M, et. al Alcohol and cocaine interactions in humans. J Pharm Exp Ther;266(3):1364-73, 1993.

16. von Martius, C.F. Philip Travels in Brazil, in the years 1817-1820. Undertaken by command of His Majesty the King of Bavaria. By Dr. Joh. bapt. von spix and Dr. C. F. Phil. von Martius. London. Longman, Hurst, Rees, Orme, Brown and Green, 1824.

17. von Tschudi J. Travels in Peru during the years 1838-1842. New York: Wiley & Putnam, 1847.

18. Shuttleworth E. Some experiments on the physiological effects of coca. Pharm J Trans, reprinted from Canadian Pharm J, (September 22):221-222, 1877.

19. Anon. Mont Blanc. Therapeutic Gazette, ii:165-165, 1882.

20. Christison R. Observations of cuca, or coca, the leaves of Erythroxylon Coca. Br Med J;(April 29, 1876):527-531, 1876.

21. Edmonston Charles T. Cocaine. Pharm J Trans; (Sept 2) 185-185, 1882.

22. Anrep V. B. Uber die physiologische Wirkung des Cocain. Archv fur Physiologi, 38-77, 1880.

23. Holmstedt B, Fredga A. Sundry episodes in the history of coca and cocaine. J Ethnopharm;3:113-147, 1981.

24. Aschenbrandt T. Die physiologische Wirkung und Bedeutung des Cocain muriat. auf den menschlichen Organismus. Deutsche Medixinsche Wochenschrift;50:730-732, 1883.

25. Kramer J. Opium rampant: medical use, misuse, and abuse in Britain and the West in the 17th and 18th centuries. Br J Addict; 74:377-389, 1979.

26. Macht D. The history of opium and some of its preparations and alkaloids. JAMA 64(6):477-481, 1915.

27. Berridge V. Opium and the people. Opiate use in nineteenth-century England. London and New Haven: Yale University Press, 1987.

28. Terry C, Pellens M. The opium problem. New York: Committee on Drug Addictions, Bureau of Social Hygiene, Inc., 1928.

29. Wood A. New method of treating neuralgia by the direct application of opiates to painful spots. Edinburgh Med Surg; 82: 265-273, 1855.

30. Bartholow R. A manual of hypodermatic medication: the treatment of disease by the hypodermatic or subcutaneous method. (Fifth ed.) London: J. B. Lippincott, 1892.

31. Billings J. Medical reminiscences of the Civil War. Trans Coll Phys
    Phil;xxvii:115-121, 1905.
32. Anstie. The hypodermic injection of remedies. Practitioner; 1:32-41, 1868.

CHAPTER 4

General Sources: The most useful book for further information
about the subjects discussed in this chapter is Hans Maier's monograph, Cocaine Addiction. Parts of the book were finally translated into
English several years ago by a Canadian drug researcher named Oriana
Kalant. Maier's book remains the single most comprehensive, most
accurate, and most useful book on the etiology and dissemination of
cocaine and cocaine-related disease. Unfortunately, the portions of the
book dealing with cocaine's botany and forensics were not included in
the English edition. Copies can be ordered from the Addiction Research
Foundation in Toronto. If you can wade through Mortimer's effusive
praise for the drug, his *History of Coca* contains some very accurate
descriptions of coca botany and cultivation, and some interesting information about the history of coca in the Andes. A facsimile edition was
published in 1974, and the book is in many libraries.

To learn more about Freud and Koller, read the medical papers
from that period. Most are in German, but many of Freud's papers have
been translated. *The Cocaine Papers and Sigmund Freud*, edited by Robert
Byck, contains a very useful collection of translations, including Freud's
multiple papers on cocaine, and other papers from that period. Another
collection, *The Coca Leaf and Cocaine Papers*, edited by George Andrews
and David Solomon, contains some additional important papers from
that period. However, neither book is still in print.

1. Erlenmeyer A. Die Morphiumsucht und ihre Behandlung, (3rd ed.) Berlin:
   Heusser, pg 154, 1887.
2. Gaedecke F. Archives de Pharmacie 1855; LXXXII, cited in Mortimer (see
   Reference 3).
3. Mortimer W. History of coca. "The Divine Plant" of the Incas. New York,
   1901. Reissued by And/Or Press, Fitz Hugh Ludlow Memorial Library Edition, San Francisco, 1974.
4. Maier H. Der Kokainismus-Geschichte/Pathologie Medizinische und
   behördliche Bekämpfung. Leipzig: Georg Thieme Verlag, 1926. Edited and
   translated version reissued by the Addiction Research Foundation, Toronto,
   O.J. Kalant, editor, 1987.
5. Hirschmüller A. E. Merck und das Kokain: zu Sigmund Freuds kokainstudien
   und ihren Beziehungen zu der Darmstädter Firma. Gesnerus;52:116-132, 1995.
6. Schroff C. Vorläfige Mittheilungen über Cocäin. Wochenbladt d.k.k. Gesellsch.
   d. Aerzte in Wein; XVIII:233-241, 1862.
7. Maiz M Y. Recherches Chimiques et Physiologiques sur l'Erythroxylon Coca
   du Pérou et la Cocaine, Paris: A. Parent, 1868.

8. Siegel R, Hirschman A. Moreno and the first study on cocaine: a historical note and translation. J Psychoactive Drug;15(3):219-220, 1983.

9. Fauvel C. E. Coca Gazette des Hopitaux,(427), 1877. Cited in Reference #3.

10. Julien P. Angelo Mariani et son Vin de coca: mécénat et publcité. In: Sarmiento F, ed. Farmacia e inductrializacion. Libro homenaje al Doctor Guillermo Folch Jou. Madrid: Sociedad Española de Historia de la Farmcaia, 1985.

11. Anrep v. B. Uber die physiologische Wirkung des Cocain. Archv fur Physiologie:38-77, 1880.

12. Holmstedt B, Fredga A. Sundry episodes in the history of coca and cocaine. J Ethnopharm;3:113-147, 1891.

13. Martindale W. Coca and cocaine: their history, medical and economic uses, and medicinal preparations. London: H.K. Lewis, 1892.

14. Squibb E. Erythroxylon Coca. Ephemeris; 599-602, 1885.

15. Goldberg M. Cocaine: the first local anesthetic and the 'third scourge of humanity', a centennial melodrama. Arch Opthalmol; 102:1443-1447, 1984.

16. Freud S. Über coca. Wein Centralblatt fúr die ges Therapie 1884;2 (translated and reprinted in Cocaine Papers by Sigmund Freud (see Reference #38), also in J Substance Abuse Treatment 1: 205-217:289-314, 1984.

17. Bartholow R. Cartwright Lectures: On the physiological antagonism between medicines, and between remedies and diseases. Med Record 1880;XVIII (December 11):645-647, 1880.

18. Anon. Morphia and cocaine, theine, caffeine and guaranine. Med Rec:647, 1880.

19. Thornton E. Freud and cocaine. The Freudian Fallacy. London: Blond & Briggs, 1983.

20. Aschenbrandt T. Die physiologische Wirkung und Bedeutung des Cocain. muriat. auf den menschlichen Organismus. Deutsche Medicinsche Wochenschrift;50:730-732, 1883.

21. Jones E. The life and work of Sigmund Freud, Chapter VI, "The cocaine episode." New York City: Basic Books, 1953.

22. Bentley W. Erythroxylon Coca. Therapeutic Gazette;i:253, 1880.

23. Huse E. Coca erythroxylon - a new cure for the opium habit. Therapeutic Gazette;i:256-257, 1880.

24. Palmer E. Coca in fatigue. Am Practitioner;31:69-74, 1885.

25. Clark R. Freud: The man and the cause. New York: Random House, 1981.

26. Jones E. The life and work of Sigmund Freud. Vol 1: The formative years and the great discoveries, 1856-1900. London: Hogarth Press, 1953.

27. Merck E. Cocaine and its salts. Druggists Circular Chem Gaz (December 12):179-179, 1884.

28. Merck E. Cocaine and its salts. Pharm J Trans (November 29):426-427, 1884.

29. Merck E. Einen offenen Brief von E. Merck. Weiner med Presse; 26:1373, 1885.

30. Erlenmeyer. Über die Wirkung des Kokains bei der Morphiumentziehung. Zentralbl f Nervhk Psych u gterichtl;8:289-291, 1885.

31. Freud S. Beuträge über die Anwendung des Cocaïn. Zweite Serie. I. Bemerkungen über Cocaïnsucht und Cocaïnfurcht mit Beziehung auf einem Vortrag W. A. Hammond's. Weiner Medizinische Wochenschrift;28 (July 9):929-932, 1887.

32. Schusdek A. Freud On Cocaine. Psychoanalytic Quarterly; 34:406-412, 1973.

33. Wilkinson P, Van Dyke C, Jatlow P, et al. Intranasal and oral cocaine kinetics. Clin Pharmacol Ther;27:386–394, 1980.

34. Cone E. Pharmacokinetics and pharmacodynamics of cocaine. J Analyt Toxicol;19:459-478, 1995.

35. Hutant A. Über den chronischen Kokainismus mit nasaler Anwendung. Int Zentralbl. Laryngol Rhinol;25:138-140, 1910.

36. Liljestrand G. Carl Koller and the development of local anesthesia. Acta Physiol Scand;Suppl 299:3-26, 1967.
37. Koller H. Karl Koller and Cocaine. Psychoanalytic Quart;32:304-373, 1963.
38. Freud S. Contribution to the knowledge of the effect of cocaine by Dr. Sigmund Freud, house officer of the General Hospital in Vienna. Wein Weiner Med Woch, 5:130-133, 1885. Translated and reprinted in Byck, R (ed), Cocaine Papers, Sigmund Freud. Stonehill Publishing Company, New York, 1974.
39. Becker H. Karl Koller and cocaine. Psychoanalytic Quarterly 1963;32:309-343.
40. Noyes H. Murate of cocaine as a local anesthetic to the cornea; The Ophthalmological Congress in Heidelberg. Med Rec (October 11); 417-418, 1884.
41. "Correspondent". News items, New York. Medical News (November 8), pg 6., 1884.
42. Bull C. Hydrochlorate of cocaine as a local anesthetic in ophthalmic surgery. Med Rec;26:577-578, 1884.
43. Hall R. Hydrochlorate of cocaine. NY Med J;40:643-644, 1884.
44. Knapp H. Hydrochlorate of cocaine-experiments and application. Med Record(October 25):461-463, 1884.
45. Halsted W. Practical comments on the use and abuse of cocaine. NY Med J;42:294-295, 1884.
46. Wölfer A. Über die anaesthesierende Wirkung der subkutanen Cocain-injectionen. Wein Med Wochenschr;50:1531-1533, 1885.
47. Münch R, Abolson K. Carl Ludwig Schleich and the development of local anesthesia. Rev Surg;33(6):371-380, 1976.
48. Corning J. Spinal anesthesia and local medication of the cord. NY Med J;40:483-485, 1885.
49. Olch P. William S. Halsted and local anesthesia: contributions and complications. Anesthesiology;42(4):479-486, 1975.
50. Colp Jr R. Notes on Dr. William S. Halsted. Bull N.Y. Acad Med;60(9):876-887, 1984.
51. Osler W. The inner history of the Johns Hopkins Hospital, edited, annotated, and introduced by Bates, D.G., and Bensley, E.H. Johns Hopkins Med J;125:190-196, 1969.
52. Musto D. A study in cocaine: Sherlock Holmes and Sigmund Freud. JAMA;204:27-32, 1968.

CHAPTER 5

General Sources: Virtually all the supporting material comes directly from the medical literature from the 1880s forward. *The Pathology of Drug Abuse, 2nd edition,* by Steven B. Karch, may be of help to some.

1. Anon. United States, from a correspondent - Cucaine. Br Med J (January 2):40-40, 1886.
2. von Spix J.B, von Martius K.F.P. Travels in Brazil, in the years 1817-1820: undertaken by command of His Majesty the King of Bavaria, 1794-1868. (Translation of Reise in Brasilien in den Jahren 1817-1820.) London: Longman, Hurst, Rees, Orme, Brown, and Green, 1824. vol 2 v.:ill.; 24 cm.
3. Poeppig E. Travels in Chile, Peru, and on the Amazon during the years 1827-1832 (translated and extracted by William Hooker). Companion to the Botanical Magazine;I:161-175, 1835.

4. Freud S. Über coca. Wein Centralblatt fúr die ges Therapie 1884;2(translated and reprinted in Cocaine Papers by Sigmund Freud, also in J Substance Abuse Treatment 1:205-217, 1984.

5. Weddell.H.A. On the leaves of the coca of Peru (Erythroxylon Coca, Lamarck. "Extracted" from Voyage dans le nord de la Bolivie, Paris, 1853. Pharm J:162,213, 1854.

6. von Tschudi J. Travels in Peru during the years 1838-1842. New York: Wiley & Putnam, 1847.

7. Holmstedt B, Fredga A. Sundry episodes in the history of coca and cocaine. J Ethnopharm;3:113-147, 1981.

8. Mantegazza P. Sulle virtú igieniche e medicinali della coca. Annali Universali di Medicine e Chirugia, but also translated and reprinted the American Journal of Pharmacy, 1860, 32:415-421; and in Andrews & Solomon (eds): The Coca Leaf and Cocaine Papers.

9. Anon. Erythroxylon Coca. Bulletin of Miscellaneous Information, Royal Botanical Gardens, Kew:72-73, 1892.

10. Plowman T, Rivier L. Cocaine and cinnamoyl-cocaine of Erythroxylum species. Ann Botany;51:641-659, 1983.

11. Paly D, Jatlow P, Van Dyke C, et al., Plasma levels of cocaine in native Peruvian coca chewers. In: Juri F, ed. Cocaine 1980, Proceedings of the Interamerican Seminar on Coca and Cocaine. Lima: Pacific Press; 86-89, 1980.

12. Cone E. Pharmacokinetics and pharmacodynamics of cocaine. J Analyt Toxicol;19:459-478, 1995.

13. Fischman M, Schuster C, Rajfer S. A comparison of the subjective and cardiovascular effects of cocaine and procaine in humans. Pharm Biochem Behav;18:711-716, 1983.

14. Foltin R, Fischman M. Smoked and intravenous cocaine in humans - acute tolerance, cardiovascular and subjective effects. J Pharmacol Exp Ther;257(1):247-261, 1991.

15. Vilensky W. Illicit and licit drugs causing perforation of the nasal septum: a case report. J Forensic Sci;27(4):958-962, 1982.

16. Hautant A. Über den chronischen Kokainismus mit nasaler Anwendung. Int Zentralbl Laryngol Rhinol;25(138-139), 1910.

17. Noyes H. Murate of cocaine as a local anesthetic to the cornea; The Opthalmological Congress in Heidelberg. Med Rec(October 11), pg 417-418, 1884.

18. Knapp H. Hydrochlorate of cocaine-experiments and application. Med Record(October 25):461-463, 1884.

19. MacCormack M. Cucaine in prostatic disease. Br Med J 1886 (January 23), 1886.

20. Anon. Cucaine in hayfever. Br Med J;(May 8):393-393, 1886.

21. Anon. United States - from a correspondent. Br Med J 1886 (March 27):614-614, 1886.

22. Anon. Toxic action of cocaine. Br Med J; (November 21):963-963, 1885.

23. Thompson A. Toxic action of cucaine. Br Med J;(January 9):67-67, 1886.

24. Anon. On cocaine poisoning. Lancet;ii (November 7):863-863, 1895.

25. Stewart J. Another case of epileptiform convulsions following the use of cocaine as an urethral anesthetic. Med News (August 18) :182-182, 1888.

26. Chalmers J. Proceedings of the Philadelphia Neurological Society; Four cases of cocaine delirium. Med News (April 6):387-387, 1889.

27. Chetwood C. The toxic effect of cocaine hydrochlorate with report of a case. Med Rec; (August 10):144-145, 1889.

28. Anon. Doctors as coroners' jurors. Interesting verdicts in an ether and a cocaine case. New York Times, September 16, 1892, pg 8.

29. Anon. Fatal case of cocaine poisoning. Lancet; i. (February 9):292-292, 1889.
30. Anon. A surgeon's suicide and the dose of cocaine. Med Rec; (January 1):17-17, 1887.
31. Ettinger T, Stine R. Sudden death temporally related to vaginal cocaine abuse. Am J Emerg Med;7(1):129-130, 1989.
32. Greenland V, Delke I, Minkoff H. Vaginally administered cocaine overdose in a pregnant woman. Obstet Gynecol;74:476-477, 1989.
33. Mittleman R, Wetli C. Death caused by recreational cocaine use, an update. JAMA;252:1889-1893, 1984.
34. Halsted W. Practical comments on the use and abuse of cocaine. NY Med J;42:294-295, 1884.
35. Mattison J. Cocaine dosage and cocaine addiction. Pacific Med Surg J & West Lancet;XXX(4):191-213, 1887.
36. Karch S, Green G, Young S. Myocardial hypertrophy and coronary artery disease in male cocaine users. J Forensic Sci;40(4):591-596, 1995.
37. Anon. The Soho cocaine fatality. Pharm J 1908 (February 1):135-135, 1908.
38. Mattison J. Communications. Cocaine poisoning. Med Rec; lxv (October 24):645-650, 1891.
39. Anon. Death from Cocaine. Br J Dent Sci;45:1073-1073, 1902.
40. Garland O. Fatal acute poisoning by cocaine. Lancet;ii:1104-1105, 1895.
41. Mayer E. The toxic effects following use of local anesthetics. JAMA;876-885, 1924.
42. Jones E. The life and work of Sigmund Freud. Vol 1: The formative years and the great discoveries, 1856-1900. London: Hogarth Press, 1953.
43. Maier H. Der Kokainismus-Geschichte/Pathologie Medizinische und behördliche Bekämpfung. Leipzig: Georg Thieme Verlag, 1926.
44. Anon. The confessions of a cocainist. Sci Am;(March 20):17695-17696, 1897.
45. Williams E. Negro cocaine "fiends" are a new Southern menace. New York Times, 1908 February 8, 1914: Magazine Section, pg 12.
46. Knopf S. The one million drug addicts in the United States. A defense of and suggestion to the medical profession. Med J Rec; 119:135-139, 1924.
47. Wetli C, Fishbain, D. Cocaine-induced psychosis and sudden death in recreational cocaine users. J Forensic Sci;30(3):873-880, 1985.
48. Wetli C, Mash D, Karch S. Cocaine-associated agitated delirium and the neuroleptic malignant syndrome. Am J Emerg Med 1996;14:425-428.
49. Staley J, Hearn L, Ruttenber A, et al. High affinity cocaine recognition sites on the dopamine transporter are elevated in fatal cocaine overdose victims. J Pharm Exp Ther;271:1678-1685, 1994.
50. Staley J, Wetli C, Ruttenber A, et al. Altered Dopaminergic synaptic markers in cocaine psychosis and sudden death. NIDA Res. Monograph;153:491- 504, 1995.

CHAPTER 6

General Sources: Botanists at the Royal Botanical Gardens at Kew oversaw the distribution of coca plants around the world, and documented the results in a series of papers published in their *Bulletin of Miscellaneous Information*. The Botanical Gardens in Java had their own journal, called *Tesymannia*. It details many of the early experiments with growing coca in Java. Information on coca cultivation in Java can be obtained from a number of sources, including the Minutes of the League of Nations Opium Committee (available in many depository libraries), and in a Ph.D. thesis written in 1919, *La Coca de Java*. There are only two copies in the United States, one in the National Library of Medicine and one at Yale University. Another source is the Netherlands National Archives in the Hague. Many of the records dealing with the NCF and the Coca Growers Cartel are in English. The most definitive work on the Dutch cocaine industry is by Marcel deKort (see Reference 28 below), however, it has not yet been translated into English.

Japan's cocaine and drug trafficking is described, though not in sufficient detail, in the trial transcripts from the Tokyo War Crimes Trials. The best source is the recently declassified material from Henry Anslingers' old Bureau of Narcotics. Anslinger supplied drug intelligence officers to General Douglas MacArthur's occupation forces, and kept copies of the reports for his own files. Bureau of Narcotics records from the 1930s were taken over by the DEA and were still classified when we filed a freedom of information request in 1993. The documents of most interest, are contained in RG 170 - Records of the DEA, Acc #71-A-3554, cartons #10 through 30. Interesting information is also to be found in the "SCAP" records (Supreme Commander Allied Pacific). The Public Health section deals with drug-related problems. However, some of the files still remain classified. These records, along with Anslinger's papers, are now located in the new Archives Center in suburban Maryland.

1. Anon. Cocaine hydrochlorate. Pharmaceutical Record; 465,1885.
2. Anon. Cheap cocaine. Chemist and Druggist; (March 14):412-413, 1908.
3. Mansvelt, WMF (ed) Changing economy in Indonesia, a selection of statistical source material from the early 19th Century up to 1940, Volume 1, Indonesia's export crops, 1816-1840. Martinus Nijhoff, The Hague.
4. Anon. Erythroxylon Coca. Bulletin of miscellaneous information, Royal Botanical Gardens, Kew;72-73, 1892.
5. Anon. The Java Coca Plant. Pharm J and Transactions;(February 28), 1891.
6. Holland J. The useful plants of Nigeria. Bulletin of miscellaneous information, Royal Botanical Gardens, Kew; Additional Series, IX:116-121, 1909.
7. McNair J. Botanical Station at Lagos. Bulletin of miscellaneous information, Royal Botanical Gardens, Kew; 162-162, 1890.
8. Anon. Cocaine in India. Chemist and Druggist; (March 26, 1904): 504-505, 1904.
9. Reens E. La coca de Java. Monmographie historique, botanique, chimique et pharmacoligique [pour l'obtention du diplome de Docteur de l'Universite de Paris, Pharmacie]: Ecole Superieure de Pharmacie, 1919.
10. Feldwick, W (ED), Present day impressions of the Far East and prominent and progressive Chinese at home and abroad. Globe Encyclopedia Co, London and Shanghai, 1917, pg, 1047-1048.
11. de Jong D. Cultivation of coca in Java. Teysmannia; 233, 1908.
12. Anon. The cultivation of coca. Chemist and Druggist;(January 26):122-124, 1889.

13. Mortimer W. History of coca. "The Divine Plant" of the Incas. New York, 1901. Reissued by And/Or Press, Fitz Hugh Ludlow Memorial Library Edition, San Francisco, 1974.

14. Anon. Parke, Davis & Company, 1866-1966, a backward glance. Detroit: Parke, Davis & Company, 1966.

15. Rusby H. Jungle Memories. New York and London: Whittlesey House, McGraw-Hill Book Company, Inc, 1933.

16. Kawell, Jo Ann, The "essentially peruvian" industry: legal cocaine production in the 19th century. Read at "The historical and global transformations of cocaine: 1860-1960, Russell Sage Foundation, May 1997.

17. Anon. Cocaine from Peru. Chemist and Druggist;(May 29):507-507, 1886.

18. Anon. Coca leaves and crude cocaine. Chemist and Druggist; (January 28):136-137, 1888.

19. Anon. The American cocaine duty. Chemist and Druggist; (October 17):591-591, 1891.

20. Anon. Exportation of coca-leaves and cocaine from Peru. Chemist and Druggist; (August 19):344-344, 1899.

21. Anon. The coca plants in cultivation. Pharm J Trans; (April 2):817-819, 1892.

22. Anon. Ceylon coca leaves. Bulletin of miscellaneous information, Royal Botanical Gardens, Kew; 152-153, 1890.

23. Colonial Bank, Report #29 on the Nederlandsche Cocainefabriek, omslag 928, 2.20.04. archief van de Cultuur-, Handels-en Industriebank, later Cultuurbank, N.V., ARA II, 1945.

24. Anon. Cocaine-smuggling. Chemist and Druggist;(November 18):784-784, 1905.

25. Anon. Drug auction prices. Chemist and Druggist; (April 28):135 1906.

26. Hirschmüller A. E. Merck und das Kokain: zu Sigmund Freuds kokainstudien und ihren Beziehungen zu der Darmstädter Firma. Gesnerus;52:116-132, 1995.

27. Letter from Dame Rachel Crowdy to W.G. von Wettum questioning the existence of a "cocaine producers cartel." October 22, 1929. Archief van de Cultural-, Handels-en Insdustriebank, later Cultuurbank N.V., ARA II: Archief van de Cultural-, Handels-enInsdustriebank, later Cultuurbank N.V., ARA II, 1929.

28. de Kort, M. (Between patient and delinquent. The history of Drug Policy in the Netherlands). Verloren Publishers Hilversum, Amsterdam, 1995.

29. Bransky J. Survey of Production, manufacture and distribution of narcotic drugs and preparations by the Sankyo Company, Limited Reports of Joseph Bransky, Field Investigator for the Office of Counter-Intelligence, Tokyo. National Archives, RG 170: Records of the DEA, Acc #71-A-3554, carton #20, Japan Statistical Reports 1945-1946, 1946.

30. Letter from W.G. von Wettum to Dame Rachel Crowdy, November 18, 1929, the Hague. Archief van de Cultural-, Handels-en Insdustriebank, later Cultuurbank N.V., ARA II, 1929.

31. Letter from von Wettum to Dame Rachel Crowdy, League of Nations Opium Committee. Archief van de Cultural-, Handels-en Insdustriebank, later Cultuurbank N.V., ARA II. 1929.

32. Anon. Jaarverslag Coca Producenten Vereeninging. omslag 1643, 2.20.04 1928;archief van de Cultuur-, Handels-, en Industriebank, later Cultuurbank N.V., ARA II, 1928.

33. Letter from Coca Producers Association. Archief van deCultural-, Handels-en Insdustriebank, later Cultuurbank N.V., ARA II. 1929.

34. Copy of a memo from American Consulate, Taihoku, Taiwan, May 5, 1934 to Secretary of State in Washington, D.C. regarding cocaine and coca production. RG 170: Records of the DEA, Acc #71-A-3554, carton #20, Japan Statistical Reports 1945-1946, 1946.

35. Anon. Java coca and cocaine. Chemist and Druggist 1910 (July 2):50-50, 1910.

36. Atzenwiler L. Pre-War production and distribution of narcotic drugs and their raw materials. League of Nations, Permanent Central Opium Board, 1944.

37. International Military Tribunal for the Pacific, copy of Office Report for 1939, from the Third Section of the Treaty Bureau, Japanese Foreign Ministry, subtitled "The internal opium problem." Introduced at trial as Document 1045.

CHAPTER 7

General Sources: There are no general books on the topic. Two anthologies, the collection of Freud's papers edited by Byck, and the collection of miscellaneous papers edited by Andrews and Solomon, contain the most important historical documents. The material describing Freud's relationship to Merck and Parke is based, in a large part, on the recently published research by A.E. Hirschmüller (see Reference 6).

1. Guttmacher H. Neue Arzneimittel und Heilmethoden. Über die verschiedenen Cocäin-Präparate und deren Wirkung. Weiner Med Pr 1885 (August 9, 1885):1035-1038; Translated and reprinted in Cocaine Papers by Sigmund Freud, Stonehill Press, pg 121-125, 1974.

2. Anon. E. Merck, From Merck's Angel Pharmacy to the worldwide Merck group, 1668-1968. Published on the occasion of the 300th anniversary of the taking over of the Engel Apotheke in Darmstadt by Fredrich Jacob Merck on Aug. 26, 1654. Darmstadt: E. Merck Aktienges., Public Relations Department, 1968.

3. Hermann F. Aus dem Leben des Kriegsrats Joh. Heinrich Merck und seiner Kinder. Darmstadt, 1924.

4. Thorpe E. History of chemistry. London: Watts & Co, 1930.

5. Finlay M. Quackery and cookery: Justus von Liebig's extract of meat and the theory of nutrition in the Victorian age. Bull Hist Med;66:404-418, 1992.

6. Hirschmüller A. E. Merck und das Kokain: zu Sigmund Freuds kokainstudien und ihren Beziehungen zu der Darmstädter Firma. Gesnerus;52:116-132, 1995.

7. Niemann A. Über eine neue organische Base in Cocablättern. Göttingen: E.A. Huth, Inaug.-diss., 1860 Reprinted in Am J Pharmacy, 33 (third series, #9), 123-127, 1861.

8. Anon. Darmstadt. Encyclopedia Britianica. London, 1882.

9. Merck E. Cocaine and its salts. Druggists Circular Chem Gaz; (December):179-179, 1884.

10. Merck E. Cocaine and its salts. Pharm J Trans; (November):426-427, 1884.

11. Atzenwiler L. Prewar production and distribution of narcotic drugs and their raw materials. League of Nations, Permanent Central Opium Board, Geneva, 1944.

12. Rusby H. Jungle Memories. New York and London: Whittlesey House, McGraw-Hill Book Company, Inc, 1933.

13. Reens E. La coca de Java, monographie historique, botanique, chimque et pharmacologique. Paris: Lons-le-Saunier, 1919.

14. Anon. Parke, Davis, 1866-1966, a backward glance. Detroit: Parke-Davis, 1966.

15. Bentley W. Erythroxylon coca in the opium and alcohol habits. Therapeutic Gazette; 4:253-255,1880.

16. Huse E. Coca erythroxylon - a new cure for the opium habit. Therapeutic Gazette;4:256-257,1880.

17. Palmer E. The opium habit - a possible antidote. Therapeutic Gazette; 4:163-164, 1880.

18. Freud S. Über coca. Wein Centralblatt für die ges Therapie 1884;2 (translated and reprinted in Cocaine Papers of Sigmund Freud, pg 47-74 - see Reference #19); also in J Substance Abuse Treatment 1:205-217, 1984.

19. Parke DC, Scientific Department. Coca Erythroxylon and its derivatives. Promotional Brochure 1885; Reprinted in Cocaine Papers by Sigmund Freud, R. Byck, editor, Stonehill Press, 1974.

20. Anon. Coca erythroxylon and its derivatives. In: Byck R, ed. Cocaine Papers by Sigmund Freud. New York: Stonehill Publishing, 127-150, 1974.

21. Jones E. Chapter VI: The cocaine episode. The life and work of Sigmund Freud. (1st ed.). New York: Basic Books, 1953; The 60 guilder fee is mentioned in a letter to Martha Bernays.

22. Merck E. Einen offenen Brief von E. Merck. Weiner med Presse; 26:1373, 1885.

23. Crowdy DR. Letter from Dame Rachel Crowdy to W.G. Van Wettum questioning the existence of a "cocaine producers cartel." October 22, 1929. Archief van de Cultural-, Handels-en Insdustriebank, later Cultuurbank N.V., ARA II: Archief van de Cultural-, Handels-en Insdustriebank, later Cultuurbank N.V., ARA II, 1929.

24. Van Wettum WG. Letter from Van Wettum to Dame Rachel Crowdy, November 18, 1929, the Hague. Archief van de Cultural-, Handels-en Insdustriebank, later Cultuurbank N.V., ARA II, 1929.

25. Van Wettum WG. Letter from Van Wettum to Dame Rachel Crowdy, December 24, 1929, the Hague. Archief van de Cultural-, Handels-en Insdustriebank, later Cultuurbank N.V., ARA II, 1929.

26. Van Wettum V. Letter from Van Wettum to Dame Rachel Crowdy, League of Nation Opium Committee. Archief van de Cultural-, Handels-en Insdustriebank, later Cultuurbank N.V., ARA II. 1929.

27. League of Nations, Opium Committee. O.C.Document #445, 1925; Articles of Association of the Coca Producers Association approved by Royal Decrees, November 2, 1925 (Decree #54), 1925.

28. Atzenwiler L. Prewar production and distribution of narcotic drugs and their raw materials. League of Nations, Permanent Central Opium Board, 1944.

29. League of Nations, Opium Committee. O.C. Document # 372, 1926.

30. League of Nations Opium Committee, Report to the Council on the Work of the Twelfth Session, Advisory Committee on Traffic in Opium and Dangerous Drugs, February 2, 1929.

31. League of Nations Opium Committee, O.C.Document # 756, Letter from the Netherlands Minister for Foreign Affairs on enforcement of the export certificate system. League of Nations: 1928.

32. Feldwick W, ed. Present Day Impressions of Japan. London: Globe Encyclopedia, 1919.

CHAPTER 8

General Sources: Mark Pendergrast's book on Coca-Cola is probably the definitive work on that subject, and it also has the merit of being highly readable. Unfortunately, the *Atlanta Constitution* is not indexed for the period of the Coca-Cola trials, and a manual search failed to disclose much coverage. *The Commercial Appeal,* printed in Chattanooga had some interesting material on the trial, but it appears that the trial transcript itself was never printed. Anderson's book on Harvey W. Wiley is informative, but is more concerned with political and social issues than with Wiley's very bad science. The articles and editorials in *Scientific American* and *Colliers* Magazine are interesting and informative. Copies of both magazines should be available at large libraries. Otherwise, most of the material in this chapter came from the newspapers of the time and the printed court judgments.

1. United States District Court EDT, S.D, Judge Edward Terry Sanford. 191 Fed. Rep. 431; United States v Forty Barrels and Twenty Kegs of Coca-Cola. 1911.
2. Anon. Drugs sap nation's vigor, says Wiley. New York Times;12-12, 1911.
3. Anderson O, Jr. The health of a nation. Harvey W. Wiley and the fight for pure food. Chicago: University of Chicago Press, 1958.
4. Adams S. The great American Fraud, II: Peruna and the "Bracers". Collier's:17-18, 1905.
5. Hearn WL, Flynn D, Hime D, et.al. Cocaethylene - a unique cocaine metabolite displays high affinity for the dopamine transporter. J Neurochem,. J Neurochem; 56(2): 698–701, 1991.
6. Mash D. Paper read at College on the Problems of Drug Dependency annual meeting, Richmond, VA. NIDA monograph 1989.
7. Pendergrast M. For God, country, and Coca-Cola. The unauthorized history of the great American soft drink and the company that makes it. New York: Collier Books, 1993.
8. Allen F. Secret formula: how brilliant marketing and relentless salesmanship made Coca-Cola the best-known product in the world. New York: Frederick Allen. 1st ed., Harper Business, 1994.
9. King M. Dr. John S. Pemberton: originator of Coca-Cola. Pharm Hist;29:85-89, 1987.
10. Freud S. Über coca. Wein Centralblatt fúr die ges Therapie 1884;(translated and reprinted in Cocaine Papers by SigmundFreud), also in J Substance Abuse Treatment 1:205-217, 1984.
11. Riley JJ. A history of the American soft drink industry; bottled carbonated beverages, 1807-1957. Washington, American Bottlers of Carbonated Beverages, 1958.
12. Adams S. The great American fraud, part IV - the subtle poisons. Collier's:16-18, 1905.
13. Blochman L. Doctor Squibb, the life and times of a rugged idealist. New York: Simon and Schuster, 1958.
14. Sinclair U. The Jungle. New York: Reprinted Version 1990, Signet Classic, Penguin Books, 1905.
15. Adams S. The great American fraud. Colliers; 14-15, 1905.

16. Anon. Nostrums and Quackeries: Articles on the nostrum evil and quackery reprinted, with additions and modifications from the Journal of the American Medical Association. (2nd ed.) Chicago: American Medical Association, 1912.

17. Wiley H. Influence of food preservatives and artificial colors on digestion and health. Washington, D.C.: Government Printing Office, U.S. Dept. Agriculture, Bureau of Chemistry, Bulletin No 84, Pt 1, 1904.

18. Tremblay G, Qureshi I. The biochemistry and toxicology of benzoic acid metabolism and its relationship to the elimination of waste nitrogen. Pharmac Ther;60:63-90, 1993.

19. Wiechowski W. Die gesetze de Hippursauresynthese. Beitr chem Physiol;7:204-272, 1905.

20. Editorial. The bureau of chemistry and its work. Scientific American; 439-439, 1912.

21. Freud S. Beitrag zu Kenntniss der Cocawirkung. (Contribution to the knowledge of the effect of cocaine). Wien Wiener Med Wochenschrift 1885 (January 31, 1985):130-133. Translated and reprinted in Byck (ed), Cocaine Papers of Sigmund Freud.

22. Young J. The toadstool millionaires: a social history of patent medicines in America before regulation. Princeton: Princeton University Press, 1974.

23. Anon. Pure food work a failure. New York Times, November 21, 18:2, 1911.

24. Circuit Court of Appeals SC. 215 Fed. Rep. 535; United States v Forty Barrels and Twenty Kegs of Coca Cola. 1914.

25. Bunker M, McWilliams M. Caffeine content of common beverages. J Am Dietetic Assn;74:28-32, 1979.

26. Anon. Drink it straight? Only alternative - U.S. starts war on soft drinks. Commercial Appeal, Chattanooga, Tennessee, March 21, pg 5, 1911.

27. Anon. Coca-Cola wins case. Judge instructs for verdict for defendant - U.S. will appeal. Commercial Appeal, Chattanooga, Tennessee, page 3, April 17, 1911.

CHAPTER 9

General Sources: The files of the British Foreign Office offer a goldmine of information about how international drug regulations came to be enacted, especially when it came to the commercial interests of the countries involved. All Foreign Office correspondence regarding drug issues, from 1910 to 1941, have been collated and released as a six volume set, available at some large libraries. There are two standard books on the topic of narcotic control: David Musto's "American Disease" (Yale University Press, 1973) focuses on domestic control measures, while Arnold Taylor's, American Diplomacy and the Narcotics Traffic (Duke University Press, 1969) book deals more extensively with the relations between the United States and the League of Nations. Musto deals in some detail with the actions of Dr. Wright, and the conditions in the United States which nutured Wright's approach. The remainder of the materials come from the League of Nations, Opium Committee files. Regrettably, they are very hard to come by. The main collections are housed in New York and Geneva.

1. British Foreign Office. Letter from Max Muller. FO 371/1076/461. 1912.
2. Brent C. The opium problem in the Philippine islands. Speech delivered before the League of Nations, Advisory Committee on Traffic in Opium, May 29, 1923. The traffic in habit-forming narcotic drugs. Statement of the attitude of the government of the United States with documents relating thereto. Washington, DC. Government Printing Office, 1923.
3. Stein S. International diplomacy, state administrators and narcotics control. The origins of a social problem. London: London School of Economics and Gower Publishing Company, 1985.
4. Musto D. The American disease. New Haven: Yale University Press, 1973.
5. Eisenlohr LES. International narcotics control. London: George Allen & Unwin Ltd, 1934.
6. Committee on Traffic in Opium. International control of the traffic in opium. Summary of the Opium Conferences held at Geneva, November, 1924 to February, 1925 with appendices containing complete texts of final agreements, and the Hague Convention of 1912. New York: Foreign Policy Association, reprinted in 1981 by Arno Press, Inc, 1925.
7. Briitish Foreign Office. Memorandum by Mr. Brunyate, Enclosure 2 in No. 55, from India Office to Foreign Office, dated August 9, 1910 [29029]. 1910.
8. Wright H. Document #377, The International Opium Commission and its results. Washington, D.C.: United States Senate, 61st Congress, 2nd session, 1910.
9. British Foreign Office Letter from FA Campbell, Foreign Office, to Sir C. Clementi Smith [29029]. 1910.
10. British Foreign Office, Telegram from James Bryce to Sir Edward Grey, September 6, 1911 [35280]. 1911.
11. British Foreign Office, Letter from James Bryce to Edward Grey, Washington, March 12, 1910 [10010]. 1910.
12. British Foreign Office, Letter from Sir Edward Grey to Mr. Whitelaw Reid, U.S. State Department [33412]. 1910.
13. Atzenwiler L. Pre-war production and distribution of narcotic drugs and their raw materials. League of Nations, Permanent Central Opium Board, Geneva, 1944.
14. Noble G. Policies and opinions at Paris 1919: Wilsonian diplomacy, the Versailles Peace and French public opinion. New York: Howard Fertig, 1968.
15. Temperley H, ed. A history of the Peace Conference of Paris. London: Henry Froude, Hodder and Stroughton, 4 volumes, 1920.
16. Opium Committee. Minutes of the First Session of the Advisory Committee on Traffic in Opium and Dangerous Drugs, First session. Geneva: League of Nations, 1921.
17. British Foreign Office. Question asked in the House of Commons, by H. Clynes, November 25, 1929. F 6142/6142/87. 1929.
18. United States Congress. Public Resolution 96, March 2, 1923. The traffic in habit-forming narcotic drugs. Statement of the attitude of the governmnet of the United States with documents relating thereto. Washington, DC: Government Printing Office, 1923.
19. Porter S. Memorandum from U.S. Representative Stephen G. Porter to M. Zahle, President of the Second Hague Conference. Contained in the "Summary of the Opium Conferences held in Geneva, November 1924 to February 1925. The Committee on Traffic in Opium of the Foreign Policy Association, 1925, with Appendicies containing complete texts of final agreements, and

the Hague Convention of 1912." Originally published by the Foreign Policy Association, Pamphlet No. 33, Series of 1924-1925, New York, 1925. Reprinted Edition 1981 by Arno Press, under the title of Narcotic addiction and American foreign policy., G. Grob, Ed. 1925.

20. Frimans, H. Richard. Narcodiplomacy. Cornell University Press, Ithica and New York, 1996.

CHAPTER 10

General sources: Material for this section came from three primary sources: (1) the transcript of the War Crimes Tribunal held in Tokyo after World War II (the International Military Tribunal for the Far East), (2) recently declassified records from the old Bureau of Narcotics, which was absorbed into the Drug Enforcement Agency, and (3) the records of the British Foreign Office. Copies of the transcript are available at major research libraries. The Bureau of Narcotic Records form a part of Records Group #170 (RG 170: Records of the DEA, acc #71-A-3554, carton #10-20 Japan Statistical Reports 1945-1946). In 1974, a facsimile reproduction of Foreign Office Correspondence on drug-related issues, from 1910 to 1941 (Foreign Office Collection #415) was published by Scholarly Resources, Inc. It, too, should be available in most major research libraries. League of Nations documents were also used. A few of the relevant League documents can be found in depository libraries around the United States, but most are at U.N. Headquarters in New York and Geneva. Special permission is required for access.

1. British Foreign Service, Dispatch 31 from the British Consulate in Tamsui, Formosa to Sir J Tilley, British Embassy in Tokyo. Dated September 20, 1929 [F 6622/375/87]. 1929.

2. Feldwick W, ed. Present Day Impressions of Japan. London: Globe Encyclopedia, 1919.

3. International Military Tribunal for the Far East. The Tokyo judgment: the International Military Tribunal for the Far East (I.M.T.F.E.), 29 April 1946 - 12 November 1948 / edited by B. V. A. Roling and C. F. Ruter. Amsterdam: APA-University Press Amsterdam, 1977. Nicholson R. Puppet opium monopoly in Shanghai. IMTFE Exhibit 428, Introduced September 4, 1946; Letter sent from Nicholson, U.S. Treasury Attache to U.S. Commissioner of Customs, 1939.

4. International Military Tribunal for the Far East (I.M.T.F.E.), Exhibit 376; Manchukuoan lean promulgation - KYC Ordinance No. 109 on opium monopoly. 1946.

5. British Foreign Service, Letter from C. Dormer, British Embassy in Tokyo to Sir Austen Chamberlin, Foreign Office. F 1556/201/87. 1928.

6. Morikawa H. Zaibatsu:the rise and fall of family enterprise groups in Japan. Tokyo, Japan: University of Tokyo Press, 1992.

7. Bisson TA. Zaibatsu dissolution in Japan. Berkeley: University of California Press, 1954.

8. Anon, The 100 year history of Mitsui & Co., Ltd., 1876-1976. Tokyo: Mitsui, 1977. (Translated by Elliot, T., Ed.)

9. Mitsubishi PAC. A Brief history of Mitsubishi. Tokyo: Mitsubishi, 1990.

10. Hadley E. Antitrust in Japan. Princeton: Princeton University Press, 1970.

11. Eisenlohr L.E.. International narcotics control. London: George Allen & Unwin Ltd, 1934.

12. Anon. The drug situation and the control of narcotic drugs in Japan. Note by the Drug Control Service of the Secretariat. League of Nations, Opium Committee, 1944.

13. Anon. Japan and Narcotic Drugs. RG 170: Records of the DEA, acc #71-A-3554, carton #20 Japan Statistical Reports 1945-1946. Tokyo, Ministry of Foreign Affairs, Japanese Government 1950.

14. Anon. Traffic in opium and dangerous drugs. The control of narcotic drugs and of opium smoking and the drug situation in Formosa (Taiwan). Note by the Drug Control Service of the Secretariat. League of Nations, 1944.

15. Anon. Organized bands of traffickers in cocaine from Japan to India. Letter from the British Representative dated July 11, 1932. League of Nations, Advisory Committee on Traffic in Opium and Other Dangerous Drugs, 1932.

16. League of Nations, Advisory Committee on Traffic in Opium and Other Dangerous Drugs, Report to the Council on the Work of the Thirteenth Session, Geneva, January 30, 1930; Speech by Sir John Campbell, India's representative to the Committee. 1930.

17. Letter from Wayland Speer to J. Henry Anslinger regarding origin of "Fujitsuru" brand. RG 170: Records of the DEA, acc #71-A-3554, carton #20 Japan Statistical Reports 1945-1946, 1946.

18. British Foreign Office, Memorandum from C. Peake on the Report by the Government of Japan for the year 1926 on the traffic in dangerous drugs. Included as enclosure #14 in a dispatch from the British Ambassador in Tokyo to Austin Chamberlin in the Foreign Office [F 1556/201/87]. 1928.

19. Morton W. Japan, its history and culture. New York City: Crowell Press, 1970.

20. Lockwood W. The economic growth of Japan. Princeton: Princeton University Press, pg 64-68, 1954.

21. Memo from American Consulate, Taihoku, Taiwan, May 5, 1934 to Secretary of State in Washington, re cocaine and coca production. US Government, 1934 Records of the DEA, acc #71-A-3554, carton #20 Japan Statistical Reports 1945-1946, 1946.

22. British Foreign Office, Traffic in dangerous drugs. Enclosure #2 in Dispatch #43 from G. Patton, His Majesty's consul in Tamsui, Formosa. [F 471/469/87]. 1929.

23. Speer, W, Information concerning narcotics in Taiwan. Report sent by Agent Speer to General Headquarters, Supreme Commander for the Allied Powers (SCAP), Public Health & Welfare Section, 1946

24. Nicholson R. Formosan cocaine factory. Report from Treasury Attache Nicholson; Introduced as Exhibit #388, IMTFE, September 3, 1946; Copied to J. Henry Anslinger, 1939, copies also in DEA records, box 20.

25. International Military Tribunal for the Far East (I.M.T.F.E.) testimony

26. Bransky J. Survey of production, manufacture and distribution of narcotic drugs and preparations by the Sankyo Company, Limited (Sankyo Kabushiki Kaisha). Reports of Joseph Bransky, Field Investigator for the Office of Counter-Intelligence, Tokyo RG 170: Records of the DEA, acc #71-A-3554, carton #20 Japan Statistical Reports 1945-1946, 1946.

27. Anon. Parke, Davis, 1866-1966, a backward glance. Detroit: Parke, Davis, 1966.

28. Anon. Agreement between Taiwan Shoyaku and Koto Pharmaceutical, et al., for the delivery of cocaine. Signed July 14, 1926; copies held in SCAP, RG 170 1926.

29. Speer W. Memorandum for record: Questionnaire on coca leaf production - Japan. General Headquarters, Supreme Commander for the Allied Powers; Public Health and Welfare Section, 1948.

30. Meeting notes of the Colonial Development Bank, 1929. Archief van de Cultural-, Handels-en Industriebank, later Cultuurbank N.V., ARA II, 1929.

31. British Foreign Office, Memorandum from A. Ovens, on the production of dried coca leaves and drugs derived therefrom, in Formosa. Enclosure #2 in memorandum from British Ambassador in Tokyo to the Foreign Office [F 8/8/87]. 1930.

32. Bransky J. Survey of Hoshi Pharmaceutical Company, RG 170: Records of the DEA, acc #71-A-3554, carton #20 Japan Statistical Reports 1945-1946, 1946.

33. Bransky J. Survey of Shionogi Pharmaceutical Manufacturing Co., Ltd. RG 170: Records of the DEA, acc #71-A-3554, carton #20 Japan Statistical Reports 1945-1946.

34. Anon. The coca plant in India. Chemist and Druggist 1888 (February 25):254-255, 1888.

35. Walger T. Die Coca, ihre geschichte, geographische verbreitung und wirtschaftliche bedeutung: Ludwigs-Universität zu Giessen, 1917.

36. Reens E. La coca de Java. Monmographie historique, botanique, chimique et pharmacoligique [pour l'obtention du diplome de Docteur de l'Universite de Paris, Pharmacie]: Ecole Superieure de Pharmacie, 1919.

37. Report #29 from the Colonial Bank on the Nederlandsche Cocainefabriek, omslag 928,2.20.04. archief van de Cultuur-, Handels-en Industriebank, later Cultuurbank, N.V., ARA II, 1945.

38. League of Nations. The Geneva Opium Convention, Signed at Geneva February 19,1925. Chapter 1.-Definitions, Article 1. 1925.

39. Anon. Coca cultivation in the East Indies. Chemist and Druggist 1889 (September 28, 1889).

40. Anon. Java coca and cocaine. Chemist and Druggist 1910 (July 2, 1910):50-50.

41. Abruzzese R. Coca-leaf production in the countries of the Andean subregion. Bull Narc 1989;41(1&2):95-98.

42. British Foreign Office. Question asked by H.Clynes in the House of Commons, November 25, 1929. F 6142/6142/87. 1929.

43. Yasumi Y. Translation of a written statement submitted by Yasumi relative to the fraudulent figures furnished the League of Nations and the Manchurian affair.71-A-3554, carton #20 Japan Statistical Reports 1945-1946.

44. International Military Tribunal for the Far East (I.M.T.F.E.). Exhibit 427. 1939.

45. Office of National Drug Control Police, The national Drug Control Strategy: 1996, Drug Related Data. NCJ #160086, Washington, D.C.

CHAPTER 11

General Sources: These are essentially the same as those in the preceding chapter, but with the edition of the "Red" intercepts. The actual exhibits presented at the Tokyo War Crimes Trials are available for viewing at the National Archives, and they have been microfilmed. Copies of the film can be purchased for a nominal fee from the Archives. Arnold Brackman, who attended the Tokyo Trials, has written a very readable book that gives a good overview of the trial, although the section dealing with drugs is very brief. Brackman's book is sold in paperback and can still be purchased in general book stores. Röling's three volume analysis of the Trials is the most authoritative source, but the book is not really indexed, and copies are not readily available.

American code-breakers began to read these transmissions several years before the war began, although often many days after the cables had been sent. These intercepts can be read only at the National Archives (Record Group 456, National Security Agency/Central Security Service). They are entitled "Translations of Japanese Diplomatic Messages, 1934-1938 ("Red machine"), boxes 1-4 1938. Even though very few of the cables deal directly with drug-related issues, they reveal a tremendous amount about the prewar Japanese government. One cable, from the Foreign office in Tokyo to its Embassy in Washington (January 17, 1938 from Tokyo (Hirota) to Washington, Intercept #1263) clearly shows that Japan's Army had not even bothered to tell its diplomats what was going on in Nanking!

> *Since return (to) Shanghai (a) few days ago I investigated reported atrocities committed by Japanese Army in Nanking and elsewhere. Verbal accounts (pf) reliable eye-witnesses and letters from individuals whose credibility (is) beyond question afford convincing proof (that) Japanese Army behaves and (is) continuing (to) behave in (a) fashion reminiscent (of) Atilla (and) his Huns. (Not) less than three hundred thousand Chinese civilians slaughtered, many cases (in) cold blood. Robbery, rape, including children (of) tender years, and insensate brutality towards civilians continues (to) be reported from areas where actual hostilities ceased weeks ago. Deep shame which better type (of) Japanese civilians here feel — reprehensible conduct (of) Japanese troops elsewhere heightened by series (of) local incidents where Japanese soldiers run amuck (in) Shanghai itself. Today's North China Daily News reports (a) particularly revolting cases where (a) drunken Japanese soldier, unable (to) obtain women and drink he demanded, shot (and) killed three Chinese women over sixty and wounded several other harmless civilians.*

1. Röling BVA, Rüter CF, eds. The Tokyo judgment. The International Military Tribunal for the Far East (IMTFE), 29 April 1946 - 12 November 1948. Introduction by Dr. V.A. Röling. Amsterdam: APA University Press, 1977. vol 1, pg 53-193.
2. Paton GP. Dispatch 31 from the British Consulate in Tamsui, Formosa to Sir J Tilley, British Embassy in Tokyo. Dated September 20, 1929 [F 6622/375/87]. 1929.

3. Brackman A. The other Nuremberg. The untold story of the Tokyo war crimes trials. New York: Quill, William Morrow, 1987.

4. Opium Committee, Minutes of the Twenty-fourth Session of the Advisory Committee on Traffic in Opium and Dangerous Drugs; Geneva, May 24th to June 12, 1939. League of Nations, 1939.

5. International Military Tribunal for the Far East. The Tokyo judgment: the International Military Tribunal for the Far East (I.M.T.F.E.), 29 April 1946 - 12 November 1948 / edited by B. V. A. Roling and C. F. Ruter. Amsterdam: APA-University Press Amsterdam, 1977.

6. Anon. Japan and Narcotic Drugs. RG 170: Records of the DEA, Acc #71-A-3554, carton #20 Japan Statistical Reports 1945-1946. Tokyo, Ministry of Foreign Affairs, Japanese Government 1950.

7. Anon. Traffic in opium and dangerous drugs. The control of narcotic drugs and of opium smoking and the drug situation in Formosa (Taiwan). Note by the Drug Control Service of the Secretariat. League of Nations, 1944.

8. Morton W. Japan, its history and culture. New York City: Crowell Press, 1970.

9. British Foreign Office, The Opium Trade, 1910-1941. A facsimile reproduction of The Foreign Office Collection (F.O. 415) in the Public Records Office, London. [F 1556/201/87]. Wilmington, Delaware and London: Scholarly Resources, Inc, 1974.

10. Tilley SJ. Dispatch #32 from the British Consul in Taiwan, Dated December 3, 1929. [F6623/375/87]. 1929.

11. Bransky J. Letter of June 10, 1946 from Joseph Bransky to Henry Anslinger. Records of the DEA, Acc #71-A-3554, carton #20 Japan Statistical Reports 1945-1946.

12. British Foreign Office. "Fujitsuru brand cocaine seized in India port." Letter from the second secretary at the British Tokyo embassy, included in dispatch from J. Dormer to Sir Austen Chamberlain April 2, 1928. [F 1556/201/87]

13. British Foreign Office. "Fujitsuru brand cocaine seized in India port." Letter from the second secretary at the British Tokyo embassy, included in dispatch from J. Dormer to Sir Austen Chamberlain April 2, 1928. [F 6622/375/87]

14. Editorial. Triumph over evil. New York Times 1946 June 24, 1946.

15. Archer A. Report from Consul Archer to Viscount Halifax, Peking, Dated July 1, 1938. 1938.

16. Nicholson M, U.S. Treasury Attache, Shanghai, Letter to the Commissioner of Customs, Re: Japanese Narcotic Factories in Mukden, dated March 30, 1935. Records of the DEA, Acc #71-A-3554, carton #20 Japan Statistical Reports 1935-1946.

17. Oyler R. Memo to General Thorpe (Chief of Counter Intelligence): Preliminary Report on Japan's Monopolies of Opium Traffic. Records of the DEA, Acc #71-A-3554, carton #20 Japan Statistical Reports 1935-1946.

18. Nishiki, S, Deposition taken by Joseph Bransky for the Chief of Public Health Section, Division of Police Affairs, Korea. Records of the DEA, Acc #71-A-3554, carton #20 Japan Statistical Reports 1935-1946.

19. Homeyer A, Chief Chemists, Malinkrodt Chemical Works, St. Louis, Missouri. Letter to J. Henry Anslinger, Re "Narcotic factory in Mukden" St. Louis, Missouri. Records of the DEA, Acc #71-A-3554, carton #20 Japan Statistical Reports 1935-1946.

20. Rehe A. Investigation of opium situation in Manchuria, 1924-1944. AG 441.1 (23 Apr 48) PH, General Headquarters, Supreme Commander for the Allied Powers. 1948, copied to J. H. Anslinger, Records of the DEA, Acc #71-A-3554, carton #20 Japan Statistical Reports 1935-1946.

21. The National Narcotics Intelligence Consumers Committee (NNICC); The supply of illicit drugs to the United States. Drug Enforcement Agency, Report #DEA-94066, August 1994.

22. Office of National Drug Control Policy, Executive Office of the President. The national drug control strategy: 1996. Washington, D.C. The White House, 1996.

23. Cable from Mitsui, Sitencho to the Mitsui Berlin Office. Cable intercepted and translated by British Information & Records Branch, ref: No H 36957, 1942 RG 170: Records of the DEA, Acc #71-A-3554, carton #20 Japan Statistical Reports 1945-1946.

24. League of Nations. The drug situation and the control of narcotic drugs in Japan. Note by the Drug Control Service of the Secretariat. League of Nations, Opium Committee, 1944.

25. Shunichi I. Translation of report submitted by Ikawa, Sunichi to the twelfth Preliminary Conference of the (Japanese) Opium Committee held at the home of Minister of Public Welfare on 12 December 1938. Records of the DEA, Acc #71-A-3554, carton #22 Japan Statistical Reports 1945-1946.

26. International Military Tribunal for the Far East. The Tokyo judgment: the International Military Tribunal for the Far East (I.M.T.F.E.), 29 April 1946 - 12 November 1948. Edited by B. V. A. Roling and C. F. Ruter. Amsterdam: APA-University Press Amsterdam, 1977, pg 4761-4764.

27. ibid, pages 4896 to 4903.

28. Yasumi Y. Translation of a written statement submitted by Yasumi relative to the fraudulent figures furnished the League of Nations and the Manchurian affair. Records of the DEA, Acc #71-A-3554, carton #22 Japan Statistical Reports 1945-1946.

29. ibid. Exhibit 375; Contract for Underwriting the Subscription of the Manchuko Governments National Founding, 1946.

30. Anon. Cable Intercept #2824, Dated September 8, 1938, from Japanese Embassy Shanghai to Tokyo FO, translated 10/4/38. In: National Archives Record Group 456 of the National Security Agency/Central Security Service. Translations of Japanese Diplomatic Messages - "Red machine" (RM), boxes 1-4, ed. 1938.

31. Anon. Cable Intercept 3140. Translated 11/15/38 from Tokyo Foreign Office to Japanese Ambassador to the League. National Archives Record Group 456 of the National Security Agency/Central Security Service. Translations of Japanese Diplomatic Messages, 1934-1938 "Red machine" (RM), boxes 1-4 1938.

32. International Military Tribunal for the Far East. The Tokyo judgment: the International Military Tribunal for the Far East (I.M.T.F.E.), 29 April 1946 - 12 November 1948. Edited by B. V. A. Roling and C. F. Ruter. Amsterdam: APA-University Press Amsterdam, 1977, "Office Report for 1939 of the Third Section of the Treaty Bureau, Foreign Ministry: the internal opium problem." Document 1045, 1939.

33. Anon. Cable Intercept #554, Dated April 13, 1938, from Japanese Embassy Shanghai to Tokyo FO, translated 10/4/38. In: National Archives Record Group 456 of the National Security Agency/Central Security Service. Translations of Japanese Diplomatic Messages - "Red machine" (RM), boxes 1-4, 1938.

34. Anon. Cable Intercept #1785, Dated April 15, 1938, from Japanese Embassy Shanghai to Tokyo FO, translated 10/4/38. In: National Archives Record Group 456 of the National Security Agency/Central Security Service. Translations of Japanese Diplomatic Messages - "Red machine" (RM), boxes 1-4, 1938.

35. Langdon W. Report from the American Consul in Darien, Manchuria to the Secretary of State, Washington, D.C. Records of the DEA, Acc #71-A-3554, carton #22 Japan Statistical Reports 1945-1946.

36. League of Nations, Organized bands of traffickers in cocaine from Japan to India. Letter from the British Representative dated July 11, 1932. League of Nations, Advisory Committee on Traffic in Opium and Other Dangerous Drugs, 1932.

37. Anon. Circular #426, intercept #1598, dated March 22, 1938, translated 4/7/38. From Shanghai to Tientsin. Forwarded to Tokyo as #942. In: National Archives Record Group 456 of the National Security Agency/Central Security Service. Translations of Japanese Diplomatic Messages - RM, boxes 1-4, ed. 1938.

38. News clipping (paper not specified) dated November 30, 1938, Japan's narcotization policy in full swing in Shanghai. Copy retained in Bureau of Narcotic Files. Records of the DEA, Acc #71-A-3554, carton #22 Japan Statistical Reports 1945-1946.

39. International Military Tribunal for the Far East. The Tokyo judgment: the International Military Tribunal for the Far East (I.M.T.F.E.), 29 April 1946-12 November 1948. Edited by B. V. A. Roling and C. F. Ruter. Amsterdam: APA-University Press Amsterdam, 1977, "Office Report for 1939 of the Third Section of the Treaty Bureau, Foreign Ministry: the internal opium problem." Document 1045 1939, Exhibit 427. 1939.

40. British Foreign Office. Letter from Max Muller to Foreign Office, FO 371/1076/461. 1912.

AFTERWORD

1. British Foreign Office. Letter from Sir Edward Grey to Mr. Whitelaw Reid, U.S. State Department [33412]. 1910.

2. United Nations Demographic Yearbook, eleventh issue. New York City: United Nations, Department of Economic and Social Affairs, 1959.

3. Atzenwiler L. Prewar production and distribution of narcotic drugs and their raw materials. League of Nations, Permanent Central Opium Board, 1944.

4. British Foreign Office. Clynes H. Question asked in the House of Commons, November 25, 1929. F 6142/6142/87. 1929.

5. Drug Enforcement Agency Operation Breakthrough. Coca Cultivation & Cocaine Base Production in Bolivia. Drug Intelligence Report. Washington, D.C.: DEA, 1993. Report #DEA-94032.

6. Painter J. Bolivia and coca; a study in dependency. Boulder, Colorado: Lynne Rienner Publishers, 1994.

7. Tullis L. Unintended consequences. Illegal drugs & drug policies in nine countries. Boulder, Colorado: Lynne Rienner Publishers, 1995. (Tullis L, ed. Studies on the impact of the illegal drug trade).

8. Anon. A drug tale of two cites, Mexico City and Bogota. Economist 1996(April 6):41-42.

9. The National Narcotics Intelligence Consumers Committee (NNICC); The supply of illicit drugs to the United States. DEA, 1994.

10. Office of National Drug Control Policy. The national drug control strategy: 1996. Washington, D.C., The White House, 1996.

INDEX